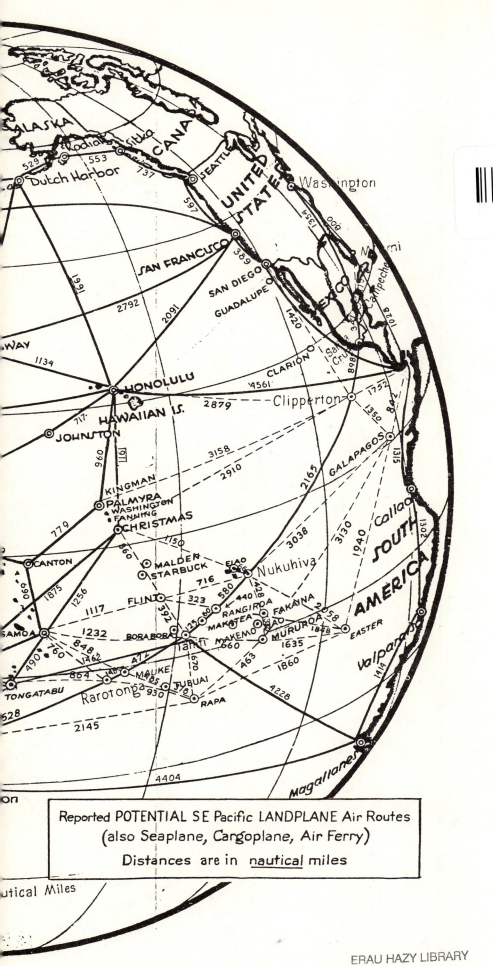

Reported POTENTIAL SE Pacific LANDPLANE Air Routes
(also Seaplane, Cargoplane, Air Ferry)

Distances are in <u>nautical</u> miles

The Earhart Disappearance
The British Connection

by
J. A. Donahue

The Earhart Disappearance
The British Connection

by
J. A. Donahue

A story about the disappearance of Amelia Earhart
and the cover-up which followed

Published as part of the
"Aviation Heritage Library Series"

by
SunShine House, Inc.
P.O. Box 2065
Terre Haute, IN 47802
(812) 232-3076

The Earhart Disappearance
The British Connection
by
J. A. Donahue

Foreword
by
Paul Rafford, Jr.

A story about the disappearance of Amelia Earhart
and the cover-up which followed

Published as part of the
"Aviation Heritage Library Series"
by

SunShine House
P.O. Box 2065
Terre Haute, IN 47802

First Edition, First Printing
Printed in the United States of America

Library of Congress
Catalog Card Number 87-061635

ISBN 0-943691-01-X

This book is the fourth in the **Aviation Heritage Library Series** published by
SunShine House, Inc.

The **Aviation Heritage Library Series** is published to preserve, for future generations,
the history of the men and women, and of their airplanes,
during the era of the Golden Years of Aviation.

The **Aviation Heritage Library Series**:
First Book: *The Welch Airplane Story* by Drina Welch Abel
Second Book: *It's a Funk!* by G. Dale Beach
Third Book: *The Luscombe Story* by John C. Swick
Fourth Book: *The Earhart Disappearance - The British Connection* by James A. Donahue

DEDICATION

This book is dedicated to my talented and loving daughter
Laura Lee Donahue.

Without her spirited assistance, this book would not have
been attempted or completed.

In Commemoration of the *50th Anniversary*
of the Disappearance of Amelia Earhart
1937 - 1987

Amelia Mary Earhart
(1897 - 1938)
A legend in her own time;
An inspiration for all time.

CONTENTS

FOREWORD
by Paul Rafford, Jr.

When Amelia Earhart and her navigator, Fred Noonan, vanished a half century ago, their disappearance touched off one of the world's greatest air/sea searches. The planes and ships have long since been called back from their missions but the search goes on. Although the "searchers" come from all walks of life and hold widely differing opinions, they are motivated by a common goal: "The missing in action - we want them accounted for!"

There are almost as many theories about what finally happened to Amelia and Fred as there are would-be investigators attempting to find out. With "official" information extremely sparse, any writer can postulate his own theory with little fear of formal contradiction.

Any serious student of the Earhart mystery must judge each theory on its own merits. Ultimately, the strength and acceptance of any theory must depend on the amount and quality of the evidence supporting it.

The only official information released to the public on the Earhart disappearance in the past fifty years has been the Navy's file on its search, declassified in 1962. All other information has been uncovered only through the diligence and dedication of private individuals.

Jim Donahue, retired aerospace engineer, is one of them. For the past several years he has devoted full time to his Earhart research. Using the skills of his profession, he has unearthed and analyzed a prodigious amount of evidence on which to base his theories. A surprising spin-off from his work has been the discovery that Earhart's Pacific flight was only one of several "covert" scouting missions carried out by the Allies in that area during the mid-1930s.

Jim first called on me for help in 1985, having come across my paper in the Smithsonian Air and Space Museum's library. In it, I outline my analysis of Earhart's radio activities during the last hours before she made her final transmission.

In 1940 I joined Pan American Airways as a Flight Radio Officer on the flying boat Clippers. As a result, I am well acquainted with the radio equipment and operating procedures of the Earhart era. Then, during the Mercury, Gemini and Apollo programs I served as a Communications Manager on the Astronaut Recovery Team. My specialty was the analysis and forecasting of radio communication with the ships and planes supporting the astronaut landings.

It was while I was at my console in Mission Control that I became impressed with the parallels between the Navy's astronaut search and recovery operations in the mid-Pacific and its vast search for Amelia Earhart in the same area thirty years before. In 1980, I decided to apply space-age, computer-aided investigative techniques to the problem of unraveling aviation's greatest mystery.

Jim was greatly impressed by my evidence that Amelia had used the giant lights on Nauru Island as a navigational checkpoint and did *not* fly a straight course from New Guinea to Howland Island as presumed by the news media. He was also intrigued by my analysis of her radio calls to the U.S. Coast Guard cutter *Itasca* that indicated she never came closer than 125 miles when she flew past Howland. Then, he asked me if I would apply my radio analysis techniques to his theory that Amelia deliberately by-passed Howland and flew directly from Jaluit, in the Marshalls, to Hull, in the Phoenix Group.

When I finished my analysis and plotted her positions, I almost fell off my chair! There, staring me in the face, was the answer to a question that had kept investigators guessing for years. In her last, enigmatic, radio transmission she declared, "We are on the line of position 157-337..." What did she mean by this? She was now crossing a line on her chart connecting Howland and Gardner Islands. To her secret listeners, armed with the same chart, it was like telling them, "We are on highway I-10, just crossing I-95." She had arrived at her last checkpoint. Having done so, she announced that she was discontinuing transmissions on her night radio frequency. The *Itasca* never heard her again.

Fifty years later, Jim Donahue had won a new convert!

August 1987

Part One

World Flight Attempts

Earhart Electra over San Francisco Bay - 1937
Photo credit - © Clyde Sunderland

WORLD FLIGHT ATTEMPTS

Amelia Earhart prepared herself well to become the right woman at the right time by inspiring national enthusiasm in the late 1920s and 1930s. She was the perfect counterpart to Charles A. Lindbergh, and the public admired both for their being tall, slender, attractive, modest human beings and competent pilots. Earhart was a complex, sensitive individual, and realized her record flights were stunts subject to diminishing returns. She enjoyed flying more than public acclaim but managed both to help aviation progress. Although not a feminist in the traditional sense, she proved that women were capable of becoming proficient and professional pilots.

Born in Atchison, Kansas, on 24 July 1897, she was the daughter of an attorney who worked for the railroad. As the family traveled, she acquired a broad perspective and more independence than her friends. Although the occupations of marriage or teaching were acceptable for young women of that era, her parents approved her more adventurous spirit. In Toronto, she served as a Red Cross nurse's aide. While there in 1918, she saw a flight exhibition and became aware that she was fascinated by the airplanes themselves as well as flying. She took a course in engine mechanics, something which would serve her well in later years. After World War I ended, she entered Columbia University to study medicine. This was interrupted by a trip to California and her first airplane ride, after which she decided to learn to fly. To pay for the lessons given by Neta Snook, Amelia worked for the Los Angeles Telephone Company. She soloed and obtained her pilot's license in 1921.

Amelia Earhart as a young pilot
*Photo credit - Smithsonian Institution's
National Air & Space Museum Negative #45906F*

During the following years, Amelia built up flying time and took a wide variety of employment, including being a social worker in Boston's Denison House for $60 a month in 1928. At that time, she became the first woman passenger to fly the Atlantic. Although receiving wide acclaim for this, she was discontented at not having piloted during the 20 hours and 40 minutes. Aware that her newfound fame and fortune would enable her to make aviation a career, she began preparing for a solo flight across the Atlantic. She was asked to lecture, write articles, and make demonstration flights. Also, she flew solo flights back and forth across this country, always trying to improve her techniques and learn as much as possible about instrument flying and fuel management, both important in long-distance attempts.

George Palmer Putnam had advised and encouraged Earhart since her first flight across the Atlantic as a passenger and went on to provide the business experience she needed to undertake record flights. They married in 1931. On 20 May 1932, she departed Newfoundland in a Lockheed Vega and landed in Ireland 15 hours and 18 minutes later, the first woman to solo across the Atlantic, the fulfillment of her dream. In August of that year, she became the first woman to solo from Los Angeles to Newark, a feat accomplished in 19 hours and 5 minutes. For the following few years, she received many honors and set even more records, always aware that these flights were necessary to maintain public interest in aviation, and eventually would become routine flights over the same routes.

Her next major record, in a new and improved Vega, was a solo flight from Honolulu to Oakland, accomplished on 11 January 1935 in 18 hours and 16 minutes, the first person to do so. In April 1936 she flew nonstop from Mexico City to New York. She became a visiting faculty member at Purdue University, West Lafayette, Indiana. Ostensibly, the Purdue Research Foundation provided her with a flying laboratory, a twin-engine Lockheed Electra. Having the best and most suitable aircraft available fitted with long-range tanks allowed her to dream of a flight around the world, done as nearly as possible at the equator. A westerly direction was chosen for the flight and plans were made with meticulous care. In March 1937, the Lockheed was damaged during her takeoff from Honolulu, the result of an unintentional groundloop. While waiting for the second attempt, Earhart and her navigator, Fred Noonan, opted for a June departure, more favorable weatherwise, and flying in the opposite direction.

On 1 June 1937, Earhart left Miami, and followed her planned route (see chart on next page) until reaching Lae, New Guinea, some 22,000 miles and 146 flying hours later. They had reached the most hazardous part of their flight, purportedly a 2,556-mile leg to tiny Howland Island. The Lockheed was performing well, but, supposedly, Noonan was unable to obtain perfect radio reception so as to synchronize his chronometers. On 1 July 1937, they departed Lae, at first sending ordinary radio messages. According to official records of the past fifty years, the airplane missed Howland Island and went down in the ocean, taking the famed pilot and navigator with it. A massive air search was made of the area by the U. S. Navy. By 18 July the effort had ended, and the pair

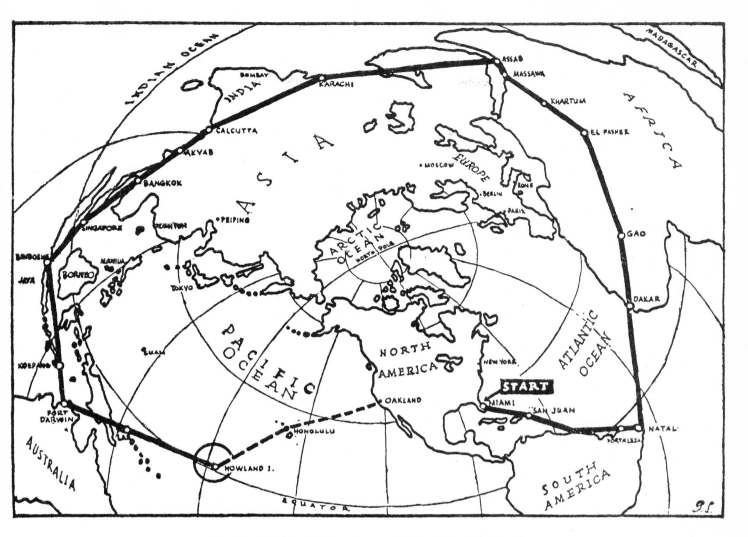

World Flight Path, June 1937 (West-to-East)

were officially presumed lost at sea. Since 1937, numerous theories about what happened to Earhart have surfaced periodically. Her career stirred the hearts and imaginations of millions of persons around the world and will continue to do so for generations to come.

Perhaps the most intimate views and significant items regarding Earhart's global flight appear in her book, *Last Flight*. On those pages are the beginnings of the world flight: the oceanic flights, the acquisition of the Lockheed 10, and the preparations for what became her final public flight.

In May 1935, when flying from Mexico City to New York, she thought about her earlier record flights which had been done mostly at night or with heavy cloud cover during daylight hours. Thus, when viewing the endless waters of the Gulf of Mexico, she made a decision. "So, on that sunny morning out of sight of land, I promised my lovely red Vega I'd fly her across no more water. And I promised myself that any further over-ocean flying would be attempted in a plane with more than one motor, capable of keeping aloft with a single engine. Just in case."

Realizing that persons in the aviation industry had been concerned with mechanical and economic problems and had not given the effect of flying on human beings the attention it deserved, Earhart wrote, "I am interested in finding out whether one kind of food is better than another during flight, i.e., the effects of altitude on metabolism. Also I should like to know the rate at which fatigue is induced by the myriad instruments a modern pilot must use. What will stratosphere flying do to creatures accustomed to the dense air of lower altitudes? Are men and women different in their reactions to air travel? If so how? And perhaps, why?"

Her association with Purdue University, which had an aviation department and a landing field, as a "periodic and rather peripatetic faculty member," made her dream of having a twin engine Lockheed a reality. "One day in early 1936, President Edward C. Elliott asked my husband what most interested me beyond immediate academic matters. He divulged my suppressed pilot's yearning for a bigger and better airplane, not only to go to far places farther and faster and more safely, but essentially for pioneering in aviation education and technical experimentation."

Earhart wrote that the purchase of her Lockheed Electra "was made possible chiefly through the Purdue Research Foundation, aided by such friends as J. K. Lilly, Vincent Bendix, and others, mostly within the aviation industry, and by the generosity of manufacturers who seemed to feel that my activities were helpful in promoting aviation, and especially, perhaps in overcoming women's 'sales resistance' to air travel."

Classic photograph of Amelia Earhart and her Electra used on United States postage stamp
Photo credit - Lockheed Aircraft Corporation

At the conclusion of a week's visit on the campus of Purdue University, on April 19, 1936, Earhart announced her acquisition of a "flying laboratory." It was to be equipped to include the latest devices evolved in modern air transport and was to literally become a "flying laboratory" for practical flight research in scientific aeronautics. Purdue was already a notable pioneer, being America's only university with its own fully-equipped airport providing for day and night flying.

Announced at the same time was that Earhart, who during the 1936 academic year had been the University's consultant in Careers for Women and in Aeronautics, would continue to be associated in these fields. Although the famed flier would own the plane and would be entirely responsible for its use, she would cooperate with Purdue and the Foundation in the expansion of research and education in the field of aeronautics.

The purpose of the "Amelia Earhart Research Fund" was to provide ways and means for pure and applied aeronautical research and education predicated on the facilities already established at Purdue. In due time, the Research Fund would provide activities both stimulating to students and of commercial value to the aeronautical industry.

Amelia Earhart's Lockheed Electra, Model 10E, on delivery day, May 1936
Photo credit - Lockheed Aircraft Corporation

Amelia Earhart and Fred Noonan discuss trans-Pacific route
Photo credit - Seaver Center,
Los Angeles Natural History Museum

Amelia Earhart in her working environment
Photo credit - Smithsonian Institution's
National Air & Space Museum Negative #85-14509

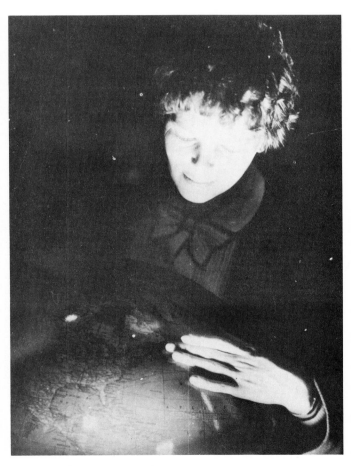

Amelia Earhart contemplates her final challenge, circumnavigation of the world
Photo credit - Smithsonian Institution's
National Air & Space Museum Negative # 85-14508

In his discussion, President Elliott declared: "We who have observed the effect of Earhart's words and work realize what she is accomplishing for the fundamental promotion of sound aeronautics. Even aside from her pioneering feats, she seems to me today the most potent single influence in encouraging American air travel. Certainly she is pre-eminent in breaking down feminine sales resistance. Much of the aeronautical industry, I think, recognizes the debt to her. We of Purdue welcome the opportunity to cooperate with Earhart who is an inspiring example for youth and a fine technician of the air."

Earhart expressed the following sentiment during the interview: "I am exceedingly grateful to President Elliott and the friends of Purdue who are making possible my new plane. I hope its use may result in constructive accomplishment—both for Purdue and for women in general. For it is not often we of the feminine persuasion are given such opportunities to pioneer in our chosen fields. I appreciate deeply, too, the generous help given by those in the industry. As they know, aviation is a business to me, and my ambition is that the project shall produce practical results. It should focus further attention upon aviation developments which are making flying the most modern, convenient, and attractive form of transportation." (Much of the above information was in a news release dated April 19, 1936.)

Earhart had intended "to undertake a year's research with my plane and thereafter plan some interesting flight. But circumstances made it appear wiser to postpone the research and attempt the flight first."

In May, Earhart and her husband, George Palmer Putnam, returned to the Pacific coast where she supervised the completion and equipping of the plane. As with all her previous flights, Putnam managed the administrative aspects of the new project.

The airplane, Lockheed Electra, Model 10E, with Civil Aeronautics Administration (CAA) identification number NR16020 was completed and delivered to Amelia Earhart in May 1936. It was moved to the Paul Mantz hangar at Union Air Terminal, Burbank, where it was prepared for its intended round-the-world flight. Under Mantz's expert guidance, Earhart had ten months to become familiar with her airplane and equip it with the necessities for a world flight.

Then followed a period of testing and trial flights in southern California and at Purdue. Experimental work included fuel consumption tests; speed and fuel consumption under varying conditions; the use of oxygen; radio communication and navigation instruments and methods; and human fatigue and endurance in relation to altitude, diet, sleep, eyestrain, etc. Periodic "field tests" on actual flights were planned. Such flights included continental crossings and an overseas journey.

Amelia Earhart and Paul Mantz after test flight of Electra in 1936
Photo credit - Paul Mantz Collection

Amelia Earhart and her Lockheed 10E at Union Air Terminal, Burbank, California
*Photo credit - Seaver Center,
Los Angeles Natural History Museum*

The plane had been fitted with special windows for the navigator's work. He had a good-sized table to hold necessary charts. Chronometers were beside the table, shock-mounted on rubber. Earhart wrote, "Other 'chart-room' equipment included altimeter, air-speed and drift indicators, pelorus and compass. The navigator had access to any part of the plane, for a catwalk over the large gasoline tanks connected the cabin in the rear with the cockpit."

About the Lockheed, Earhart wrote, "The plane itself is a two-motor, all-metal monoplane, with retractable landing gear. It is a big brother to the two Lockheed Vegas which I have used on previous flights. It has a normal cruising speed of about 180 miles an hour and at top speed in excess of 200. With the special gasoline tanks that have been installed in the fuselage, capable of carrying 1,150 gallons, it has a cruising radius in excess of 4,000 miles. With full load the ship weighs about 15,000 pounds. It is powered with two Wasp 'H' engines, developing 1,100 horsepower."

Auxiliary fuselage tanks installed for range of 4,000 miles
Photo credit - Lockheed Aircraft Corporation

About the equipment installed in her "flying laboratory," she wrote it was equipped with "a Sperry Gyro-Pilot, an automatic device which actually flies the ship unaided. There is a Bendix radio direction finder which points the way to any selected broadcasting station within its range. There is the finest two-way voice and code Western Electric communication equipment in whose installation the Bell Laboratories, under the aegis of Dr. Frank B. Jewett, co-operated."

AIRCRAFT REGISTRATION: 16020

Mfg. Serial # (c/n): 1055 Model: Electra 10-E Make: LOCKHEED

ATC #: 590 Mfg. Date: 7/36 Engine(s) No.: 2 Make: P&W

Engine Model: Wasp S3 H 1' H.P.: 550 each Engine(s) Serial #: (R) 6149 (L) 6150

General Descrip: 2 PCLM Wts: Empty 7340 Gross 10500 Other:

License Appl.: by mfg. 7/19/36 Ident. # Issued: Approved Exper.: X to L/A/C for factory test work Approved Comm.:

Mfgr.: Lockheed Aircraft Corporation, Burbank, Calif.

Sold to: Amelia Earhart, 50 West 45th St., N.Y.C.
(1/22/37 to: Locust Avenue, Rye, N.Y.)

Date: 7/24/36

Subsequent History: R Lic. to Earhart to exp. 8/15/37, "for long-distance flights and research." NR okayed on 9/21/36. 1148 gal. cap tanks installed (diagram in original file folder), 12 tanks.

Round-the World Flight to be attempted by Earhart, and navigator Harry Manning 362 Riverside Drive, New York, N.Y., who held Priv. lic.# 17063. Earhart's Transport Lic. # 5716 expired 10/15/36. (She was notified to renew it on 10/2C

Flight permit from CAA sent to Earhart 3/12/37

Accident: Luke Field, Hawaii, 3/20/37. Earhart failed to submit accident report, and was subject to a $500 fine. As of 4/19/36, Dept. of Commerce inspector Emil Williams of Honolulu recommended "no actior

Aircraft returned to factory and repairs consisting of new right wing and repairs to landing gear and center fuselage section completed 5/19/37.

Second Round-the-World flight permission from CAA granted 5/14/37.
R Lic. to exp. 12/22/36, 8/19/37 and with crew of 4 to exp. 6/5/37.

Final Disposition: Accompanied by navigator Fred Noonan, Amelia Earhart took off from Lae, New Guinea at 10 A.M. 7/2/37, bound for Howland Island, a distance of 2550 miles. Carried 1100 gals fuel, 75 gals oil, Using 53 gals per hr., th Approx. time to Howland should have been 20 hrs. 46 min. Wind was a 25 knots. Also estimated as 20 hrs, 16 min. Flyers never arrived and radioed "30 min. fuel left." Thought to have missed island and gone down in ocean. No traces. Reg. cancelled in CAA records 7/12/38, due to disappearance.

NASM/Historical A/C Listing Date: 1/21/81 RSA

Model 10 Identification
(National Air and Space Museum)

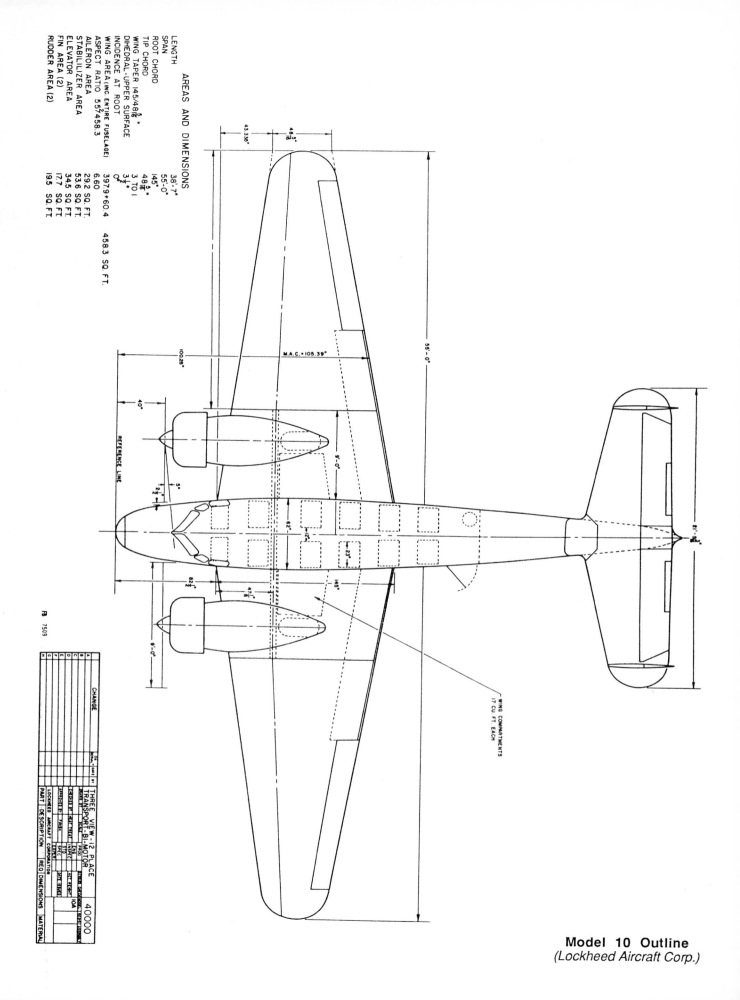

AREAS AND DIMENSIONS

LENGTH .... 38'-7"
SPAN .... 55'-0"
ROOT CHORD .... 145"
TIP CHORD .... 48 5/16"
WING TAPER 145/48 5/16 .... 3 TO I
DIHEDRAL—UPPER SURFACE .... 3 1/2°
INCIDENCE AT ROOT .... 0°
WING AREA (INC ENTIRE FUSELAGE) .... 397.9+60.4   458.3 SQ. FT.
ASPECT RATIO 55²/458.3 .... 6.60
AILERON AREA .... 29.2 SQ. FT.
STABILIZER AREA .... 53.6 SQ. FT.
ELEVATOR AREA .... 34.5 SQ. FT.
FIN AREA (2) .... 17.7 SQ. FT.
RUDDER AREA (2) .... 19.5 SQ. FT.

FB 7509

THREE VIEW - 12 PLACE
TRANSPORT - BI-MOTOR

LOCKHEED AIRCRAFT CORPORATION

40000

Model 10 Outline
(Lockheed Aircraft Corp.)

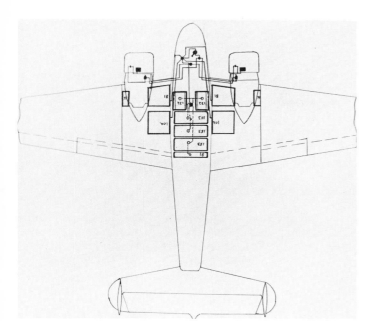

Fuel tank schematic of Earhart's Electra
Photo credit - Paul Mantz Collection

"Preparation," Earhart wrote, "is often two-thirds of any venture. Preparation for the world flight occupied many months. There were the mechanical problems of the ship and its operations and far-flung arrangements for the journey."

On a flight around the world, "much of it off the beaten paths of established air transport, there are complexities. It took many weeks to get all the maps and charts we needed. Once secured, the courses to be followed were laid out in detail on them, mostly by Commander Clarence Williams of Los Angeles, who had helped me plot previous flights.

"In assembling the precious data a tower of helpfulness was Jacques de Sibour, an old friend of ours who, with his wife, Violette (both pilots), is intimately familiar with flying conditions in much of the most difficult territory involved.

"All important in our budding campaign were the arrangements for fuel and service. As our plans progressed, the world-wide organization of the Standard Oil Company of New Jersey and its associates cooperated in assembling information and in 'spotting' fuel supplies at designated points. At certain fields scattered here and there, competent mechanics were provided for and spare parts assembled."

At the end of 1936 Earhart had been flying her Electra for eight months since its delivery in May of that year. Prior to May she had also been checked out in the flying characteristics of the Model 10 by Lockheed test pilots in company-owned airplanes. Company tests of her specially modified Model 10E included variable load testing, takeoff and landing characteristics, flight performance, fuel consumption evaluation, etc. These tests were necessary to verify contractual performance guarantees specified by the purchaser. Paul Mantz oversaw the many special features which were incorporated at the factory during manufacture.

During this period, approximately one year, Earhart became a proficient pilot of the aircraft under Paul Mantz's technical supervision. Several trans-continental flights had been completed along with extensive over-water flying off the California coast and numerous local flights in California.

The initial year also included a one-month period when the airplane was "loaned" to the U.S. Air Corps at the Wright Field test center near Dayton, Ohio. Tests included evaluation of airborne radio direction finders and radio range (navigation) equipment.

At the beginning of 1937, world flight preparations went into high gear. Two significant developments solidified the east-to-west route. The Roosevelt administration provided funds and personnel to construct a rudimentary airfield on Howland Island near the equator, 1,800 miles southwest of Hawaii. The British also granted Earhart access to the Royal Air Force Base at Aden (near the mouth of the Red Sea) so that she could travel across equatorial Africa through Khartoum, Anglo Egyptian Sudan to Dakar on Africa's west coast.

Technical modifications to the airplane were accelerated to meet a March departure date. Paul Mantz devoted his efforts full time to the Earhart flight, first at his hangar at Burbank's Union Air Terminal and later at the Navy Reserve hangar at Oakland's Municipal Airport. Concurrent with route refinement and airplane permanence and equipment enhancement, fuel and supplies were provisioned at all anticipated stops around the world route, technical support arranged and State Department clearances obtained to visit countries en route.

During an East Coast visit in early 1937, Earhart finally revealed her world flight plans to the press. Highlights of the press conference included introducing Merchant Marine mariner Harry Manning as her navigator and acknowledging that tiny and remote Howland Island

**The heavy black line across the face of the two hemispheres shows
the intended course of Amelia Earhart's world flight**

near the equator would be a difficult island to locate. The inclusion of Fred Noonan as the *de facto* navigator and using Paul Mantz as co-pilot came as last minute surprises.

Final preparations at Burbank included the installation of a government supplied all wave (frequency) airborne radio receiver of the latest design. This Bendix RA-1 unit provided long-range receiving capability and improved radio direction finder sensitivity. Lt. Commander Clarence Williams, USNR, completed piloting the revised route on aeronautical charts along the entire worldwide route.

Publicity photograph of Amelia Earhart with radio direction finder loop
Photo credit - Smithsonian Institution's National Air & Space Museum Negative #71-1055

After flight preparation shifted to the Naval Reserve hangar at Oakland, security tightened. Earhart was kept in the dark on many of the special equipment provisions. A high capacity emergency electrical storage battery was installed in the navigation compartment to enable emergency radio transmissions. Air Corps technicians from Hamilton Field across San Francisco Bay appeared on the scene to install the latest in military aerial camera equipment, including General George W. Goddard's perfected nighttime photoflash technology. By mid-March, the airplane had been changed into a high technology, long-range photo reconnaissance aircraft using the very latest in technological equipment. Newly activated Hamilton Field near San Rafael, California, included a bombing squadron transferred from March Field, Riverside, California, and an observation squadron

transferred from Crissy Field at San Francisco. General Goddard's photoflash technology was in operation at observation squadrons in the United States in 1936 and 1937. Final provisions included installation of a separate gasoline tank for the recently perfected 100-octane gasoline which was later to give the Allies an edge in aircraft performance in World War II.

Finally, all preparations were completed and March 15 designated for departure day. Winter weather in the area prevented takeoffs on the 15th. Two Pan American clippers scheduled for departure from nearby Alameda on San Francisco Bay were also grounded by the inclement weather. Finally, on the afternoon of March 17, weather clearance was given by the government weather department in San Francisco and all three airplanes departed for Hawaii. One of the PAA clippers was the regularly scheduled trans-Pacific (Manila) clipper. The other flight was headed by Pacific Ocean flying pioneer Captain Edwin Musick and selected crew on a survey flight to Auckland, New Zealand, to fly the Pacific Ocean via Kingman Reef (just north of the equator) and Pago Pago harbor at American Samoa.

Although Earhart departed later than the lumbering flying boats with their parasitic (high aerodynamic drag) seaplane hulls, she quickly caught up and passed them before night fall and set an east-to-west crossing record from the west coast to Hawaii, over a 2,400-mile distance. The PAA survey route to the Southwest Pacific has important parallels with the Earhart flight. The PAA route became an airline. The Earhart route was an excuse for the government to build an airfield on Howland Island which was close to the Japanese Marshall Islands.

The PAA flight was eminently successful. Airline technicians left nothing to chance and had a chartered merchant ship, S.S. *Northwind,* which was outfitted to serve as an airway support vessel at Kingman Reef where no facilities were available. Communications, fuel, overnight lodgings, radio direction finding equipment, food, supplies, mechanics and weather technicians were all provided on the sea mobile clipper tender. Also, in the event that the clipper had to land at sea en route, the S.S. *Northwind* could launch an immediate rescue effort knowing in advance exactly where the ship had ditched.

When the clipper came into Kingman Reef on the southbound flight, the area was in the middle of a 300-mile tropical depression. Despite the adverse weather, Musick brought the clipper right into the lagoon at Kingman Reef without a hitch. One can only marvel at this display of airline efficiency as compared to the makeshift provisions for Earhart at Howland Island in an operation one senior naval officer was to summarize as a "tragedy of errors".

It is significant to note that a commercial merchant vessel had been converted to act as a mother ship for aeronautical oceanic operations in March 1937. The ship was provided with all the necessary equipment to support an airplane in an isolated oceanic area by serving as an en route airbase. A British merchant ship was also provided in a similar fashion a few months later while operating to the east of the Japanese Marshall Islands.

After obtaining weather clearance, Earhart left Oakland Airport at 4:30 p.m. for the 2,400-mile over water flight to the Hawaiian Islands. She had a full crew with Paul Mantz as co-pilot, late arrival Fred J. Noonan as navigator and Harry Manning relegated to radio operating duties.

Amelia Earhart's Electra at Oakland Airport, March 1937 - Note military guard
Photo credit - National Archives

Amelia Earhart taking off from Oakland for flight to Hawaii, 17 March 1937
Photo credit - National Archives

Amelia Earhart taking off for Hawaii - Note military hangar in background
Photo credit - Seaver Center, Los Angeles Natural History Museum

Oakland to Hawaii Flight crew, 17 March 1937
Left to right: Paul Mantz, Amelia Earhart,
Harry Manning and Fred Noonan
Photo credit - Smithsonian Institution's
National Air & Space Museum Negative #A334

The story behind Fred J. Noonan's last-minute substitution has never been told. The connection between Lt. Commander Noonan, USNR, and the final secret modifications to the airplane in the U.S. Naval Reserve Hangar at Oakland Airport are rather obvious. Noonan, after leaving the employment of Pan American Airways, lived in Oakland and soon became acquainted with the officer in charge of the local Naval Reserve activities. He was the go-between who brought Earhart and Noonan together.

Earhart was not completely satisfied with Manning's marine (15 knot, sea level) capability and equipment for aerial navigation. Fred Noonan had pioneered PAA's trans-Pacific flight and had made 12 Pacific Ocean crossings plus trained junior navigators for the airline. As Noonan was looking for a job he was soon hired by Earhart.

The takeoff, burning high performance 100 octane gasoline (87 octane was the standard gasoline rating in 1937), enabled the 14,000 pound heavily overloaded airplane to become airborne in a remarkable measured distance of 1,897 feet. High test 100 octane gasoline was in limited production in the United States in 1937 and special arrangements had to be made to obtain it. On the initial flight from Oakland, Earhart carried 100 gallons although less than 50 gallons were required for the 30-40 second full power phase of takeoff. The remainder was scheduled for use on the short runway at Howland Island and the near maximum takeoff weight required for the long 2,556-mile flight to Lae, New Guinea.

The flight across the Eastern Pacific was uneventful. The two PAA flying boats which had left Alameda earlier in the afternoon were soon overtaken and left behind. A speed of 150 mph was maintained for a planned arrival at Oahu's Wheeler Field after dawn on March 18.

Two malfunctions occurred during the flight; the right hand propeller froze in a fixed pitch due to a faulty lubricant having been used and the radio transmitter's

dynamotor burned out due to prolonged high power application by Harry Manning. Oahu's Diamond Head was sighted soon after dawn after "riding in" the radio beam at Makapuu, Hawaii. Earhart acknowledged that this was a first experience using her radio direction finder but under Fred Noonan's expert navigation, Oahu Island was located without trouble.

Paul Mantz, Amelia Earhart and Fred Noonan
after arrival in Hawaii on 18 March 1937
Photo credit - Paul Mantz Collection

The Earhart Electra landed at U.S. Army Wheeler Field near Schofield Barracks in the Interior of Oahu Island, Hawaii, shortly after daybreak on 18 March 1937.

The lapsed time from Oakland to Honolulu was 15 hours 47 minutes which was a new record for the east-to-west crossing. A planned late afternoon takeoff for Howland Island had to be postponed for one day until the propellers were overhauled by Air Corps military depot personnel and the radio dynamotor replaced.

Co-pilot Paul Mantz noted that Earhart appeared to be seriously fatigued, even though she had his expert help plus an autopilot as well as the two other crew members, Noonan and Manning. Earhart was in poor shape physically, but evolving events precluded her from another night at the controls. First were the necessary correction of mechanical problems occurring on the flight. Depot overhaul of the propeller required overnight tear down, repair of internal parts and regreasing with the correct lubricant. By the following afternoon (March 19) the airplane was ready for late afternoon takeoff 24 hours behind the original schedule. At noon on the 19th, Earhart cancelled the flight "due to unsatisfactory weather." As a test flight was necessary to verify satisfactory propeller operation after the overhaul, Paul Mantz took the airplane aloft and flew over to the U.S. Army airstrip on Ford Island at the Navy base in Pearl Harbor. The reason for the change of takeoff sites was said to have been due to a better airstrip on Ford Island than at Wheeler Field.

Actually, the shift to Ford Island was an improvision to adjust to mission requirements. It is now known that the weather was satisfactory from Hawaii to Howland on the 19th. The weather was unsatisfactory not on her publicly announced route but her unannounced covert route over the Marshall Islands. The late afternoon takeoff was changed to early morning, which left very little time to find Howland Island before nighttime.

Preparing for the take-off from Ford Island, Hawaii, on 20 March 1937
Photo credit - National Archives

Subsequent events also provided that takeoff at Ford Island was not better but worse than at Wheeler. Paul Mantz took off from Wheeler without any trouble, but Earhart ground looped at Ford Island when the right landing gear support gave way over an improvised runway section of grass covered by metal mats (according to the U.S. Army Air Corps accident investigation conducted shortly after the accident). There is but little doubt that all these last minute shifts in plans were predicated on one covert reason: namely, that the weather over the target area was unsatisfactory for an overflight of the Marshall Islands. With "unsatisfactory weather," a late afternoon departure was unnecessary and takeoff from the interior of Oahu on an isolated military reservation (18 miles from Honolulu) for security reasons was unnecessary.

Crack-up at Ford Island on 20 March 1937 ended east to west world flight attempt
Photo credit - National Archives

Collapse of right main landing gear support caused ground loop
Photo credit - National Archives

Lt. Arnold True, USN, Patrol Wing Two aerologist, was aboard the USCG cutter *Shoshone* as weather forecaster. His March 19 forecast to Hawaii was clear weather all the way along the 1,800-mile flight path from Oahu to Howland Island. Imagine his surprise when Earhart cancelled the flight saying the weather was "unsatisfactory". The weather was in fact satisfactory along the announced (overt) course; it was "unsatisfactory" over the Marshall Island (covert) route.

On the next day when announcement of a surprise dawn takeoff was relayed to *Shoshone*, everyone on board could hardly believe the switch to a morning departure. An afternoon arrival in the Howland vicinity with a navigation error could cause the flight to miss Howland and force a night landing for which provisions had not been made. This eventuality didn't occur because the airplane never got airborne from Ford Island airfield.

There has been considerable debate about the March 20 aborted takeoff due to landing gear support failure and ensuing ground loop. Various "experts" have suggested over a dozen reasons for the accident ranging from overly simplistic (cross wind) to absurdly ridiculous (deliberate induced ground loop at 90 mph). This would very likely mean suicide for herself and the murder of her traveling companions in the heavily overloaded flying gasoline tank.

Earhart's own assessment that the right hand landing gear support gave way was the real reason for the ground loop. This is supported by the knowledge that the airstrip was defective where the metal mats were layed over a grass covered stretch midway down the runway where a large gap existed in the noncontinuous concrete.

After an assessment of ground loop damages, it was decided to ship the airplane back to Lockheed's Burbank factory for extensive remanufacturing of damaged airframe components.

WORLD FLIGHT ATTEMPT
(EAST TO WEST: 17 — 20 MARCH 1937)
COVERT ACTIVITIES

The overt activities of the Earhart world flight are well known from countless documented sources which have become available throughout the past half century. The covert aspects of the flights are not well known; nevertheless, over the past five decades sufficient evidence has surfaced from a multitude of credible sources to define the operation with assurance. So much of the activity is now known that the remaining (still classified) gaps are quite discernible. The situation is similar to the well-understood "jigsaw puzzle" in that as the majority of the pieces are linked together, the few remaining pieces can be readily put in place.

A logical division of the covert activities in the initial flight can be made between the Electra pre-flight preparation from the May 1936 delivery date to the 17 March 1937 departure from California in the first world-girdling flight attempt and the operational activities associated with the flight and the airplane support services provided. All of these activities have been reported by participants and documented by a score of civilian and military individuals who have voluntarily come forward and recounted the extent of their participation in this activity. These persons are not braggers or publicity seekers, but highly technical, dedicated professionals who were doing their assigned duties. These technological individuals converted the Lockheed Model 10E Electra into an extremely long-range, high-technology reconnaissance aircraft with the latest techniques and equipment. There is an exact parallel between Earhart's airplane and the later Lockheed U-2 "spy plane" used by the CIA and flown by Francis Gary Powers on 1 May 1960 over the strategic heartlands of Russia.

The conversion of the Earhart Electra occurred over a period of ten months from May 1936 delivery date to the first world flight date of March 1937. When delivered in May 1936, the airplane was a "bare-bone" configuration with the exception of a multitude of auxiliary fuselage fuel tanks which would give the airplane a cruising range of more than 4,000 miles. The chronological sequence of modifications to the basic airframe into a hi-tech machine is as follows:

Note: The sequence of major modifications includes the persons involved and their affiliation.

Summer 1936: Installation of basic aeronautical radio equipment by Western Electric including W.E. Model 13 (CB) transmitter and W.E. Model 20 receiver (and appropriate antenna) at Newark, New Jersey. W. C. Tinus, Western Electric, was the project engineer.

October 1936: At Wright Field (near Dayton, Ohio) test installations of Type Z, 75-Mc (radio range) Marker Beacon receiver (with antennas on underbelly of forward fuselage). Installation of prototype Bendix Radio Compass by company personnel and Wright Field radio technicians. (This installation included a streamlined D\F loop on top of the fuselage with a "sense" antenna on the underside of the fuselage.) Internal equipment was subsequently removed after Air Corps tests, but the underbelly "sense" antenna and "Z" type (75 Mc) Marker Beacon antenna were left installed. (Frederick J. Hooven, Bendix Vice President and Chief Engineer, Radio Products Division.)

Late 1936: Modified fuel selector transfer system to single valve control. Clarence Belinn, (National Airways, Boston, fuel management expert) also provided special fuel feed from 100-gallon wing tank to carry 100-octane gasoline for takeoff boost.

Early 1937: Modified Earhart's Wasp (Type "H") engines to burn 100-octane gasoline on takeoff for boost power for short jungle and island airstrips which would be encountered around the world.

January 1937: Installed high-capacity auxiliary storage battery in aft cabin navigation compartment for emergency radio power. (Oakland Municipal Airport, Naval Reserve hangar, Robert Myers).

February 1937: Installation of a Bendix RA-1 multi-band airborne receiver (supplied by the USN) by Joseph Gurr at Paul Mantz's Union Air Terminal hangar. According to Vernon Moore, Bendix project engineer, on the RA-1, three receivers of this advanced type were procured; one went to Earhart, the other two went to Dr. Archbold of the New York Natural History Museum, whose civilian version of a Consolidated PBY (USN long-range patrol airplane) would be flown across the Pacific to New Guinea. On the final leg, Archbold flew through the Japanese Caroline Islands over strategic Truk Atoll.

February and March 1937: U.S. Army Air Corps aerial photography specialist from Hamilton Field, San Rafael, California, installed Air Corps-developed (see General George W. Goddard's U.S. patent 1,936,595, dated 28 November 1933 on pages 155 and 156) synchronizing equipment and photoflash bomb design for aerial nighttime photography.

February 1937: U.S. Air Corps' Lt. Col. Joseph J. Pelligrini, then with the first photo mapping group at Bolling Field (Washington, D.C.), completed the sensitive assignment of drawing the guidelines on a map of some Pacific islands for cameras to be installed in a civilian aircraft "to be flown by a woman pilot . . . to take photographs in the Pacific."

Reconstruction of airplane and overhaul of equipment cost $25,000 and delayed second world flight attempt for three months
Photo credit - National Archives Negative #80-G-410136

Note: This Bolling Field photo mapping group effort to put a camera in a civilian airplane for a woman aviator to photograph Pacific Islands is important because it depicts the involvement of the U.S. Air Corps in oceanic aerial reconnaissance in 1937. This particular project was not for Earhart or her Electra because they were being aided by the photo mapping group at nearby Hamilton Field on the West Coast of the United States. Pelligrini's guidelines were for a much closer camera installation on a foreign commercial aircraft at the Naval Airfield at Norfolk, Virginia, perennial home of the U.S. fleet. The civilian aircraft was neither a U.S.-built airplane nor was its pilot an American aviatrix. (See Part Four, "The British Connection" in this volume.) Joseph Klaas/Joseph Gervais, *Amelia Earhart Lives*, pages 13-14.

OPERATIONAL PHASE

Many covert aspects were connected with the operational phase of the east-to-west world flight attempt. The departure from Oakland Airport on 100-octane gasoline was to test takeoff performance. It was remarkable, taking only 1,897 feet of runway. Less than half of the high octane gas in a special wing fuel tank was used, leaving the remainder for use on short airstrips on Howland Island, or other islands or jungle airstrips. See Earhart: *Last Flight* (p. 58)

Oahu Flight: With four fliers, role shifting had Paul Mantz flying right seat as relief pilot. New arrival Fred Noonan became main aerial navigator while Harry Manning became radio operator and check navigator. There were two military (reserve) officers aboard and they were privy to the assigned tasks. Mantz and Manning were civilians. With Mantz as relief pilot coming over, Earhart was scheduled for late afternoon departure from Oahu. Takeoff was canceled because of "unsatisfactory weather." Where the unsuitable weather was located was not stated. March 18 saw the installation of a military vertical camera in aft compartment below floorboards at U.S. Army Air Corps Wheeler Field near Schofield barracks in the interior of Oahu. March 20: After Luke Field crack-up, the airplane was defueled, engine cowling and bent propellers removed, and the airplane lifted by crane onto a flat-bed trailer and transported into an Air Corps hangar where it was placed under guard. After dark, U.S. Navy (aerial) photographer's mate Thurman Wade was detailed from Patrol Wing Two (PatWing2) to remove a military aerial camera from Earhart's airplane and transfer it to USN storage. When Thurman Wade was asked by this author, "What was she going to photograph?" he replied, "The Marshall Islands." Asked why he was so certain, he stated, "Because that was also PatWing2's mission at that time." Thurman Wade's testimony is important in that it establishes conclusively that pilots of both civilian aircraft and the PBY patrol bombers of PatWing2 were engaged in covert flying and taking aerial photographs of designated Marshall Island installations.

Aboard the USCG cutter *Shoshone*, stationed off Howland Islands, Navy PatWing2 aerologist Lt. Arnold E. True sent an en route weather report to Pearl Harbor on March 19, "Clear weather over entire route except for minor rain squalls southwest of Oahu." Lt. True was flabbergasted to hear on 1200 Honolulu radio broadcast that Earhart had canceled the flight on the 19th because of unfavorable weather at destination. In his four-page memo to the Commander of PatWing2, Lt. True could only say, "weather en route satisfactory, flight cancelled for other reason." Here is concrete evidence of using weather conditions as a cover story for actual abort reasons. What Earhart meant was that weather was unsatisfactory over the target area, which wasn't along the route to Howland, but over the Japanese Marshall Islands. This revelation from USN records is particularly significant because how did the USN know that the weather over the designated target was unsatisfactory? The only way was to have an observer on the scene and that was only feasible in 1937 by having a fleet submarine off the designated island to report local weather by radio to Pearl Harbor. (This was an assignment the silent submarine service was well equipped to provide because there were more fleet submarines at Pearl Harbor than at other U.S. naval bases.) Forward observation was the primary operational duty of submarines at Pearl Harbor in 1937.

In addition to the coal-burning tug U.S.S. *Ontario* on station halfway between Howland Island and Lae, New Guinea, there were other unreported navy ships nearby in the South Seas. Two of these were the new *Mahan* Class destroyers, the U.S.S. *Preston* (DD-379) and the U.S.S. *Smith* (DD-378). This two-ship destroyer flotilla, with Captain Charles D. Swain in command, was on a shake-down cruise from the West Coast to the South Seas and Australia and return which was the usual shake-down cruise after commissioning. Captain Swain, in recounting this cruise to this author, stated that they were under the Chief of Naval Operations (CNO) and not yet assigned to the fleet destroyers command. He said that they were "talked around by OPNAV" (Chief of Naval Operations). Instead of the usual departure date and return-to-port date with stopovers optional, they were directed from each port of call on a Washington-prescribed schedule. It can easily be seen why this was done. Checking the U.S.S. *Preston* log, the destroyers were directed to be near Suva, Fiji, the morning of March 20, which was Earhart's departure date from Hawaii.

The *Preston* and the *Smith* were only 18 hours fast steaming from Canton Island in the Phoenix Group and 24 hours from Howland. The ships had refueled at Sydney, Australia, and were topped off at Nouma, New Caledonia (not a usual port of call for United States naval ships on shake-down cruises). It is quite obvious that these two 40-knot destroyers were standing by to render assistance (if needed) to a United States airplane which might happen to end up in their vicinity. After the Luke Field crack-up, they weren't needed and were put into Suva, port city and capital of the Fiji Islands. En route home, while passing by Canton Island in the Phoenix Group, Capt. Swain called his flotilla to General Quarters (this is not a drill) and opened fire with their main batteries against designated targets. General Quarters in mid-ocean in peace time seems odd, but perhaps Capt. Swain had his reasons. It is not difficult to see what he was doing in the Howland/Baker/Canton Island area. What is much more important is that the U.S.S. *Preston* would return to these same waters later in the year on a really important mission which was subsequently completed.

In summary, based on the extensive evidence accumulated over the past half century, the overt/covert aspects of the Earhart flights can now be stated. The late afternoon takeoff of the Howland flight was predicated on an overflight of the Marshall Islands. After a delay of two days attributed to unsatisfactory weather, the overflight was cancelled and, much to the surprise of the personnel aboard the USCG cutter *Shoshone*, the following morning an unscheduled takeoff was attempted.

Although the designated targets in the Marshalls for the March 1937 flight are not precisely known, an approach from the northeast suggests that Wotje Island was the prime target with Jaluit Island a possible second location. After the overflight detour, the Electra would be flown to either Baker Island or Canton Island in the nearby Phoenix Group so the actual elapsed time of the flight could be concealed.

The importance of the "weather factor" over the photographic target can be clearly seen in that the weather along the "announced" course could not have forced a mission postponement but only covertly reported unsuitable local weather over the target which could only be known from the silent (submarine) service on the scene.

Finally, knowledge that there were naval ships unreported to the public in a position to support the final phases of the flight is significant and would be an important factor in the second world flight attempt and the Earhart disappearance.

Amelia Earhart signing flight covers.
Operational costs of flights were defrayed by
commercialization and donations.
Photo credit - Smithsonian Institution's
National Air & Space Museum Negative #71-1056

INTERLUDE

The fliers returned to the West Coast aboard S.S. *Malolo* (Matson liner) the same day as the accident. The airplane was prepared for ocean shipment aboard the S.S. *Lurline* as deck cargo. The U.S. Army presented a bill to the Putnams of $1,048 for the work performed on the aircraft. George Putnam eventually sent a letter and check to the U.S. Army. Off-loaded on a dock at Wilmington, California, the airplane was trucked across Los Angeles to the San Fernando Valley and the Lockheed plant at Burbank.

Clarence "Kelly" Johnson and Harvey Christen headed up an engineering team to rebuild (restore) the airplane to tiptop shape. A number of changes were made. Heavier landing gear supports and tires were installed. Appropriate parts of the airplane structure were X-rayed with special portable industrial X-ray equipment. The right wing was replaced by one from a production line Electra.

The Wasp commercial engines were sent to Pacific Airmotive at the nearby Union Air Terminal for disassembly and overhaul. The damaged propellers were replaced. The reported cost was $25,000 and took about six weeks although the required engineering started soon after the decision to rebuild had been reached and Lockheed notified.

The remanufacture was conducted in a separate hangar on a two-shift basis. Several people who were active on the program have reported that they were pledged to secrecy. Lockheed refused to give an itemized accounting of the repairs accomplished, the costs and who actually paid for the repairs. Neither the Putmans nor Purdue paid these capital costs, and Lockheed wasn't a non-profit institution. The only conclusion is that the U.S. Government paid the costs for the remanufacture ($25,000) and probably the costs were absorbed on existing U.S. Air Corps contracts for Electra aircraft.

Those workers interviewed, who were willing to talk, mentioned engine changes, an aerial camera mount, electrical control equipment for camera operation and radio equipment modifications including a lengthened "Vee" antenna on top of the fuselage. Obviously, structural repair of an airplane which had ground looped was not reason enough for pledging secrecy. It was some specialized secret equipment which had been installed in the airplane under government direction which made the entire operation classified.

Earhart has accounted for the three months' interlude between the first east-to-west flight (March) and the west-to-east final flight (June). It can be shown using Earhart's own text *Last Flight* that the "weather" factor to which she attributed the directional change was little more than a cover story.

It is true that initially a west-to-east course was planned possibly because of the use of established airline routes all the way to Lae, New Guinea. As the route shifted to an equatorial route across the mid-section of Africa, it became evident that leaving the Pacific crossing as the final phase of the flight would "introduce a fatigue factor of unknown magnitude." Other factors like the known prevailing headwinds westbound to Honolulu which grounded many clipper flights were negated with the more efficient land airplane. By late 1936 or early 1937, the westerly route was firmly established and provisions to satisfy its requirements accomplished. In mid-March weather such as hurricanes, monsoons and typhoons along the equatorial route finally selected were not major problems, but by June when the second flight started they were a more significant factor. However, by itself, "weather" was not of such a magnitude as to be a flight path reversal factor. It was just a convenient "half truth" useful as a cover story. Why this is apparent is as follows:

The significant weather factors were, in order of importance:

1. The monsoon "season", beginning in June in the eastern Indian Ocean, particularly the Bay of Bengal.

2. The Gulf of Mexico spawn hurricanes summer and early fall. Easily avoided by using the Central America route.

3. Completely unpredictable typhoons in the South Seas. Recently, Fiji, which might experience one every three to five years on the average had three typhoons in one year. They occur in the summer but when they happen one worries about them and detours around them.

4. Equatorial Africa and India develop sand storms. French and British airways across Africa had adequate weather forecasting and the airplane had adequate range, height capability and performance to fly around or over any adverse weather encountered on this route.

One of the more perplexing features of the Earhart second round-the-world attempt was the switch from the earlier March east-to-west direction to the June west-to-east course. The reason given for this shift of direction was anticipated weather to be encountered en route. Crossing the Carribean in early June would dodge the summer hurricane period and in southeast Asia the monsoon/typhoon season would be negated. This sounds good but is in fact the usual "cover story." In the first place, she would have flown through the monsoon/typhoon belt (the most serious weather problems) sooner by staying with the original east-to-west route. As far as Carribean hurricanes, she had already planned out an alternate course following the Central American airways which bypassed the Carribean completely. Other seasonal weather; such as the rainy season in northeast South America, equatorial Africa's sandstorms and the Arabian area monsoon winds were variable and unpredictable. While weather was a factor, it was only one of several. Much more important were (1) personnel fatigue, (2) airplane condition, (3) engine reliability, (4) radio coordination, (5) weather forecasting (Pacific Ocean), (6) long over water stretches, (7) nighttime flying, and (8) approach to Marshall Islands delayed an additional month.

Regardless of the noted, repeated delays en route almost caused Earhart to be weathered in for two months at Burma due to the monsoon season. Only a fortunate and timely break in the monsoon deluge allowed her to pass through and skirt the weather by flying around it. Desert dust storms were also encountered in India and southwestern United States which she simply flew over. The serious weather problems she encountered clearly show the route reversal actually compounded rather than alleviated the problem. Therefore, some other reason was behind the change of direction.

One of the main reasons weather became a problem was that instead of using the long-range capability of the airplane as the flight progressed, Earhart reverted more and more to short legs; dawn to noon, dawn to dusk. This forced her to use inadequate airfields and carry less fuel and impaired her capability of dodging bad weather. Consider the following essentially unnecessary stops: Caripito, Fortaleza, St. Louis, El Flasher, Messawa, Assab, Sourabya and Koepang. These eight stops added over a week to her itinerary. Instead of taking off from Lae, New Guinea for the Pacific legs on June 25 as originally planned, it was July 2 before she finally departed for the Pacific Ocean crossing.

Several Earhart researchers have surmised that the weather alibi for the route reverse was a sham but have not attempted to establish a rationale to verify its falsity and establish the true reason why it was accomplished. One reason given was to facilitate overflight of Japanese territory. If the Japanese had been seriously concerned by an Earhart overflight, the three months delay (April-June) would have given them extra time to get ships, high frequency D\F equipment and float-equipped aircraft into the eastern Carolinas and Marshalls. We now know that instead of bringing anything in, ships there were recalled to Japan in support of the invasion of the Chinese mainland.

Why then the course change that caused such consternation, cost, and disruption? Why her leisurely dawn-to-dusk routine, using an airplane with a 3,000-4,000 mile range for 150-500 mile short hops? Did she suddenly become a Sunday pilot or weekend aviatrix on a sightseeing tour as she seems to portray in her book, *Last Flight*? Absolutely not! She was on a mission which was being externally directed by others. The British military was interested in the airfields of Eritrea: Asmara, Massawa and Assab from 1935 until Italian East Africa was conquered in World War II. She almost blew this assignment by late afternoon photography of Asmara airplanes. External sources had pushed back her takeoff date from Lae, New Guinea, from June 25 to July 2, 1937. An extra week was needed for some corollary activity to her flight. The *Itasca*, *Ontario* and *Swan* were "on station" on June 25 and were treading water.

The week's delay was caused by the British connection. Available evidence indicates that in late March the British had decided to participate in the Marshalls overflight, with Wotje Island as their designated target. They had to procure and prepare a suitable airplane, ship it to its takeoff point, train its crew and be ready for a Marshall Island overflight in three short months.

The three-month interlude between the two world flights is indicative of the entire Earhart episode. There are many legitimate questions which can be asked and no satisfactory answers available after half a century. Questions asked herein include:

1. Who really paid the capital costs of $25,000 to rebuild the airplane?

2. Were "weather factors" the real reason for the course reversal when actual weather encountered en route refute this rationale?

3. Based on multiple testimony of individuals involved in the refurbishing of the airplane, why were secrecy pledges demanded of the restorers?

This series of unanswered questions are representative of the entire episode. From the initial capital costs of the airplane and its expensive equipment ($85,000) until the final landing (splashdown) and subsequent deaths of the fliers, there are many questions and few answers. The respective abilities of the fliers, Noonan as a navigator and Earhart as a pilot, were discredited by the government to support its contention that they got lost and died at sea. Justice cannot be served until every shred of evidence is examined in detail and the truth is established.

WEST-TO-EAST WORLD FLIGHT ATTEMPT

The remanufacture of the Earhart Electra was completed at Lockheed on 19 May 1937 and test flown by the company's check pilot Marshall Healey. The airplane was then delivered to Earhart at the Paul Mantz hangar facility at Union Air Terminal. The following day, 20 May, Earhart, Paul Mantz and mechanic R. D. "Bo" McKneely departed from Burbank for Oakland to check out the repaired airplane. At Oakland, the post office delivered the second group of "Flight Covers" to help defray the operational costs of the rescheduled flight. Fred Noonan remained behind at Burbank making final corrections and updates to his world aeronautical charts. After loading the flight covers, Earhart and crew returned to Burbank after an overnight stay. Earhart and Bo McKneely were joined by navigator Noonan and George Putnam. Paul Mantz departed the same day for an aeronautical show with stunt flier Tex Rankin in the middle west. Paul Mantz's duties as technical advisor for Earhart were finished but he didn't realize it at the time.

**Amelia Earhart with mechanic
R. D. "Bo" McKneely and Fred Noonan
at Miami on 31 May 1937**
*Photo credit - Smithsonian Institution's
National Air & Space Museum Negative #71-1059*

The eastward flight flew to Tucson, Arizona, where an engine fire was quickly extinguished with an onboard Lox fire bottle. Inspection and minor repairs to the nacelle components delayed the flight east until the following day. Morning departure encountered a southwestern desert sandstorm. Trouble was avoided by flying high over the blowing sand. Arriving at New Orleans, George Putnam departed the flight for a business appointment in New York City and later joined the crew on the nine-day layover at Miami, Florida. At Miami, last minute modifications were made to the airplane equipment. The principal attention was given to the radio installation which was considered unsatisfactory. Also the Sperry autopilot was overhauled. Bo McKneely gave the engines a good tuneup and checked mechanical systems operation. Several test flights were made to verify the

adequacy of the repair/modifications to the airplane. Unneeded and redundant equipment was removed.

**Amelia Earhart testing radio receiver
in Electra cockpit**
*Photo credit - Smithsonian Institution's
National Air & Space Museum Negative #71-1052*

**Amelia Earhart in the Electra cockpit on
1 June 1937 - prior to overseas departure**
*Photo credit - Smithsonian Institution's
National Air & Space Museum Negative #80-3187*

32

Before beginning a week long modification to the radio equipment, antennas and radio navigation equipment, a two-hour conference was held between Pan American radio personnel and Earhart. Pan American employees led by Al Gray told her there was no way that satisfactory communication and D\F work could be maintained for the flight she intended to make with inadequate equipment installed. (In stripping the plane for the long flight, the trailing antenna and weight were removed as a weight-saving measure, leaving only a small "V" communication antenna strung between the forward fuselage and twin tails.)

After the 500 kc emergency frequency was deactivated, Pan American personnel suggested their Pacific Ocean frequency be utilized so that their highly efficient radio direction finding equipment could track her course. Earhart's response was, "I don't need that, I have my own navigator." On May 31, Miami Pan American Airways technicians completed eight days of effort preparing the airplane for the overseas flight. On June 1, Amelia Earhart's silver airplane was ready on the concrete runway at Miami. Bo McKneely had just finished the last job on it and would accompany the plane no further. Noonan climbed into the cockpit, and Amelia's husband wished her well.

After a routine takeoff, they headed for Puerto Rico with the bright morning sun shining in their eyes. An hour later they were over Andros Island, and from the islands of the Bahamas would appear continuously until they were all flown over. A one o'clock landing was made without incident at San Juan, Puerto Rico. They remained the night at the residence of a friend and departed at seven the next morning across the Caribbean for Caripito, Venezuela. En route they saw little of the sea because of heavy clouds until the coast of Venezuela was seen through a heavy haze cover.

From San Juan, Earhart initially planned to fly nonstop to Paramaribo, Dutch Guiana, but a late takeoff (5:50 a.m. EST) and construction shortening the available runway (limiting the amount of fuel the Electra was able to carry) changed the flight plan. Instead, the trip was made in two legs, the first being 750 miles to Caripito, Venezuela. The leg from San Juan was primarily over rain forest and the Atlantic Ocean. This terrain, with its lack of emergency landing sites, persisted as far as Fortaleza, causing Earhart some concern. Other than some headwinds encountered while cruising at 8,000 feet, everything went well, and the Electra touched down four and a half hours later at the Caripito airfield, which was managed jointly by PAA and the Standard Oil Company.

Amelia Earhart departing from Caripito, Venezuela, on 3 June 1937
Photo credit - Smithsonian Institution's National Air & Space Museum Negative #71-1060

They refueled at the red tile-roofed town of Caripito and took off on the next flight leg to Paramaribo. They flew over dense jungles for many miles where an emergency landing would be very dangerous. Paramaribo, Brazil, was located on the seacoast and a landing was made on a jungle airport used by Pan American Airways. After leaving Caripito, the weather turned bad with occasional showers. Earhart once again cruised at 8,000 feet, battling headwinds to avoid the rainy weather. The rain cleared as they neared the coast of Dutch Guiana, and they landed safely at Paramaribo, a 750-mile flight.

The following day the fliers departed Paramaribo at 6:10 a.m. (EST) for the 1,330-mile flight to Fortaleza, Brazil, crossing the equator for the first time, and later the mighty Amazon River. The night was spent at a Paramaribo hotel, leaving the next morning for Fortaleza. Their route south followed the coast of Brazil and on this portion of their journey, Amelia had the thrill of both crossing the equator and the delta of the Amazon River. The Pan American Airways' facility was used at Fortaleza to prepare the airplane for a South Atlantic Ocean crossing.

At Fortaleza, final preparations were made for the cross-Atlantic flight. Earhart and Noonan stopped one day to allow PAA mechanics to do an oil change, fix a minor gasoline leak, and perform other routine maintenance. Earhart and Noonan took advantage of the stopover to rest and make personal preparations for the flight ahead.

Logistics support of world flight required fuel supplies at all potential stops. Local Stanavo representative discusses fuel requirements.
Photo credit - Smithsonian Institution's National Air & Space Museum Negative #80-3183

Departing at 4:50 (EST) the following day for the short flight to Natal, the Electra ran into some rain squalls, but still completed the trip in a little over two hours. The large airfield at Natal was the major "jumping off" point for the South Atlantic airline crossings, and Earhart planned to benefit from the facilities there. On the advice of experienced transatlantic pilots, she cancelled her planned evening takeoff, bowing to their advice to cover the first 800 miles of the route, apt to have the worst weather, during daylight hours. The next morning, they

Electra operated from primitive airfields in many parts of the world
Photo credit - Smithsonian Institution's National Air & Space Museum Negative #74-9260

flew to Natal, where they were delayed for two days by tropical rains. With clearance they departed on the long 1,900-mile overwater flight across the South Atlantic to the west coast of Africa. The dangerous flight was made without mishap, but due to a navigation error by Earhart, the plane was landed at St. Louis, Senegal, instead of Daka. The flight took thirteen hours and twelve minutes. A week prior they had been in the United States, later in South America, and then the continent of Africa.

Earhart remained in St. Louis one day so that a malfunctioning fuel-flow meter could be repaired. The next morning the Electra made the hop to Dakar, French West Africa, 163 miles north. There they prepared for the trans-African flight. Air France personnel again offered their assistance, including maps, weather forecasts, and mechanical care for the airplane.

It is now known that Earhart was suffering from dysentery during the latter stages of her trip. One of the persistent, decades-old allegations associated with her demise has this dread tropical disease being the ultimate cause of her death. It is known that the Dutch doctors at Bandoeng diagnosed her condition soon after her arrival in Java on June 21. As it takes between 10 to 14 days to tell whether the symptoms are the common "travelers curse" or the much more serious dysentery, it is evident that she must have contacted the dreaded bacteria somewhere in equatorial Africa between Dakar and El Fasher in French Africa. One pioneer airline pilot and Pan American Airways veteran of the South American pestilence ridden tropical towns had something interesting to say. In Grooch's book *Skyway to Asia,* 1936, page 14, he said, "I'd been away from the states for five years (South America) and it was grand to be home for a while where you didn't have to boil every drop of water

and where it wasn't suicide to eat fresh vegetables". Somewhere in this equatorial zone, Earhart's "shinning adventure" became tarnished.

The Electra departed eastward at six o'clock the next day. The threat of tornado-like winds along the planned southern route shifted the flight north, flying for Gao, French Sudan, 1,100 miles distant. They arrived safely after seven hours, fifty minutes in the air.

From Gao, Earhart traveled 1,140 miles over barren desert and later Lake Chad to Fort Lamy. The-Gao-to-Lamy stretch was very easy for Earhart—the weather was settled (if hot) and there were plenty of places to make a forced landing had it been necessary. But for Noonan, the poor maps made it impossible to use the "landmark to landmark" method of overland navigation. Instead, he was forced once again to rely on celestial navigation. Despite these problems the Electra landed safely at Fort Lamy at 12:55 p.m. (GMT).

From El Fasher the next day Earhart flew deeper into unmapped territory to Khartoum, crossing 500 miles of barren terrain. Earhart landed only briefly in Khartoum, then continued on to Massawa in Italian Eritrea, landing there that evening.

ERITREA AIRFIELD RECONNAISSANCE
It now appears certain that the major change of itinerary between the March and May/June flights was the Eritrea detour. This deviation from the world flight was totally unnecessary to the stated objectives of the flight. What is obvious is that it afforded an opportunity to examine all three of Italian Eritrea's military/commercial airfields: Massawa, Assam and the large strategic airfield in the suburbs of the capital city of Asmara. On the earlier flight Earhart was scheduled to land at the Royal Air Force airbase at Aden (a British protectorate near the mouth of

After being denied landing rights in Eritrea for March 1937 flight, Amelia Earhart received clearance through her friend, Italian Air Marshal Italo Balbo, in time for June flight.
Photo credit - National Archives Negative #306-NT 279C 43

Local authorities aided fliers at overnight stops in many parts of the world
Photo credit - Smithsonian Institution's National Air & Space Museum Negative #85-14511

the Red Sea). From there she was to fly across Eritrea but not land at any of the three airfields. For the June flight path, a significant alteration in itinerary was made. The RAF base was bypassed in favor of Assab on the Red Sea. The important airfield at Massawa, also on the Red Sea, was visited. Both of these locales were on the so-called British "Lifeline of Empire". In addition, the very large airfield at inland Asmara (reported as being the largest in Africa) was flown over and observed on the overflight from British Khartoum (Anglo Egyptian Sudan) which was also a Royal Air Force base. Navigator Fred Noonan's actual flight charts of the Khartoum (Sudan to Italian Massawa flight) clearly show a significant variance from a direct point-to-point flight path to fly over many strategic points of interest (not to the United States but to the British military whose generosity made the African equatorial segment of the world flight possible). This exchange of favors is known in diplomatic circles as *quid pro quo*.

The next day Earhart made a brief flight from Massawa to Assab to prepare for the long flight to India. The next morning before dawn Earhart and Noonan took off, crossing more of Eritrea, the Red Sea, and thence over southeast Arabia. Earhart followed the coast of this desolate wasteland, as British authorities were concerned about a forced landing in the middle of the desert; but the Electra landed safely in Karachi.

Earhart chose to stop at Karachi for two days so the Electra could be serviced with parts shipped from the United States. Karachi was the logical choice for repairs, since it was one of the largest airports in Asia. It was one of the main stopovers from Europe to Australia-Asia.

The Electra lifted off on schedule at dawn, headed for Dum Dum Airport, Calcutta. Navigation over this well-mapped, 1,350-mile route was easy and the weather was clear; the Electra landed safely in humid Calcutta at about four that afternoon.

During the night a monsoon struck. Monsoons are heavy rainstorms that are typical of the south of Asia from June to September. This particular storm had left the field dangerously wet. But meteorologists warned that further rain was expected, perhaps soaking the field beyond use. Earhart decided to risk going on. The takeoff was as difficult as everyone had feared, the Electra barely getting airborne in time. The flight made it to Akayab safely, barely stopping to take on fuel before again becoming airborne. Earhart had hoped to reach Bangkok, but the monsoons struck again, forcing them to return to Akayab.

Earhart and Noonan departed Akayab at about 3:30 a.m. (GMT) the next morning, again hoping to reach Bangkok, but again bad weather cut the flight short. At approximately 6:30 a.m. (GMT) the Electra set down to refuel in Rangoon, 300 miles from Akayab. A heavy rain began falling after landing, making takeoff for Bangkok hazardous, so Earhart elected to delay takeoff to the next day and spent the rest of the day sightseeing instead.

By the next morning the heavy weather had cleared and Earhart flew on over high mountain areas to Bangkok. After a brief stop there to refuel, she continued on over water and land to Singapore, arriving in the late afternoon.

Earhart and Noonan departed Singapore early the next morning for Bandoeng, Java, 646 miles distant. Their course once again took them over open sea and dense jungle, renewing Earhart's fears should a force landing be necessary during the approximately 4 1/2 hours in the air. The Electra followed the coast of Sumatra, then later crossed the equator for the third time in the flight, landing safely on the volcano-ringed isle of Java that afternoon at about 4:30 a.m. (GMT).

Once again, the Electra's engines received expert mechanical care, this time from the mechanics of KNILM (sister airline to Netherlands Airline, KLM).

The next day saw one of the few instances of mechanical delay on the flight. While preparing for takeoff at 3:45 a.m. (local time), Earhart noticed that an instrument appeared to be malfunctioning. Not until 2:00 p.m. that afternoon was the problem corrected, leaving only enough time to fly to Saurabaya, on the east coast of Java. But further instrument problems appeared on the flight, leading to a return to Bandoeng the next day so the KNILM technicians could correct the problem.

Earhart's change of itinerary from Batavia, Java (March 1937), to Bandoeng, Java (June 1937), was to use the extensive commercial and military aviation repair facilities available at the Dutch East Indies Colony. Francis Oliver Furman, Martin Airplane Company technical representative at Bandoeng was hired by Earhart to oversee mechanical work on her airplane by Dutch aviation mechanics. Furman was Martin agent to the Dutch military as a consultant on the 100 Martin twin engine bombers stationed in the Dutch East Indies. The lengthy Bandoeng stop was announced as the periodic inspection and necessary overhaul of the airplane's engines. In addition, the Cambridge Exhaust Gas Analyzer required overhaul which delayed the flight an additional two days. According to testimony by Furman, several significant events happened while the airplane and fliers were at Bandoeng. In addition to being overhauled, the engines were modified to improve their performance. High gear ratio blower gear was installed in the engines to enhance their performance under takeoff and altitude use. Minor modifications were made to enable the use of 100-octane gasoline for boosted power takeoff. In addition to these mechanical changes, relelations were reported by Furman. He has stated that Earhart's "traveler's curse" ailment had been diagnosed as dysentery which is an often fatal disease in the tropics. Furman also revealed that Earhart requested that he accompany her flight back to the United States. He declined this offer because he was under contract as a technical representative to the Martin Company and did not want to break his contract with them.

The following day, with all instruments once again functional, the Electra departed Bandoeng, hoping to reach Port Darwin, Australia. But once again the flight had to be cut short, this time at Keopang, Timor. Crossing Java, Bali, and the Arafura Sea, land masses becoming more arid as they proceeded south, the Electra landed safely in Koepang. The next day the fliers crossed the Timor Sea from Toepang to Port Darwin on the northern coast of Australia. The 3 1/2 hour flight was uneventful.

The 24 hours spent at Port Darwin, Australia, were quite eventful according to evidence accumulated over the past half century. Earhart arrived with an inoperative radio receiver. An Australia Air Force radio mechanic, Sergeant Rose identified the problem as a blown fuse in the equipment's dynamotor power source and replaced the fuse. Reportedly, the seven hours Earhart spent at the Darwin public health facility was to clarify a deficiency in her immunization record. This was obviously a cover story; actually the extensive time was to treat her dysentery ailment. Darwin was in the semi-tropics and the disease was a health problem there. It is now apparent that several items of military reconnaissance equipment were installed at Darwin in preparation for the trans-Pacific

crossing. The *quid pro quo* for this cooperation was the subsequent sharing of Mandated Islands north of the equator as revealed in a Smith's Weekly front page article (shown on page 119 of this book). Lockheed demonstration pilot Moye Stephens was in the Port Darwin area when the Earhart Electra flew through. He was hired by Lockheed to demonstrate use of the new constant speed propellers being installed in the Electras operated by Australian and later New Zealand airlines. Stephens has stated that Earhart almost clipped a row of trees at the end of the Darwin airfield on takeoff. After switching from the power boosting 100-octane gasoline used for getting airborne to the standard 87-octane gasoline, the power curve drops off and the airplane sinks temporarily until flying speed picks up. This sinking tendency was also reported at Lae, New Guinea, three days later when the airplane almost settled into the ocean after a 100-octane boost takeoff.

Amelia Earhart arrives at Lae, New Guinea, with a happy smile
Photo credit - National Archives

The next leg was the nearly eight-hour flight from Port Darwin to Lae, New Guinea. They followed the northern coast of Australia for a time, then completed the 1,200-mile flight over the Arafura Sea, flying over the capital of Port Moresby and from there on to Lae, on the eastern coast of New Guinea.

Earhart covered the 1,200-mile distance from Port Darwin, Australia to Lae, New Guinea, in seven hours and 43 minutes. She departed from Lae on her last flight on 2 July 1937 at 1000 GMT. The three days spent at Lae have been reported in considerable detail over the past five decades. The report of an Australian Civil Aviation regional officer is comprehensive and factual. He has reported every significant detail of a technical nature which transpired from touch-down to subsequent takeoff. The amount of fuel carried and the provisions for the use of 100-octane for takeoff boost are stated in his report. In addition, Guinea Airlines radio operator who ran the local radio station has described to several researchers his three-day contact with Earhart with radio details of her subsequent flight from Lae. He flew a local radio check flight with her on July 2 and was offered an opportunity to fly with her to the United States as radio operator. This offer was not consummated. A Lae radio operator did

Amelia Earhart deplanes at New Guinea prior to Pacific Ocean crossing attempt
Photo credit - National Archives

Prior to departure from Lae, New Guinea, Amelia Earhart and Fred Noonan visit with Eric Chater, manager of Guinea Air Service, and his wife
Photo credit - National Archives

maintain a lengthy eight-hour radio schedule after her departure from Lae. For over eight hours from 1000 GMT takeoff until night fall he maintained hourly scheduled communications with her. For a shocking revelation, compare this perfect example of correct radio procedure with the July 2 fiasco with the USCG cutter *Itasca* off

Howland Island. The radio experience from Lae 800 miles on course clearly shows the capability of the 6210 kc daytime frequency for which the airplane radio was optimized. When Earhart changed frequency to 3105 kc he never contacted her again. It is now known that Fred Noonan was not drunk when the flight began as has been reported. Actually, he did get little sleep the night prior to departure. He flew up to the Guinea gold fields at Wau for the joys of a typical mining town. The decision to detour the flight to Nauru Island to use its nighttime lights as a mid-course navigation check point is largely due to Harry Balfour giving the fliers a radiogram describing the availability of a light beacon and island mining lights visible during the night at Nauru Island. The decision to detour to Nauru seems certain because technical representative Furman has testified that while at Java Noonan was greatly concerned about navigating the 2,556 miles from Lae to Howland. Conversely, at Lae he was unconcerned.

Last Flight ends with the following prophetic paragraph.

"Not much more than a month ago I was on the other shore of the Pacific, looking westward. This evening, I looked eastward over the Pacific. In those fast-moving days which have intervened, the whole width of the world has passed behind us—except this broad ocean. I shall be glad when we have the hazards of its navigation behind us."

ANALYSIS OF THE SECOND WORLD FLIGHT ATTEMPT

The following sections contain information about the Electra, the route, what really occurred during specified legs of the route and at various stops on the world flight, and a probable scenario about the overflight of the Marshall Islands. Information not included in the pages of *Last Flight* is of much interest and concerns the disappearance of the famous pilot and her navigator.

EARHART'S FLIGHT LOG
(Second attempt: May - July 1937)

May 20	Oakland, California: Flight begins.
May 21	Tucson, Arizona: Left engine caught fire after refueling. Blaze quickly extinguished, and only small repairs necessary.
May 22	New Orleans, Louisiana: Overnight.
May 23-31	Miami, Florida: Final adjustments to Electra equipment.
June 1	San Juan, Puerto Rico: First 1,000 miles of flight and first stretch of ocean crossed.
June 2	Caripito, Venezuela: Overnight.
June 3	Paramaribo, Dutch Guiana: Overnight
June 4-5	Fortaleza, Brazil: Reached after flying over 950 miles of jungle and 380 miles of ocean. (10 hours) Overnight.
June 5	Short flight to Natal.
June 6	Natal, Brazil: Electra loaded with 900 gallons of gasoline for 1,900-mile leg over South Atlantic (13 hours, 12 minutes).
June 7	St. Louis, Senegal, French West Africa: Overnight.
June 8	Dakar, Senegal: Two-day layover to rest and study weather conditions and maps. Engine check, fuel meter repaired.

June 10	Gao, Mali: 1,140-mile flight from Dakar. Overnight.
June 11	Fort Lamy, Chad, French Equatorial Africa: 1,000 miles from Dakar. Overnight.
June 12	El Fasher, Anglo-Egyptian Sudan: Overnight.
June 13	Khartoum, Anglo-Egyptian Sudan.
June 13	Massawa, Eritrea.
June 13-14	Assab, Eritrea: Two-day layover.
June 15	Karachi, India (Pakistan): Two-day stop after Electra spanned two seas, the Red and Arabian, on 1,950-mile flight from Assab. Mechanics from British Imperial Airways and Royal Air Force instrument specialists put the plane back into top condition.
June 17	Calcutta, India: Overnight. After 1,400-mile flight from Karachi.
June 18-19	Akyab, Burma: Overnight.
June 20	Rangoon, Burma.
June 20	Bangkok, Siam (Thailand).
June 20	Singapore: Overnight. Reached after battling torrential rainstorms.
June 21-27	Bandoeng, Java, Dutch East Indies: An American engine specialist, Francis O. Furman, and a crew of Dutch mechanics worked on Electra engines. (On June 24, Amelia and Fred flew to Surabaya, but returned to Bandoeng because of difficulties with engine and navigation instruments. This repair took two more days. Dysentery diagnosed at Dutch medical facility (Earhart).
June 27	Koepang, Island of Timor, Indonesia: Overnight after five-hour flight from Bandoeng.
June 28	Port Darwin, Australia: Overnight. Seven hours at Darwin medical facility (dysentery treatment). Parachutes were shipped back to the United States because they would be of no use on long over-the-water flights.
June 29-30	Lae, New Guinea: About 7,000 miles remaining. Airplane repairs and test flight.
July 1	The next flight to Howland Island would be the most difficult: 2,556 miles over open water.

On the morning of 1 July 1937, Amelia Earhart enters Electra for her last flight from Lae, New Guinea

Photo credit - Smithsonian Institution's National Air & Space Museum Negative #4453

MIAMI PREPARATIONS

Earhart, Noonan, and McKneely arrived at Miami Municipal Airport on Sunday afternoon, May 23, "for a final week of preparations," for the overseas portion of the second world flight attempt. Actually, it was eight days (not including the days of arrival and departure, June 1), before she left Miami for points south. Pan American Airways president Juan Trippe had offered to make available that airline's extensive resources, including the Miami overhaul facilities (for both landplanes and seaplanes). This was an offer Earhart gladly accepted and publicly acknowledged PAA's generosity. What were these final preparations that required eight days to complete? Overtly they were:

1. Install radio range equipment (G. P. P. in *Los Angeles Times*, May 23, 1937.) (Test flight equipment performance.)
2. Remove redundant radio equipment and other unneeded equipment.
3. Simplify radio equipment operation. (Test flight.)

Underbelly radio antennas provide radio engineers with valuable clues to equipment on board the Electra
Photo credit - National Archives

4. Overhaul autopilot. (Test flight required.)
5. Repair fire-related damage in left engine nacelle and replace lox bottle. (Fire extinguisher.)
6. Final engine tune-up by "Bo" McKneely.
7. Miscellaneous unspecified minor repairs, adjustments and cargo sorting.

Many of these final preparations and the reasons they were done have not been fully understood and for good reason. In the first place, the radio range equipment available in 1937 was only operable when used domestically on established Civil Aeronautics Administration (CAA) radio ranges. Each country with radio ranges had its own type of equipment and unique frequencies. They were not compatible with each other. So this type of equipment was installed just before going overseas. Further, Earhart didn't understand how to efficiently operate the radio equipment she already had. (Noonan didn't trust radio navigational aids at all and

refused to use them.) Thus, additional problems were added.

In simplifying the radio, she maximized on the daylight channel of 6210 kilocycles, limited the nighttime channel of 3105 kilocycles to 250 miles, and essentially deactivated the 500-kilocycle emergency channel. Her logic appeared to be that she was only flying during daylight hours (except on the longer over-water segments) where voice might be understood (at the British air bases, colonies, and commercial airfields). Over the oceans where maritime radio messages were sent in Morse Code, she and Noonan couldn't communicate by telegraph key, so the keys were removed from the aircraft. Earhart had a fatalistic philosophy about flying and the risks involved. She wanted to fly and accepted the risks as inevitable. Several times she said that when she "popped off" she hoped it would be at the controls of her beloved airplane on one of her shining adventures. On the world flights, Bradford Washburn, an experienced flyer she first contacted to be her navigator/photographer, looked at her itinerary and in a matter of minutes spotted Howland Island as the critical locale. The evidence suggests Earhart never did and trusted to luck in finding this needle in a haystack.

MIAMI, FLORIDA, RADIO CHANGES

A "Z" type marker beacon receiver was installed.

It was well known that Earhart, Putnam, and their technical advisor Paul Mantz were not satisfied with the low-power Western Electric radio gear and its installation. (Actually, Earhart herself was part of the problem.) At the PAA base for landplanes at Miami, radio shop employees were asked to "optimize the radio equipment" in a week's time.

Earhart told them she was going to mainly make short daytime hops, and would maintain limited schedules en route. She would transmit at 0015 and 0045, listen on the hour and half hour (0000 and 0030), and transmit (voice) on the quarter hour.

On the South Atlantic leg she would take off shortly after midnight to arrive at Africa in the late afternoon. Apparently, little thought was given at this stage to the 2,556 miles from Lae, New Guinea, to Howland Island or the 2,400 miles from Honolulu to Oakland (the latter being somewhat of a milk run by 1937).

The point is that she, with her acquired "logic," ignored the really dangerous leg to make it easy on herself by optimizing her equipment for the majority of daytime flights.

In the air, in space, and on the sea, it is wise to plan for the "worst case" possibility—that's what will kill you. A chain is only as strong as its weakest link. Earhart, a stunt flier, counted on luck to get her to Howland. From the very start she had been warned that Howland Island (her designated mid-Pacific landfall) was the "crux" of the flight. That advice went unheeded. Twice she tried and twice she failed to reach Howland for whatever reason.

In catering to her stated wishes, the PAA radio personnel optimized her "V" antenna to tune to her daytime frequency of 6210 kilocycles for maximum strength because it would be used most of the time. This is borne out by Balfour's experience at Lae, New Guinea. He copied her on 6210 kilocycles for 800 miles, and when she switched to 3105, she was gone. In other words, the radiation power in the mismatched nighttime frequency was only 250 miles (ground wave). As far as 500 kilocycles was concerned, the radiated power was nil. This was a marine frequency and code was used almost exclusively. She couldn't send Morse Code and thus failed to use the international distress frequency. The PAA radio technicians gave her what she wanted, maximum power on 6210 kilocycles, moderate power on 3105, and minimum power on 500.

SOUTH ATLANTIC CROSSING (7 JUNE 1937)

Second only to the Lae, New Guinea, to Howland Island "final flight," the South Atlantic crossing from South America to the west coast of Africa has received the most comments during the past decades. The principal reason for this is that Earhart's apparent disregard for Noonan's instructions resulted in missing their designated landfall by 163 miles. Instead of landing at the announced destination of Dakar, French West Africa, they did, in fact, land at St. Louis, Senegal, 163 miles northward along the African coast. In her record of the flight she acknowledged that the navigational error was her fault and that if she had followed Noonan's directions, they would have reached Dakar. Obviously, if the combination of their combined skills resulted in an error of this magnitude, what chance was there of locating an island (Howland) in mid-Pacific that was two miles long and a half mile wide?

This example of Earhart overriding her navigator's professional expertise has been cited by many authors as sheer folly and a sure sign of her incompetence to attempt such a dangerous stunt flight in the first place. These Earhart commentators are obviously accepting her overt declaration as factual when, in fact, many of her chronologically previous and subsequent declarations are now known to be "cover stories" for actual covert reasons. Stated another way, the appearance (overt) and reality (covert) meaning were by design diametrically opposed. As a result of this indiscretion, Earhart was soundly ridiculed by many authors. The gist of these comments—why carry a professional navigator if at the decisive moment you disregard his experienced judgment when "it seemed to her they should turn north" when, in fact, they should have followed his suggested course?

After the lapse of a half century and the ensuing accumulation of large amounts of evidence, it is evident that Earhart's publicly-acknowledged indiscretion was not necessarily what really happened. Foremost among the indicators is that Noonan did not abandon the flight at St. Louis or Dakar and take a freighter home. Furthermore, as the premier overwater navigator of the period with 12 trans-Pacific crossings aboard PAA flying clippers, Noonan was the most certain to recognize the seriousness of the indiscretion. Based on what is now known, there is a valid explanation of what really happened. Leaving all other rhetoric aside, what was behind the St. Louis episode was that it was a time-consuming detour. This can't be denied from the obvious facts. The St. Louis "detour" added two days to her already-stretched itinerary. The forced overnight stop at St. Louis and the 163-mile (one hour) flight to her original destination of Dakar were a neatly-contrived delay explained away by a false cover story. By looking back along her previous course and subsequently forward (as can be done with hindsight), a number of induced delays and other detours can be seen which accumulatively added days to her flight. These delays added to the one-

week stopover at Miami before flying overseas and the week delay at Bandoeng resulted in a sizeable postponement of the Lae, New Guinea, takeoff (along with alleged weather delays forcing postponements).

In fact, the original June 25 date of departure from Lae, when the supporting Coast Guard ship and the United States Navy vessels had to be deployed on station to support the flight, had been eclipsed by more than a week.

Available evidence now known strongly suggests that all these detours, short half-day flights, flight delays, and alleged weather problems were all part of cleverly-programed itinerary juggling to delay the ultimate departure from Lae, New Guinea, until the scene in the Central Pacific was satisfactory for the planned events.

A lengthy exposition of this *fait accompli* could be made, but the facts are self-evident to honest appraisal. Therefore, only a brief synopsis will be given. Looking at both sides of the South Atlantic flight path, it can be seen that Fortaleza, Brazil, was another unscheduled stop a few hundred miles from Natal, Brazil (the over-ocean departure point). This resulted in another induced delay plus a very short flight (to Natal) with more delay. The triteness of an airplane with a 4,000-mile range making a series of flights under 500 miles is suspicious to say the least. Finally, both Harry Manning and Fred Noonan had very similar backgrounds as Merchant Marine seamen. It was learned shortly before Manning's demise that he abandoned the Earhart flight after the Ford Island crackup because he feared risking his life any further. So he used the excuse of "his leave being up" as an alibi to leave the flight when he could have had his leave extended. Noonan must also have had serious misgivings at this time but, as he said, "he needed this flight" for business and personal reasons. After the St. Louis fiasco, Noonan must have had misgivings a second time. He publicly said absolutely nothing but did, in fact, shortly thereafter write a gushing letter to his new bride (which has been made public) of how competent Earhart was and what a perfect traveling companion she had turned out to be, etc. Something doesn't ring true at all, unless Noonan was himself privy to the delaying tactic which, as a Lt. Commander in the USN Reserve, he, of course, undoubtedly was. What this personal letter to his wife suggests is that Noonan was discreetly attempting to tell her not to believe all she read in the newspapers about Earhart's "mistakes" and that there was a (secret) reason for them.

ERITREA OVERFLIGHT

Readily seen from the Gasoline and Oil Provisioning Chart (*Last Flight*, p. 147) is that the three airports in Eritrea were all projected for Earhart's attention. None of them had been approved by the Italian government for the initial March flight. On that occasion, her route was from the RAF base at Aden to Khartoum, which also had an RAF base, as was a portion of the Karachi, Western India, airbase used by the RAF.

When approval was not forthcoming from the Italian government prior to March 1937, Earhart appealed directly to her friend, Italian Air Force Marshal Italo Balbo, to intercede with the Italian government in her behalf to open up the Eritrea airports. Eventually, the Red Sea airports of Massawa and Assab were approved, but permission was denied to land at the military airport at the Italian capital of Asmara, 40 miles inland. Asmara, reported to be the largest airfield in Africa,[1] was high on the African plateau stretching into Ethiopia and was the key bombing base used against Addis Ababa in the recently completed 1935-36 Italo-Ethiopian war. It was also the principal threat to the British "lifeline of empire" through the Red Sea and the airport they couldn't photograph well from the air (as they had been attempting to do since 1935[2]) by flying up and down the Red Sea (eight miles offshore in international waters) from the RAF base at Aden.

Little doubt remains but that the Eritrea detour on the final flight was to accommodate British intelligence interests. The United States had little or no interest in Asmara or Eritrea, for that matter. The British had a vital interest as evidenced by aerial espionage agent Cotton's 1939 flight over Italian East Africa (Eritrea)[3] in his Lockheed Electra equipped for photographic reconnaissance.

Not being allowed to land at Asmara was no deterrent to Earhart and Noonan. Flying from Khartoum to Massawa, they would have used the two cities of Kassala and Asmara en route as check points for "navigation" purposes. The Asmara airport was only nine kilometers south-southwest of Asmara so oblique aerial photographs could readily be taken as their Lockheed flew overhead. A standard RAF aerial camera would have been taken aboard at Khartoum at the RAF base, photographs taken en route, and the camera stowed in the secure compartment under the floorboards where the vertical camera mount was installed. When they reached Karachi, the camera and film (exposed) would have been turned over to RAF personnel.

If further proof is necessary, consider the "get away" provisions from Massawa, Eritrea, if the Italians got too inquisitive about her overflight of Asmara. In her *New York Herald Tribune* write-up, she stated that the option for a direct flight across Arabia (which was forbidden) to Karachi, India, was still a possibility. In other words, if the military authorities began asking questions of an embarrassing nature, she was to hop in the airplane and fly across the Arabian badlands with the Italians not daring to create an international incident by following.

As it happened, the Italian military officials at Massawa did not question the Asmara overflight or at least did not associate it with oblique photography of nearby Maddalena Airfield. By limiting her stay at Khartoum to a two-hour refueling stop, she was able to fly over the strategic part of Italian Eritrea during the early afternoon hours which are best-suited for aerial photography. Earhart researcher Charles N. Hill checked Noonan's navigation charts, part of the special Earhart collection at Purdue University, for the flight from Khartoum to Massawa. These actual charts show conclusively that the Earhart Electra did not fly a direct course, but followed the Italian railroad from the border of Anglo-Egyptian Sudan to

.

the Red Sea through Asmara. (Refer to the Italian Eritrea Overflight Chart by Charles N. Hill in Appendix A on page 160.) By crossing Eritrea on Sunday, it was felt that neither the military garrison would be on alert status nor would military aircraft likely be flying during siesta time after the noon hour. In World War II, the Italians used this railroad to invade British Sudan and in 1941 British Field Marshal Wavell followed this same railroad into Asmara to defeat the Italian garrison in Northeast Africa. The crucial battle was fought at Karim on the rail route a few miles from Asmara, Eritrea.

Noonan's actual flight chart of this intelligence-gathering mission proves beyond any doubt that the Earhart flight was, in part, to obtain military information of strategic importance not to the United States but to Great Britain. This occurred thousands of miles before Earhart ever reached the Pacific and the Mandated Islands of Japan. The Eritrea overflight of Karim and Asmara are irrefutable proof of the British Connection.

AIRPLANE CHANGES

In addition to an engine change or modification, some prior authors have speculated on airplane switches, either during the remanufacture at Burbank, California, in April-May 1937 or somewhere during the world flight. Either an alternate Model 10E with "souped up" engines and aerial camera was substituted, most likely at Port Darwin, Australia, or a second (covert) XC-35 had been secretly constructed by Lockheed before the (overt) XC-35 airplane was even tested, and flown thousands of miles over water by a crew who hadn't even been checked out in its flight characteristics.

Clarence J. "Kelly" Johnson, Lockheed project engineer on the Earhart Electra, has stated in answer to a direct question that the original Earhart Electra Model 10E, Registration Number NR16020, was returned to Lockheed from Hawaii and remanufactured to incorporate structural improvements deemed necessary for the heavily-overloaded conditions under which the Earhart airplane operated.

Only one XC-35 was built, and it is at the Silver Hill, Maryland, storage facility (Gerber facility of the Smithsonian's National Air and Space Museum) awaiting possible restoration at some future date.

Although never acknowledged officially, Lockheed Electra military variant, the XC-35, had high-altitude reconnaissance capability.
Photo credit - Lockheed Aircraft Corporation

---

[1] Lechenberg, H.P., "With the Italians in Africa," *National Geographic*, September 1935, pp. 265-295.

[2] Hinsley, F. H., *et al. British Intelligence in the Second World War*, Volume 1, p. 26.

[3] *Ibid*. p. 498, East Africa, including Eritrea.

Pictorial evidence exists that while Earhart's Wasp engines were undergoing overhaul at the Union Air Port hangar of Pacific Airmotive (an authorized West Coast Pratt & Whitney overhaul facility), Lockheed personnel fitted a pair of R-1340-43 Pratt & Whitney military Wasp engines to the Earhart Electra.

These were the same military Wasps used on the XC-35, but without the turbo superchargers. Existent photographs show this installation in the Lockheed overhaul hangar which was used during the remanufacturing.

In 1937, Lockheed was a small company trying to sell a militarized version of its commercial airplane to United States and foreign military purchasers. They had a long-range reconnaissance airplane in the Model 10E (with auxiliary fuselage fuel tanks) and a high-altitude reconnaissance configuration in the XC-35. This is the best explanation for the military Wasps on the Earhart Electra. While the Earhart Wasp engines were being overhauled at Pacific Airmotive, other military engines from the XC-35 program with new exhaust collector rings were temporarily installed in the Earhart Electra to take photographs for military sales brochures.

Military versions of Lockheed Electra were sold in limited numbers to all service branches in 1930s. In a number of cases civilian airplanes had higher performance than military service types. United States Air Corps version shown.
Photo credit - Lockheed Aircraft Corporation

Lockheed Electra as delivered to United States Navy
Photo credit - Lockheed Aircraft Corporation

Lockheed Electra for overseas air transport service
Photo credit - Lockheed Aircraft Corporation

There may have been some consideration given to using the military Pratt & Whitney XR-1340-43 on the Earhart Electra, but none was available on the West Coast. Additionally, timely air transport of two Wasp engines across the Pacific to Hong Kong and south to Bandoeng, Java, in the time available was impractical.

What was practical was installing the higher (military) ratio blower gears in the Earhart Wasps. Supporting evidence exists that this was, in fact, accomplished during the scheduled engine "overhaul" at Bandoeng, Java. The authority on this is Earhart's technical representative in charge of overhaul, Francis Oliver Furman, technical representative for the Martin Company on the 100 B-10 twin-engine bombers, export version, sold to the Dutch East Indies Air Force. Furman, when interviewed by this author, said that the higher gear ratio (13.5 to 1 military gears) replaced the standard 10:1 commercial blower gears on the "H" series Wasp engines. Feasibly, the gears could have been shipped by priority air mail from West Hartford, Connecticut, to Bandoeng by air via PAA clipper across the Pacific to Hong Kong and thence to Singapore and Bandoeng by commercial carrier.

A second very important source supporting the gear ratio switch is Clarence "Kelly" Johnson, Lockheed project engineer on the Electra. In his book, he wrote of supplying Earhart with a complete "new" set of fuel consumption curves for her Wasp engines in March 1937. Obviously, Earhart and Paul Mantz had worked almost a year from May 1936 to March 1937 using the specially-installed Cambridge fuel analyzer to perfect fuel management technique. This had been checked on several cross-country flights and lengthy overwater ones, including the 2,400-mile flight from Oakland to Hawaii. Therefore, Earhart hardly had any use for a "new" set of fuel consumption curves (numbers). That is, unless some basic alteration, such as installing the blower reduction gears to the engines which would affect fuel consumption, had been done.

Furman, who accomplished the change at Bandoeng, Java, and "Kelly" Johnson, who gave Earhart the revised fuel performance numbers, both contributed supportive evidence to the likelihood of an important engine modification accomplished en route during the last flight.

The higher blower gear ratio would enhance engine performance, particularly at higher altitudes, by providing an elementary form of supercharging.

Another decided indication was delaying the flight for repair requirements for the Cambridge fuel flow analyzer. This was the "instrument" which required overhaul by the Dutch mechanics at Bandoeng, Java. With other major overwater crossings behind her, and additional thousands of transcontinental miles behind her, the Exhaust Gas Analyzer (EGA), was not vital for the remaining flight segments, especially with the 100-octane boost for takeoff, with high-ratio blower assist, so that a vast fuel reserve for all legs could be carried.

The EGA then was vital because a new aspect had been added and fuel monitoring was all the more important. While having some "supercharging" effect, upgrading the impeller gear ratio would not significantly, in itself, improve overall performance. The top speed, or cruising speed, would not be significantly increased. Improvement would be primarily in takeoff enhancement and performance at altitude would be noticeably improved.

In conjunction with the 100-octane gas, the high ratio blower would improve takeoff, but thereafter a sinking into the heavy air cushion up to ten feet above ground would be noticed. This "ground effects" problem immediately after takeoff was noted by many observers at both Darwin, Australia, and Lae, New Guinea.

Mission enhancement for takeoffs from jungle airstrips such as Lae and short island airstrips such as at Howland had been provided for Earhart. In the event of an intrusion over unfriendly territory, the high-ratio gears would enable a more rapid climb to altitude to outdistance any hot pursuit. The oxygen-equipped Electra could then operate in oxygen-deficient altitudes where unequipped aircraft could not follow.

The sequence of events from final takeoff to final signoff are captured by Paul Rafford, Jr., in a flight chart of the flight from Lae, New Guinea, to Hull Island. (This flight chart may be found in Appendix B on page 163.)

LAE, NEW GUINEA, ENROUTE NAURU
James A. Collopy, District Superintendent of Civil Aviation at Australian New Guinea, filed a factual memo with the Civil Aviation Board regarding Amelia Earhart's three days at Lae, New Guinea, from landing to takeoff. In the next section is his summary of events, which is followed by comments of others who were involved.

"As District Superintendent, I was present during the time Amelia Earhart and Fred Noonan were at Lae to assist them in any way I could. They arrived at Lae at 3:00 p.m. on 29 June and left at 10:00 a.m. on 2 July. Practically the entire time the aircraft was at Lae, Guinea Airways mechanics were carrying out maintenance work on the aircraft, engines, and instruments. No serious defects were reported by the fliers or found by Guinea Airways personnel. A test flight was carried out by Earhart on the morning of 1 July, after which she reported the aircraft was operating satisfactorily. The main cause of the delay at Lae was because they awaited a satisfactory weather report and an accurate check on time signals for setting the chronometers.

"According to Fred Noonan, the total fuel capacity of the aircraft was 1,150 United States gallons. Oil capacity was 64 United States gallons. They left Lae with a total of 1,100 gallons of fuel and 64 gallons of oil. One tank contained only 50 gallons of its total capacity of 100 gallons. This tank contained 100-octane fuel and they considered 50 gallons of this fuel sufficient for the Lae departure. The takeoff was hair-raising as after taking every yard of the 3,000-foot runway from the northwest end of the aerodrome toward the sea, the aircraft had not left the ground 150 feet from the end of the runway. When the airplane did leave the ground, it sank, but was by this time over the sea. It continued to sink to about five or six feet above the water and had not climbed to more than 100 feet before disappearing from sight over the horizon. It was obvious that the aircraft was well handled and pilots of Guinea Airways, who had flown Lockheed aircraft, were loud in their praise of the takeoff with such an overload.

"As the result of conversations with Mr. E. Chater, manager of Guinea Airways, and Harry Balfour, the Lae radio operator, it is very apparent that the weak link in the combination was the crew's lack of expert knowledge of radio. Their Morse was very slow and they preferred to use telephony as much as possible. Balfour stated that they advised him they would change the wave length at nightfall. Balfour advised them by radio just before nightfall not to change as their signals were coming through quite strong. They apparently changed, however, as Balfour never heard them again. At about 3:00 p.m., a message came though to the effect that they were at 10,000 feet, but were going to reduce altitude because of thick banks of cumulus clouds. The next and last message was to the effect that they were at 7,000 feet and making 150 knots. This message was received at approximately 5:00 p.m.

"Mr. Noonan told me that he was confident about the flight to Howland Island and was quite certain that he would have little difficulty in locating it. One can only have opinions as to what actually happened to them, but in the light of the foregoing regarding radio, and the confusion which arose during the search in connection with all the radio messages which were supposed to have emanated from the aircraft, I do think that had an expert radio operator been included in the plane crew, the conclusion may have been different." (J.A.C.).

LAE TO NAURU
Seemingly clear now is that the preflight strategy was to fly a great circle course from Lae, New Guinea, toward Howland during the daylight hours. Balfour, radio operator at Lae, has testified that during Earhart's and Noonan's hourly radio contacts from the mid-morning takeoff until sunset, Earhart consistently gave altitude, position, and occasional weather information. Only one of these daytime positions became available to the ship and shore stations which comprised the flight support group. By what channel that became known is uncertain, but most likely it was routed from Lae through Suva, Fiji Islands, Naval Radio Tutuila in American Samoa and United States Navy and Coast Guard personnel in Hawaii. At dark, the more efficient 6210 kc band was discontinued and with the increase of tropical nighttime static and a strong electric storm which lay over much of her flight path during the hours of darkness, radio communication from the Electra was poor, at best, until the following morning.

Now verified by a number of British residents on Nauru Island in 1937 was the fact that the Earhart Electra made a sharp alteration off course to the northeast to fly directly toward Nauru Island. The reason given for this was a radiogram sent to her at Lae advising her of a light beacon on Nauru which would be available for nighttime guidance if requested. Alternately, the open pit phosphate deposits were being mined at night using above-the-ground strings of electric lights. These could be seen for many miles at sea when one approached from any direction. Noonan had changed his outlook in the time from being at Java to the Lae stop. At Bandoeng, Noonan had expressed great concern about the navigational problems of locating Howland after 2,556 miles of night and day flight. Technical representative Francis O. Furman has commented on Noonan's concern. Conversely, at Lae, the new knowledge of a mid-course navigational checkpoint came as a big relief and the use of the lights at the phosphate mines would be incorporated in the flight plan.

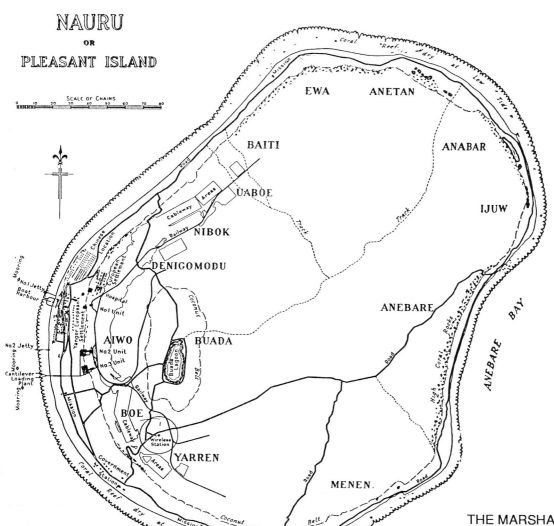

NAURU
OR
PLEASANT ISLAND

SCALE OF CHAINS

EWA   ANETAN

BAITI   ANABAR

UABOE   IJUW

NIBOK

DENIGOMODU

ANEBARE

AIWO   BUADA

BOE

Wireless
Station

YARREN

MENEN.

ANEBARE BAY

Nauru Island Chart
Proof of Nauru Island fly by clearly shows that straight line course to Howland Island had been changed for a detour to the northeast towards the Japanese Marshall Islands.

From relatively recent testimony made available more than 30 years after the event, it is now known that Earhart approached and flew by Nauru between 10:00 and 11:00 p.m. local time. This has been attested to by Nauru's (1937) Director of Police who heard her radio transmissions on an all-wave radio receiver. Although she did not fly directly over the island, other members of the local white colony heard her as well. If Noonan intended to use Nauru as a checkpoint and take off to the east with a new departure point halfway between Lae and Howland, their presence would have been known by the white residents of Nauru who waited outdoors to see the aircraft lights or hear the sound of the engines. If Earhart and Noonan had been en route to Howland, they would have wanted to establish their time of arrival at Nauru so that the radio network operators along the equatorial islands would have an accurate midcourse fix on her progress and location. Obviously, exactly the opposite is the case,

for she did not want her itinerary known by those on the ground and for good reason. The Japanese Marshall Islands were only a few hundred miles away and all the deception exercised since receiving the airplane as a gift to conduct research for interested parties was on the line.

For the first part of the Lae-to-Howland flight (to the vicinity of Nauru Island), a considerable amount of information has been collected. Her basic altitude, course, and speed were known. Altitudes were from 5,000 feet to 8,000 feet. A speed of 110 knots, slightly under normal cruise, was maintained until nightfall. With the lightening gasoline load, the cruising speed gradually increased to reflect the lower gross weight.

THE MARSHALL ISLANDS
During 1937 the United States Government was interested in only three atolls in the Marshall Islands. One of these, Eniwetok, was administratively attached to the Eastern Carolines. The other two were Wotje and Jaluit. While true that Japanese float aircraft would land and take off in surveyed and marked areas in the lagoons of many of the atolls in the Marshall Islands, there were no shore facilities to support extended operations and a seaplane tender was required to facilitate prolonged military activity. That these three atolls were of interest was known from many sources, including open literature and classified naval documents.[4]

Eniwetok had fueling facilities for submarines and limited supplies and facilities for staging submarines on reconnaissance patrols to nearby Wake Island, Midway Island, and the islands in the Hawaiian chain.

Geographically, Wotje was the Japanese possession closest to Hawaii and the west coast of the United States. During the 1930s it was a radio surveillance facility with direction-finding equipment. At one time there was an 834-foot tower on the eastern end of Wotje. This gigantic tower was one of eight obtained from Germany in the 1920s as World War I reparation for

---

[4] H. O. No. 184, Naval Air Pilot—Pacific Islands, January 1936, U.S. Navy Hydrographic Office, Washington, D.C.

use in Japan's radio facilities. As noted by personnel in United States submarines patrolling the Marshall Island area, it was tested but later removed for higher priority military installations.

In 1937 Jaluit Atoll was the administrative center of the Japanese Marshall Islands as it had been for the governments of previous owners of the islands prior to World War I. The settlement on Jaluit was the largest in the Marshalls and the trading center was also housed there. Jaluit was of particular interest as a pseudo-military target because it was the announced eastern terminus of the Japanese Mandates Airline which was designated to interconnect the Marianas, Carolines, Marshalls, and Peleliu with Japan. This north-south and west-east airline was first announced in the mid-1930s, but was slow in developing. In 1937, the United States Government was interested in determining whether or not seaplane ramps were being prepared and facilities being built on shore to support this airline. If these accommodations were being constructed, the airline would soon be activated. The often-repeated Japanese declarations were not to be believed, but their deeds would be discernible. If the facilities were ready, the airline would follow. Thus, in 1937, the United States Government had three targets of interest in the Marshall Islands: Eniwetok and Wotje were military installations; Jaluit was pseudo-military in that military ships in transit could use its harbor and shore facilities. The airline facilities would serve both civil and military aircraft just as the PAA facilities at Midway and Wake were used by United States naval patrol aircraft.

WEATHER NETWORK EAST AND WEST OF WAKE ISLAND

Due to the proximity of the military target, Eniwetok, to Wake Island, it was obviously a PatWing2 target. That Navy group was operating PBYs in and out of Wake with three squadrons of PBYs (36 total) available by the end of 1937. Had Earhart been approaching the Marshalls flying southwest from Hawaii, she would have taken a look at Wotje Island.

This leaves the military target of Wotje in the eastern portion of the Marshalls susceptible to an eastern approach and a third, so far unidentified, aircraft could best overfly this target. The "two islands" designated in the article in *Smith's Weekly* have been identified as Eniwetok and Wotje Islands. The distance from Nauru to Jaluit in the southern Marshalls was short, but the estimated time of arrival would have been about midnight. Earhart had trouble navigating in the day and help offered from the PAA Adcock direction-finding stations across the Pacific had been refused. Nauru as a navigational checkpoint was quite convenient at the approximate midpoint of her flight. After flying several hundred miles from this checkpoint, however, unknown winds, unknown magnetic variations, unknown island shapes, mislocated island coordinates, pitch darkness, clouds, thunderstorms, and tropical squalls would have made finding the exact island(s) difficult. Clearly, some navigational aid of an electronic type was needed to steer them to Jaluit. That is where the "Radio Range Equipment" installed at Miami by PAA personnel came into play. United States naval submarines, out of Pearl Harbor, patrolled these waters because they represented the closest Japanese territory to a United States possession, namely Hawaii. Radio range transmitters with appropriate antennas would be jury-rigged on a

submarine superstructure and the messages sent could be received by the radio equipment aboard the Electra. The newly-installed 75-Mc marker beacon receiver aboard the Electra would be triggered by the marker beacon transmitter aboard the submarine as the airplane flew overhead, thus giving a positive orientation of the Electra's position relative to the target, Jaluit.

Flying northeast from Nauru toward Jaluit, Earhart would have received radio range signals from the submarine when in receiving range, and thus have guided the Electra in. The marker beacon signal would mark the release zone. The submarine would then approach closer to Jaluit to detect any overt response to the photoflash "pickle" or ensuing military or civil radio traffic. Clearing Jaluit after having taken one or two photographs, Earhart would have speeded up and rapidly gained altitude to thwart any possible "hot pursuit" from Japanese naval units which might be anchored in the harbor. The course from Jaluit would be southeast to fly by (or land at) Howland Island or Baker Island.

Nighttime photography from the air depended on photoflash bombs, suitable cameras, and electrical synchronizing circuitry and devices. Brigadier General George Goddard worked out the details of a successful system between 1926 and 1929 at Wright Field, Dayton, Ohio, and by 1937, nighttime aerial photography was being used in the United States Air Corps at the operational level. (See General Goddard's autobiography entitled *Overview* for early developmental details of Goddard's "thunderclaps," as these photoflash bombs were called.)

Photoflash bombs for aerial night photography were in service test use in 1937. Mark 46 photoflash bombs are shown stowed in USN Lockheed PV-1 patrol plane
Photo credit - National Archives Negative #80-G-225498

The installation of radio-range equipment in the Electra at Miami by personnel from the PAA radio department during the final week of May 1937 prior to departure for overseas has been previously cited. As evaluated by Paul Rafford, Jr., a lifetime PAA radio communication expert who flew as a radio operator in the pre-World War II clippers, this "radio-range equipment" would most likely have been a "Z" type 75-Mc marker beacon radio receiving set with "T" antenna on the underside of the Electra. As 75 Mc was a frequency peculiar to the United States at that time, there were no corresponding foreign ones. Aerial nighttime photography, using a T-1 photoflash bomb, and General George Goddard's patented [5] photocell synchronizing equipment was used. As depicted on Rafford's chart, after the Jaluit overflight, Earhart turned southeast and, with her Wasp engines equipped with "high-ratio blowers," flew away at above-cruising speed to elude any "hot pursuit." She also had oxygen equipment for emergency high-altitude flying, if necessary.

The transmitter on the submarine was to be used to send out homing signals as provided for in the Earhart "mission" plan. This is, of course, one reason a United States submarine was positioned on picket duty near the settlement of Jabor on Jaluit. Other reasons were: 1) local weather reporting, 2) mission direction, 3) on-the-scene reporting to Pearl Harbor for relay to Washington, 4) monitoring local reaction to aerial reconnaissance both visually and via military and civilian radio channels. One of the three large pre-World War II submarines at Pearl Harbor, U.S.S. *Narwahl*, or U.S.S. *Nautilus,* or the U.S.S. *Argonaut,* whichever was ready for sea duty, could have been designated for the Earhart mission. Also, any one of a dozen other smaller submarines at Pearl Harbor, including the last one out of the overhaul yard, could have been chosen. This same submarine which had been on picket duty appeared again on July 5 east of the Marshalls in the "281 miles north of Howland" subterfuge plan to fool the Japanese navy and military intelligence.

From Nauru, Earhart homed in on the signals from the submarine using her radio-range equipment. About five miles out, the marker beacon alerted them to their distance from the drop point. Available evidence indicates that just as Earhart communicated with Nauru on the "new" course, she continued talking as she flew north to Jaluit. Both Robert Myers, who had inadvertently picked up Earhart's transmissions on his father's radio and knew what he was hearing, and Karl Pierson, a radio man who was listening on more sophisticated equipment, picked up her messages from the Marshall Islands, thus revealing the covert portion of the world flight. The cover was blown on the military, or pseudo-military operations. No evidence was found that the Japanese on Jaluit, or any of the Marshall Islands, or elsewhere, intercepted any of Earhart's radio transmissions. What exists, however, is evidence of overreaction in Washington which caused hurried and unnecessarily drastic action.

HOWLAND-BAKER FLYBY

In all probability, more misinformation has been generated by the radio transmissions from the Electra heard by *Itasca* radiomen, including an undated laundered version, than from any other single source. For 30 years, from 1937 until enactment of the 1967 Freedom of Information Act, this laundered version was the only Earhart record actually released by the United States Government. In the final official abbreviated version, times of transmission were changed, so that it

Howland Island - the island in which Amelia Earhart twice missed arriving
Photo credit - National Archives Negative # 80-G-410882

was a bogus and suspect cover-up document. The purpose was to make the deficient original log more palatable to readers. For decades, Earhart buffs tried to read some sense into this laundered material. Each interpretation was different and often slanted to fit a particular viewpoint. The "half hour of gasoline left" influenced the proponents of the 20-knot-headwind advocates. Other puzzles to be solved were the following messages: "circling, we must be on you, but can't see you"; "traveling north and south, will shift to 6210 kc. Wait, listening on 6210 kc"; and "on the line of position 157-337". In addition to the radio exchange charade with the *Itasca* radiomen, the most flagrant misinterpretation is that she sent no position reports on her last flight, or only one early position report or two reports that were ambiguous. All of these conclusions are patently false and have been deliberately misrepresented to fit personal theories of Earhart researchers. The fact is that Earhart gave two excellent position reports, and by applying a sensible interpretation to them, a big step toward solving the riddle of her disappearance can be taken. The first position report was sent at nightfall and is well known. Balfour claims that Earhart gave her position and altitude on the relatively long-range frequency 6210 kc, the "daytime" frequency, until sundown when she changed to 3105 kc. This was by agreement with the United States Coast Guard. The second position report was at 8:30 a.m. the following morning when she was on the line of position 157-337.

---

[5] Goddard, General George W., U.S. Patent 1,936,595, Automatic (aerial) photographic apparatus. Application: 15 July 1929, patent granted: 28 November 1933.

The simplest explanation of this position is that the 337 reciprocal emanating from the Howland Island area covers nothing but water. On the 157-degree radial 300 to 400 miles southeast of Howland Island are numerous islands. In the laundered *Itasca* radio log, Earhart is reported to have said, "traveling north and south on the line of position 157-337."

If Noonan had been even a novice navigator, and glanced at a nautical chart of the area, he would be traveling northwest to southeast on the 157 reciprocal to the vicinity of the Phoenix Island Group. If, in this one alleged Earhart radio message, "north and south" had been interpreted to read north *to* south, the search could have concentrated in this most logical areas and not throughout the Pacific Ocean. Various authors of Earhart books have chosen to ignore the obvious and divert attention above the equator for two basic reasons:

1. It supports their contention that the two Caucasians allegedly seen "above the equator" were Earhart and Noonan. There is, however, no real proof of their identity.

2. During the search, the United States Navy reportedly found nothing south of the equator in the Phoenix Islands or elsewhere.

Information in Part Three of this book will show how false this contention actually was.

HOWLAND BAKER FLY-BY TO FINAL DESTINATION

Five decades of sporadic research by diverse individuals have provided documentary and first-party evidence carrying the Earhart Electra eastward to the Solomon Islands by nightfall of 2 July 1937. These coordinates were known during the search by United States naval personnel although the source has never been clearly established. Balfour stated that "position and altitude" reports every hour confirmed the record of her presence there between 10:00 and 11:00 p.m. (local time). Paul Rafford, Jr., as a result of a lifetime experience in the radio propagation field, picked up the "radio trail" and noted that that Nauru fly-by was carefully accomplished to avoid flying over the island when using it as an updated navigational checkpoint, a contact with the island community, and to point out a new heading. Neglecting to do these obvious things indicates that, as from the onset of the world flight, Earhart wanted to keep the important details of her activities covert. This was another manifestation of the deception, and for good reason, because her destination was not eastward direct to Howland, but northeast to the Marshall Islands.

Taking a clue from the front page of the *Smith's Weekly* article which appeared during October 1937, the number of aerial photographic targets in the southern Marshalls was small indeed. Jaluit, the administrative center of Japan's Marshall Islands, was the closest and most important target for use of General Goddard's aerial photographic system. Thunderclaps were required for this nighttime photography to mask the detonation of the photoflash bombs. Some on-site party adjacent to the area had to supply them with weather information. Of course, the "silent service" of the United States Navy provided this. Following the photo mission, a fly-by of Howland/Baker was staged to establish the contrived radio dialogue that the Electra was lost which would precipitate an official search (indicated in *Smith's Weekly* and other sources.)

Gardner Island in Phoenix Group was last navigational checkpoint for Amelia Earhart and Fred Noonan
Photo credit - National Archives Negative #80-G-410950

As shown on Paul Rafford's chart of the last flight (Appendix B), at the time of the last radio transmission, Earhart was far south of Howland and on the 157-degree course heading for Gardner Island. She might have landed there if fuel had been short, but Hull Island was her actual final flight destination. Lt. Lambrecht's report of huts on Gardner is evidence that Captain John William Jones, who was the white resident manager for the Phoenix Island Group at Hull Island, had set up the transmitter from the wrecked S.S. *Makoa* as an aerial beacon on 3105 kc. From Gardner, Earhart turned eastward for the one-hour flight to Hull. Two photographs exist from the U.S. Navy Office of Naval Information files which show the left turn at Gardner and the western approach to Hull Island. Abundant supportive evidence for this claim is found in photographs, charts, and data available from various national archives. Hull had a broad platform reef with wide sandy cover (125 yards wide on the northwest corner) admirably suited for a wheels-up landing into the prevailing wind. Captain John W. Jones was carefully chosen for this job. He was a Master Mariner from the British merchant marine and, due to service in World War I, was an officer in the Royal Navy Reserve as well. He was an experienced radio engineer and operator and his own high-powered radio equipment had recently been moved from Upolu Island in Western Samoa to Hull, ostensibly "to keep in touch with the outside world." Additionally, Jones had worked in Western Samoa for the New Zealand Reparation Estates, government coconut plantations, and directed Chinese laborers on the "Crown Estates." Jones was a well-known mariner in the Samoan and surrounding island countries from New Zealand to the Tongas and all points between. After working as a ship's officer on a number of vessels in the South Seas, he married an English woman named Margaret, who had originally resided in Australia. They were married for 12 years (1925-1936) without offspring. Their marriage was dissolved when Jones went to Hull in May 1937 for three years as resident manager. According to two of Jones' blood daughters by a later union, he was working for both British and United States military intelligence during this tour by reporting to the British High Commissioner at Suva by radio and letter and by radio to the United States Naval Station at Tutuila. He reported to the High Commissioner concerning a landing area in the western sector of Hull for British Pacific Airlines. First-person evidence of this communication to United States authorities concerned the existence of a landing site on Hull. A second interaction occurred with regard to the lagoon on Hull on 9 July 1937. Ground-level observation was necessary to verify that depth of water was adequate and that shoals and coral heads were avoidable. Crew members from the *Makoa* were used to harvest copra on Gardner Island and, while there, they installed a radio beacon for Earhart's use. A single radio operator would monitor aviation frequencies during July 1937 after the crew members returned to Hull Island.

LAST FLIGHT SUMMARY

Earhart landed into the prevailing wind on western Hull Island on a sandy portion of the broad platform reef which had adequate room for a safe wheels-up landing. The Merrill/Lambie trans-Atlantic flights during 1937 in a Lockheed Model 10E were proof that this distance (3,100 miles) was possible. Also, George Wilkins in the same airplane equalled this in the Arctic. This distance was considerably under the 4,000-mile range of the Electra. The reconnaissance target was consistent with known intelligence requirements and the pronouncement in *Smith's Weekly*.

The pre-World War II supposition that Earhart and Noonan missed Howland/Baker (either inadvertently or deliberately) and followed the 157-degree line of position reciprocal to the closest multiple landfalls in the Phoenix Group is completely justified. By expert testimony from those aboard the U.S.S. *Colorado* and, subsequently, information in the October cruise report of the United States Coast Guard cutter *Taney*, Jones was much more involved than acknowledged in July press releases. His "radio receiver" was, in fact, a high-powered communication radio set with which he could communicate with Australia. (The West Coast of the United States was a reciprocal distance, giving further credence to Karl Pierson's radio interceptions of 2-5 July 1937). As stated by Jones, the purpose of his radio was to "keep in touch with the outside world." This certainly implies current events. Earhart's presence in the South Seas in British Commonwealth territory, her presumed loss, and the search certainly would have been both current and newsworthy events. Also, Jones had an inter-island boat which he used to "travel between the various islands in the Phoenix group." All of these facts, including Jones' name, were known to United States Navy personnel yet were suppressed in news releases in which Jones remained unidentified, was out of touch with the surrounding world, was ignorant of events happening nearby, and had never heard of Amelia Earhart. All of these false and misleading "facts" were part of the cover-up to lead the Japanese into believing that the fliers had been lost at sea. According to the cruise reports of the *Taney*, first-person testimony from those aboard the *Colorado*, contemporary documents from the British High Commissioner of the Western Pacific Islands, (Suva, Fiji Islands, Western Samoan historical records, and the journalistic records in *Pacific Island Monthly*), all of the facts are contrary to the fraudulent report regarding Jones. In other words, the search of the Phoenix Group had turned up sufficient evidence to warrant a landing of search parties on Hull, Gardner, and Sydney Islands and the institution of punitive action against Jones for sending fraudulent distress signals, a serious violation of international maritime law. Of course, no charges were filed and Jones was well aware of his transgressions. He feared no reprisal by the United States Government for the rather obvious reason that, as his daughters have testified, he was working as an intelligence agent for both Britain and the United States while on Hull Island from 1937 to 1940.

The analysis of radio signal strength alone would establish that the Earhart Electra was in the immediate vicinity of Howland/Baker Islands at the approximate estimated time of arrival from Lae. Signal strength, however, can be deceptive, and after dawn when 3105 kc is being used, a significant amount of the prevalent nighttime static, in the tropics, dies away so that the Lockheed could have seemed closer after dawn than it actually was.

Noted by many Earhart analysts was that had she been approaching Howland directly on a great circle course from Lae, her 200-mile-out and 100-mile-out messages and times given were incompatible with her normal cruising speed, or fuel-economical speed. What is indicated is that these two reports were not made while she was approaching Howland, but while she was on an oblique course to the islands, as indicated on Paul Rafford's chart (Appendix B).

The final phases of the Earhart flight were undoubtedly on the 157-degree reciprocal of her only position report information received aboard the *Itasca.* "We are on the line of position 157-337." As the northwest reciprocal is 1,000 miles of very deep water, the southeast one is more logical. Also, she had flown the more than 600 miles from the Marshalls to the vicinity of Howland and another 400 miles to the Phoenix Group, claimed by the United States. From Howland, the distance to the British-owned Gilberts was 500 miles. Obviously, the multi-island Phoenix Group (on the 157-degree bearing) was the closest land to Howland. Further, since 1928, it had been known that Canton Island (the farthest north of the group) had thousands of acres of flat surface where a wheels-down landing could be accomplished safely.

A number of writers ignored the longer distance to the Marshalls by assuming that she was far north of Howland. No evidence exists to support this belief and there never has been. The assumption by the commander of the *Itasca*, Warren Thompson, that under the storm clouds to the northwest was the most likely place to search was justified by the evidence at his disposal. The "We must have been on you, but can't see you," and, "Flying at 1,000 feet," messages would have indicated to him that the Lockheed was in the vicinity, but beneath the cloud cover which forced them to a relatively low altitude and limited the distance they could see. Based on the visual evidence and the conflicting radio traffic, most ship commanders would have made the same decision of where to search.

After some 50 years, the situation can be viewed differently. The only information that Commander Thompson was given, in secret, was that the 281-miles-north message was an official notification by the 14th Naval District Headquarters in Hawaii and that he was to head north and divert both the U.S.S. *Swan* and the British freighter M.V. *Moorby* to the same empty ocean. This represented a three-day diversion of the only ships

available to search for Earhart in the crucial initial five-day period. By the time the battleship U.S.S. *Colorado* arrived at the equatorial region on 7 July, the obvious conclusion from the accumulated information was that the Phoenix Group was the most logical place to begin the search with the first aircraft available in the Central Pacific area adjacent to the equator. This was, and still is, the paramount area which should have been searched for a number of reasons.

1. On 157-degree reciprocal from Howland Island.
2. Nearest known land to Howland/Baker Islands.
3. Several identified potential landing sites (known since 1928).
4. Avid United States Government/Naval interest in the Phoenix Group.
5. Commercial airline potential later fully exploited.
6. Needed in support of Orange Plan, Navy war plan against Japan.
7. Excellent weather prevalent.
8. Pre-provisioned island during May-June 1937 naval expedition.
9. Aerial identification of Canton (white roof) and Hull (red roof) provided.

All three mid-Pacific PAA long-range Adcock high-frequency radio direction finders at Oahu, Midway, and Wake Islands had cross-bearing readings between Hull and Gardner. Coast Guard radioman Frank Cipranti, in his only bearing taken from his position on Howland Island, had a north-northwest open-water and a south-southeast Phoenix Island bearing. Most persons north of the equator assumed that the Phoenix Group was uninhabited prior to mid-1937. Due to patently false USN news release of the search of the Phoenix Islands, that locale was written off erroneously. The British in the Pacific knew that both Hull and Sydney Islands were occupied by natives who harvested copra and that the white resident manager, Captain John W. Jones, was overseeing the coconut plantations on these islands. Further, they knew that, by use of his boat, he had access to other islands in the Phoenix Group. Jones had arrived on Hull on 21 May 1937 aboard the Burns-Philp ship, *Makoa*. During the following three days the equipment was unloaded. Then, however, the ship struck a

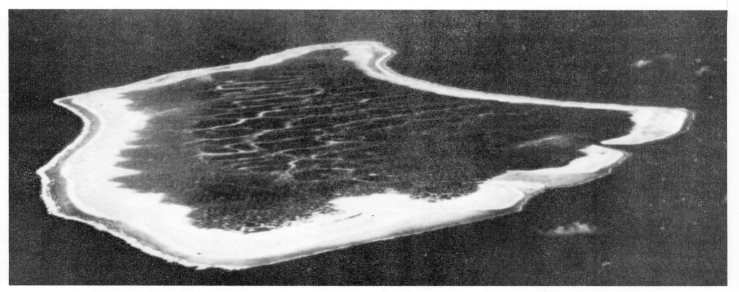

USN Patrol Wing Two aerial photograph of Gardner Island, Phoenix Group, 1939
Photo credit - National Archives Negative #80-G-410946

submerged coral head near Hull and within 12 hours was a total wreck. The crew, passengers, cargo, equipment, and most of the timber from the 100-foot ship were saved. The captain of this ship and her crew were picked up on 21 June 1937 by a re-routed British ship, the R.M.S. *Niagara*, which was en route from Honolulu to Suva in the Fiji Islands.

By July, Jones was well established on Hull and Sydney Islands with native laborers, and was also temporarily harvesting copra at Gardner to the west. In addition to bringing an inter-island boat to the Phoenix Group, Jones had also installed a high-powered radio station on Hull, along with a motor generator to provide electricity for lighting and the operation of his radio. Jones was well known in Western Samoa where he had been hired by Burns-Philp (South Seas) and Co., Ltd., to manage their Phoenix Island plantation.

Jones was a master mariner and radio enthusiast. His Western Samoan radio station, call number, ZMA11, was well known to the United States Navy brass at the Naval station. He was also known because of his frequent visits between Suva, Western (British) Samoa, and Pago Pago, American Samoa, in the early and mid-1930s. When Jones moved his domicile and radio station to Hull Island in 1937, that fact was noted by British officials at Suva, Fiji Islands, and United States Navy personnel at Tutuila, American Samoa.

Subsequently, Capt. Jones was solicited to furnish intelligence information from this strategic location by both governments via his radio station on Hull Island.

GARDNER ISLAND FLY-BY

A magnetic bearing of 157 degrees drawn on a world globe through Howland Island would pass in the vicinity of Gardner Island and, if extended a few hundred miles, would pass through the Samoan archipelago. The bearing line 157-337 was the only positional information Earhart sent in her final radio transmissions to the *Itasca*. As the 337 reciprocal northwest of Howland passed through open water for a thousand miles, obviously, Earhart was southeast of Howland. To satisfy their theories, many die-hard Earhart buffs have insisted that she had to be north of the equator.

Considerable evidence exists that Earhart followed the 157-degree bearing southeast of Howland into the Phoenix Group and "home in" on Gardner Island. This will be presented in a later section of this book. With the rejection of Howland/Baker as the initial objective, Gardner and Hull became primary destinations. Aerial photographs were taken in 1937 by an amateur photographer using an inexpensive layman's Kodak 616 camera. These two photographs pinpoint the Earhart Electra en route from Gardner to Hull. For reasons not originally certain, but now known, Gardner was bypassed and the flight continued on 160 miles east to Hull. Paul Rafford, in a comprehensive analysis of radio propagation, determined that a radio homing transmitter operating on 3105 kc was set up on Gardner for the fliers to home in on. With Gardner as a navigation checkpoint, Hull could be easily found by dead reckoning.

All of the above statements can be supported, and will be later in this book, by archival records from the United States, Fiji, Western Samoa, New Zealand, Australia, Great Britain, the Burns-Philp (South Seas) Company, Ltd., and the University of Sydney in Australia. Information relevant to the motivation for the change in

flight plan will be covered in subsequent sections of this book. Of particular significance was a major medical problem Earhart had developed in the tropics known only to a few and kept secret from the general public.

Amateur aerial photograph taken with Kodak 616 Camera of Gardner Island, Phoenix Group, from Earhart Electra on 2 July 1937
Photo credit - USN Office of Naval Intelligence Report

APPROACH TO HULL ISLAND AND TOUCHDOWN

Once Gardner Island had been reached, Noonan had no trouble identifying it from the nautical chart supplied to him by special government agents in Darwin, Australia, where the latest mission details had been given to the fliers. A quick check of remaining fuel gave assurance of sufficient gasoline for the flight to Hull. The hour's flight was made at 5,000 feet altitude. Although the horizon was obscured by haze and low-flying scud blew at low altitude over the island, Hull was easily identified by the large copra shed with the red roof on the western point of the island and the numerous islets which comprised the northern rim. Hull is unique in appearance and easily identified from the air.

The following ideas are found in Sir Gordon Taylor's *Across the Pacific*, published in 1936, regarding his 1934 trans-Pacific flight with Kingsford-Smith from Brisbane, Australia, to Oakland, California, in a Lockheed Altair, *Miss Southern Cross*. His thoughts are used in this manuscript to show a possible scenario which may have occurred during Earhart's approach to Hull.

*   *   *   *   *

Earhart said, "I think there is an island dead ahead."

His navigation job over, Noonan moved forward to the copilot's seat. "Yes, we can check to verify that it is Hull."

A couple of minutes later, Earhart saw the island below, a shallow lagoon of incredibly bright colors, snugly enclosed in a thin border of land, a perfect example of the coral island one has always read about. For a moment, the fliers gazed at the strange wild beauty of the place. Then, aroused from that momentary hypnotism by the necessity of identifying the shape that lay below, they checked on the local chart. It fit regarding shape, but there seemed to be more beach than one would expect from the chart. Noonan handed the chart to Earhart for confirmation and flew while she checked the contours of the island against the chart.

"Hull Island," she agreed.

"We should make a direct landing approach from the west into the prevailing easterly winds."

Earhart returned to the course and then began to fly the Electra in an appropriate landing pattern. Noonan had the chance to photograph something absolutely unique and pointed the Kodak toward Hull. "If only one could capture the color," he thought. "That is the whole thing."

One reads and hears of gems set in a sapphire sea. To use this expression to describe Hull Island as seen from the air seems only to destroy the impression of its incredible beauty, the mystery of its wild loneliness, and the strange uncertainty of its being; and yet that does describe it. The lagoon is a gem of infinite variety of flashing color, the ring of wooded land its setting, held in the mystery of the great depths on which it seems to rest.

From 1,000 feet above the ring of coral it does not look real. If viewed from a ship, it would, perhaps, be different, but to come upon it when one has felt the impression of space in the sea below as in the sky above, it seems only to be an illusion passing in that space. Its incredible beauty only adds to that illusion.

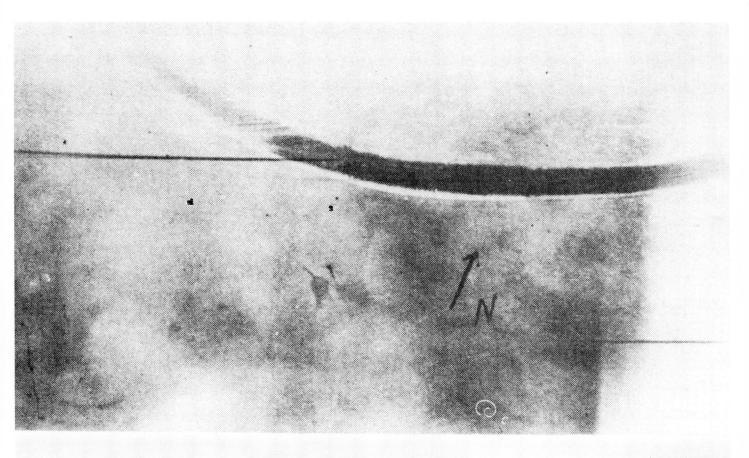

HULL Island. 1937.

CONFIDENTIAL

Amateur aerial photograph taken with Kodak 616 Camera of western approach to Hull Island, Phoenix Group, from Earhart's Electra on 2 July 1937
Photo credit - USN Office of Naval Intelligence

Slowly the Electra is flown toward Hull as Earhart traverses the downwind leg and turns onto final. The aircraft nears the glistening coraline sand and touches down midway on the sandy beach. A brief slide on the belly, and the long flight of Electra NR16020 is over.

Amelia Earhart had often been quoted as telling Eugene Vidal and others that if she couldn't find Howland, she would backtrack some 500 miles to the Gilbert Islands and, "find a nice stretch of beach to set down on and hope there is fresh water available." No official alternative landing place was ever given for the Earhart flight although nearby Baker Island would have been the most likely choice. The Gilbert Island "backtrack" story has no official status and received no consideration during the search except that she might have drifted to the Gilberts due to the prevailing trade wind and currents.

As seen from the aerial photograph of the western end of Hull Island, the broad crystalline sand on the northwest corner is so bright in the tropical sunshine that it glistens. That fact alone, established by pictorial evidence, indicates how suitable Hull was for an emergency landing.

With no trouble identifying either the island or the "landing strip" designated for her, Earhart was faced with only the relatively easy task of making a wheels-up landing on the sand. The coraline sand on most Pacific islands is too soft to allow a wheels-down landing. A direct approach from the west and touchdown along any portion of the half-mile straight stretch of beach meant that she had finished her long 3,150-mile flight from Lae in some 24 hours.

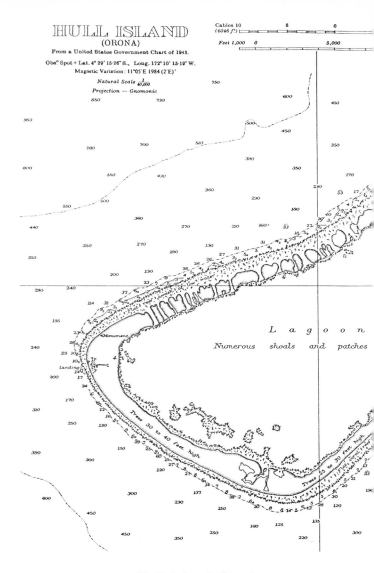

HULL ISLAND
(ORONA)
From a United States Government Chart of 1943.
Obs" Spot + Lat. 4° 29' 15·26" S., Long. 172° 10' 15·19" W.
Magnetic Variation : 11°05' E 1984 (2'E)'
Natural Scale 1/40,000
Projection — Gnomonic

Lagoon
Numerous shoals and patches

Hull Island Chart
Wide sand covered platform reef on Hull Island's northwest corner offered excellent location for safe (wheels up) landing

USN Patrol Wing Two aerial photograph of Hull Island, Phoenix Group, 1939
Photo credit - National Archives Negative 80-G-410951

The copra shed with the red roof and the suitability of the northwest strand for landing purposes were not determined from nautical charts or the Pacific Island Sailing Directions published by the United States Navy Hydrographic Office. This first-hand, current information came from only one source, the white resident manager of Hull Island, Capt. John W. Jones, RNR, who was the British Connection.

WORLD FLIGHT SUMMARY
To provide an adequate background to the disappearance of Earhart, Noonan, and the Lockheed, an accurate flight profile from the Lae, New Guinea, takeoff to the final landing must be determined. Five decades of continuing research have shown both United States and British governments as having an interest in strategic points of interest along her world-girdling route. Certainly, Italian Eritrea on the British Lifeline of Empire was of interest to the United Kingdom with another world war a distinct possibility.

The United States was predominantly (85%) against entanglement in European problems but in spite of a comparatively small share in Asian economic and political affairs, China's independence against Japan's aggression was favored. With the "first line of defense" in the Pacific, the United States was better situated for (naval) war there than in the Atlantic in 1937.

Roosevelt tried to exploit the Pacific Ocean theater with tough rhetoric as at the Chicago (Fall 1937) "Quarantine" speech and so-called "big-stick" policy toward Japan. Although some bellicose reaction occurred in the inner circles in Washington (mainly Swanson, the Secretary of the Navy), the bark was louder than the bite. Overtures to the British for joint naval action in the Pacific fell on deaf ears. Neville Chamberlain had arrived at an understanding with Italian dictator Mussolini and soon was negotiating a "peace in our time" deal with Adolph Hitler.

The intelligence communities had some choice of action. With the newly-available photoflash bombs and supercharging for high-performance aircraft engines, access to the "off limits" Japanese Mandate Islands was available. In the 1936 *Naval Air Pilot-Pacific Islands* (H. O. No. 184), almost every island in the Japanese Mandates was, or had the potential for becoming, a fortified citadel.

With the demise of Australian aviators Charles T. P. Ulm (1934) and Sir Kingsford-Smith (1935) and the employment of Harold Gatty by PAA (1936), the hope of a South Seas Airways plan to use landplanes from Brisbane to Suva never developed because of the advent of World War II in 1939.

The Howland Island failure was the death knell for flights of civilian land aircraft over water until late in the war when C-54s (and other multi-engine land planes) appeared. By the end of World War II (1945), the United States Air Transport Command had clearly established the superiority of the multi-engine land airplane for transoceanic crossings. Earhart was "missing in action" primarily because:

1.   Overreaction in Washington, D.C., was a possibility due to fear of an international incident.

2.   The desire of certain vested interests in Washington, D. C., that she wouldn't succeed.

The covert portion of each Earhart world flight was dependent upon "suitable weather" over the designated target area in the Marshall Islands. In this instance, that meant electrical storms with thunder, and lightning to mask the detonation of a photoflash bomb. In other words, the covert portion of the flight "was contingent upon" that type of weather (not unusual in the tropics) which would disguise the use of nighttime photographic reconnaissance. This was necessary in peacetime but not required in wartime.

U.S.S. *Argonaut* from naval base at Pearl Harbor, Hawaii, was submarine on picket duty offshore Jaluit Island, Marshall Islands, 1-2 July 1937
Photo credit - National Archives Negative 80-G-410066

Assuming the weather was "suitable" as it was on 1 July (but not on 20 March 1937) and the mission was performed as scheduled, the departure and landing sites were factors of either detection or non-detection by the Japanese. The picket submarine was on the surface at night five to eight miles south of Jabor, the main settlement of Jaluit Atoll. When the Electra 10E passed over its position, the submarine got underway and headed toward Jabor to see what response there was when Noonan dropped the "pickle." Of course, all the receivers aboard the submarine were tuned to the Imperial Japanese Navy frequencies to ascertain if any shipboard activity occurred. Ashore, there was no power for the radio station because the generating plant was shut down at 11:00 p.m. If the Japanese reacted to the photoflash bomb by issuing radio alerts or took defensive action ashore at Jabor, submarine personnel could have detected this activity by closing to within five miles and using a "long glass" (naval telescope).

All of these provisions were negated by Earhart's indiscreet actions. This is what Morgenthau meant by her disobeying orders (Morgenthau "Transcript").[6] She blew the cover of the mission, or so United States Navy personnel thought, by broadcasting the names of the Marshall Islands as she passed over them. Both Robert Myers and the Karl Pierson/Walter McMenamy group heard these transmissions in California. Of course, once the cover of the Earhart covert mission was blown, Howland was out of the question. Earhart and Noonan had to disappear and be presumed lost. Apparently Noonan pulled rank on Earhart and told her if she ever wanted to see the United States of America again that she better "shape up or else." So she headed for Hull Island and a wheels-up landing.

The point to all of the above is that *it was not* the United States public at large that Roosevelt was trying to deceive in 1937, but the Imperial Japanese Navy and Japanese government. The public and low-ranking persons in the military didn't have a "need to know," so they were left out. Under normal peacetime conditions, but with the tensions regarding the Japanese Mandates, getting caught over restricted territory was a serious proposition. As stated earlier, this is comparable to Francis Gary Powers going down in his U-2 airplane over central Russia in 1960.

The irony of this whole situation was that the Roosevelt administration over-reacted to the incident. No evidence exists that the Japanese detected the Earhart airplane, the photoflash bomb, or even heard the radio messages. The Imperial Japanese Navy was busy with mainland China. Naval activity in the Marshalls was nil and all military ships had left the area. No radio watch was active on merchant ships in the harbor. The generator had been shut down for the night. What did "blow the lid" was the British airplane which went down off Mili Atoll. They found out about it soon enough.

Earhart increased her speed after leaving the Marshalls for two reasons: 1) the unlikely event of a "hot pursuit" by Imperial Japanese Navy seaplanes from the harbor at Jaluit and 2) to fly back in range of Howland Island and the *Itasca* within a reasonable elapsed time after having left Lae, New Guinea, at 10:00 a.m. (0000 GCT) on 2 July 1937. A few miles after departing the Marshalls, she started scribbling a nonsense dialogue to transmit as a one-way discourse with the unseen radio operators aboard the *Itasca*. At this point, "big brother" said, "No Howland. Wheels-up on Hull Island." So Noonan directed Earhart to fly southeast and picked up the "157-337 degrees" bearing and the 3105 kc radio beacon signal sent from Gardner Island, made possible by using the salvaged radio set from the ill-fated ship, *Makoa*, which had been destroyed after striking a coral head off Hull Island's anchorage.

After the 90-degree left turn at Gardner (and amateur aerial photo taken of the island by Noonan from the optically flat observation window on the left side of the rear compartment), the Electra continued its flight to Hull Island, some 160 miles eastward. There, Captain John W. Jones could use his radio transmitter to home her in, if necessary because of adverse weather, but that probably wasn't necessary.

One very interesting part of the Karl Pierson/Walter McMenamy original script for the movie *Stand By to Die*, which was written in late 1937, was the finish during which the radio dialogue with the "navy authorities" is described as a big lie and her performance on the microphone as "play acting." Of course, this is true because both men knew the real story from hearing the United States Coast Guard intercepts and they knew the version given to the public was false. The ending was changed in the 1942 version of the movie called *Flight for Freedom*.

While deception in 1937 might have been warranted, it has continued for half a century for no discernible security reason, except perhaps the arrogant attitudes of government agency employees to keep the public uninformed. Also suspect are the economic interests of certain European nations and their citizens who classify events with no strategic security considerations at all but which might affect trading profit from former allies or enemies.

---

[6] The Morgenthau (Roosevelt's Secretary of the Treasury) "Transcript." (Morgenthau Diaries at the Hyde Park, New York, Roosevelt Library branch of the United States National Archives)

Part Two
The Searches

Officers and crew members from the U.S.C.G. Cutter *Itasca* led search for missing fliers from 2 to 18 July, 1937
Photo credit - United States Coast Guard Negative #API-04-20-37(06)

Within two hours of Earhart's last logged radio message heard aboard the *Itasca*, Commander Warren K. Thompson, United States Coast Guard, reached the conclusion that the airplane was down on the ocean and instigated a search. Thompson reasoned that she was most likely down to the northwest of Howland Island. This was based primarily on the 157-337 line of position (LOP) given in her last radio message and the clearly visible storm cover to the northwest of his location. He felt that if she had been out of this weather front, very likely she would have found Howland Island by 10:00 that morning. Based on the information he had at his disposal at that time, the importance of getting a search underway immediately and not having any assistance available for many days to come, Thompson made the logical and correct choice of the options open to him. No doubt, most skippers given the same set of circumstances would have made the same decision. Using hindsight to second guess his decision, as so many researchers have done, does little good because he had a limited amount of current information on which to base a decision.

Thompson also based his assumption on the belief that the Electra was in the vicinity of Howland Island. The less informed people are about radio propagation in the equatorial belt, the more certain they seem to be that the louder the signal strength, the closer the sending station. This is not necessarily true according to Paul Rafford, a radio propagation specialist who spent a decade arranging radio communication networks for astronauts' recovery programs in the South Seas and elsewhere as a Pan American Airways contractor to the National Air and Space Administration. He said that during the hours of darkness, night static was bad along the equator due to the major storm front going through the Marshall Islands which Earhart and the pilot of the Navy PBY from Pearl Harbor both encountered at different times and different places. After leaving the storm area at dawn, these masking effects would no longer be present so the radio signal would appear unusually loud. The point is, the radiomen aboard the *Itasca* weren't used to operating in the tropics and could easily have been fooled by the relative volume of the daytime versus the nighttime signals.

Thompson made the most logical decision based on the information available to him at the time. No other United States ship was closer than 900 miles to him, time was of the essence, and every hour of daylight available was critical. His course of action was quickly approved by San Francisco Coast Guard Headquarters. The Honolulu District Coast Guard Office and the 14th Naval District Commandant's Office at Pearl Harbor were notified. A hydro radio message to all ships and shore stations in the Central Pacific was sent on 500 kc, the international distress frequency, for those listening to be alert, and cited 500 kc, 3105 kc, and 6210 kc as radio bands to be monitored. NURI, Radio *Itasca*, was cited as the point of contact.

The response was meager. Eventually ships at sea included the United States steamer *Golden Bear*, British freighter, M.V. *Moorby*, the British Warship H.M.S. *Achilles*, and the Imperial Japanese Navy's *Koshu*. From the 14th Naval District, word was sent to Washington,

D.C., and, in due time, Rear Admiral Orin Murfin was notified publicly (overtly) that all (naval) resources were at his disposal to affect a rescue. Privately (covertly) he was directed otherwise. Of the two navy ships nearby to aid Thompson, the U.S.S. *Ontario* and the U.S.S. *Swan*, the *Ontario* was not allowed to join the search. Of the 24 long-range PBYs at Pearl Harbor, only one was sent toward Howland, and others Admiral Murfin planned to send to the equatorial region were grounded by Washington. The U.S.S. *Swan*, a seaplane tender attached to PatWing2 at Pearl Harbor, was misrepresented throughout the search as a minesweeper and was diverted, along with the *Itasca* and the M.V. *Moorby*, to a point 281 miles north of Howland by a hoax radio message heard by three USN radio operators on duty at Naval Radio Oahu. Commander Thompson referred to a request by USN personnel to investigate the 281-mile-north hoax as an "official" message. This doesn't leave much doubt as to who originated the hoax, the ones who sent it, the ones who heard it, and the ones who diverted the only three ships engaged in the search to cover a million square miles of empty ocean. This occurred on 4 and 5 July, during the crucial first five days of the search when the downed fliers would most likely have been rescued. Clearly, either Washington didn't want Earhart found or she was never lost in the first place.

Rear Admiral Orin G. Murfin, U.S.N. Commandant of 14th Naval District (Pearl Harbour), was in overall command of the Earhart search
Photo credit - National Archives Negative #80-G-410929

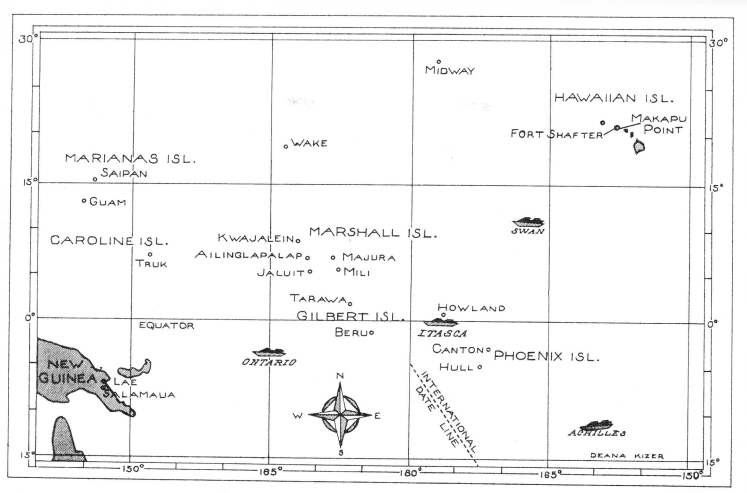

Central Pacific Ocean Chart - July 2, 1937
Graphic credit - Ann H. Pellegreno

OFFICIAL REPORT OF THE USN EARHART SEARCH,
2-18 JULY 1937

1. Amelia Earhart Putnam and Fred J. Noonan, engaged in a land plane flight around the world, departed Lae, New Guinea, at 10:00, 2 July (zone-minus-ten-time), or 0000, 1 July, Greenwich Civil Time (GCT) for Howland Island. The flight was guarded by the U.S.S. *Ontario* at approximately midpoint of the flight and by the USCG cutter *Itasca* at Howland. The U.S.S. *Swan* was on station midway between Howland and Honolulu to guard the next leg of the flight. Except for the services of the *Ontario* and the *Swan* and weather reports from the Fleet Air Base, Pearl Harbor, the Navy had no connection with the flight.

2. At 11:00 a.m. (HST), 2 July, information was received that failure of the flight was imminent and, shortly thereafter, that the plane was believed down.

Howland Island in the Central Pacific Ocean was the announced destination of Amelia Earhart
Photo credit - National Archives Negative #80-G-11883

3. At 1400, 2 July, the Commandant conferred with the Commander, Minecraft, Battle Force (the Senior Officer Present Afloat), and the Commanding Officer, Fleet Air Base, Pearl Harbor. It was agreed that no naval vessel stationed in Hawaiian waters was suitable for search operations in the distant area and that a PBY seaplane would reach Howland Island and, under favorable conditions, could start limited operations, basing on the *Itasca*. The Department was so informed. Meanwhile, the Department had directed the Commandant of the 14th Naval District to use all available naval facilities in the search. Accordingly, it was decided to dispatch a seaplane to Howland and at 1923, 2 July, patrol plane 6-P-3, Lieutenant W.W. Harvey commanding, departed from Pearl Harbor for Howland Island. The *Itasca* was directed to stand by at Howland to tend the plane and the *Swan* to proceed toward Howland.

4. The Department promptly approved the recommendation that the *Colorado*, then in Honolulu, be diverted from her ROTC cruise to join the search, and, at 2115, 2 July, the ship was ordered to proceed when fueled. In a conference with the Commanding Officer of the U.S.S. *Colorado*, prior to his departure from Pearl Harbor, he was given all information available, and it was agreed that the *Colorado* should first search the southeast quadrant from Howland and the Phoenix Islands.

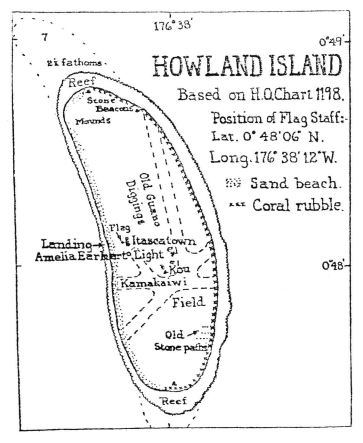

Howland Island Chart showing airstrips

5. The patrol plane, commanded by Lieutenant Harvey and manned by the following personnel, proceeded toward Howland through the night of 2-3 July. En route, contact with the *Swan* occurred on schedule.

Personnel, Patrol Plane 6-P-3
    Lieutenant W. W. Harvey, Commanding
    Lieutenant (jg) W. M. Drane
    Lieutenant (jg) E. S. Lytle
    Aviation Cadet P. W. Smith
    Aviation Cadet W. C. Curry, A.C.M.M.
    Aviation Cadet E. J. McCormick, C.R.M.
    Aviation Cadet F. M. Williams, III, R.M. 2-c.
    Aviation Cadet C. L. English, A.M.M. 2-c.
At 0710, 3 July, Lieutenant Harvey reported:

2003 APPROXIMATE POSITION LAT 06-35 LONG 72-00 PERIOD LAST TWO HOURS IN EXTREMELY BAD WEATHER BETWEEN ALTITUDE 2000 AND 12000 FEET SNOW SLEET RAIN ELECTRICAL STORMS PERIOD IN DAYLIGHT CONDITIONS LOOK EQUALLY BAD CLOUD TOPS APPEAR TO BE 18000 FEET OR MORE PERIOD AM RETURNING TO PEARL HARBOR NOW HAVE 900 GALLONS OF FUEL ON BOARD 1710

6. Vessels were dispatched from Pearl Harbor to guard the return flight of plane 6-P-3 in case of fuel exhaustion, but the prudence and skill of personnel safely returned the plane to Pearl Harbor at 1926, 3 July, after having been in the air for 24 hours and 5 minutes and flying approximately 2,570 sea miles. Faultless two-way communication was maintained throughout the flight and the navigation was accurate as evidenced by contacts with surface vessels and the sighting of landfalls, all of which occurred precisely on schedule. This performance of duty reflects great credit on Lieutenant Harvey, his officers, and his crew.

7. The Department inquired as to the feasibility of seaplane search operations basing on Johnston Island. The Commandant considered this impracticable, due to the 2,000-mile turnaround between Howland and Johnston, and stated that if a more extensive search than possible with the *Colorado*, *Itasca*, and *Swan* were desired, a carrier would be the most practicable and efficient unit.

8. The *Lexington* Group, organized on 4 July, consisted of that carrier and three destroyers, the *Lamson*, the *Cushing*, and the *Drayton*. Captain J. S. Dowell, Commander, Destroyer Squadron Two, ordered this group to assemble expeditiously, depart for Hawaii for fuel, and thence to proceed to the search area.

U.S.S. *Lamson* (DD-367) was typical of three *Mahan* class destroyers escorting the *Lexington* on Earhart search. She was normal flagship of Captain J. S. "Dad" Dowell, USN, who was Senior Officer Present Afloat. His flag was transferred to the *Lexington* during search operations.
The *Lamson* was sunk as a target ship in first Atomic Bomb Test at Bikini in July 1946.
Photo credit - Vice-Admiral L. M. Mustin, USN, retired

U.S.S. *Lexington* (CV-2) joined Earhart search on 12 July 1937. Aboard were 64 two-place observation airplanes assigned from three West Coast aircraft carriers.
Photo credit - United States Naval Institute

9. Meanwhile, *Itasca* crewmen had resumed search operations in the vicinity of Howland Island, as shown in her report and track chart. The difficulties confronting her crew may be inferred from the following dispatches:

FROM: ITASCA
TO: COMHAWSEC
INFO: COMFRANDIV
6002 YOUR 6002 1401 WE HAVE HAD NO POSITIONS COMMA SPEEDS COMMA OR COURSES FROM EARHART PLANE EXCEPT SO CALLED LINE OF POSITION AT 0843 WHICH HAD NO REF POINT PERIOD SHE GAVE US NONE OF HER BEARINGS PERIOD BELIEVE SHE PASSED TO NORTH AND WEST OF ISLAND ABOUT 0800 AND MISSED IT IN THE GLARE OF RISING SUN THOUGH WE WERE SMOKING HEAVILY AT THAT TIME PERIOD JUDGE SHE CAME DOWN BETWEEN 337 AND 90 FROM HOWLAND AND WITHIN 100 MILES PERIOD HAVE BROADCAST AS INDICATED 1402

FROM: ITASCA
TO: COMSANFRANCISCO DIVN
INTO: COMHAWN SECTION
6002 . . . EARHART ONLY ACKNOWLEDGED RECEIVING ITASCA SIGNALS ONCE AND DID NOT ANSWER QUESTIONS AS TO POSITION COURSE SPEED OR EXPECTED TIME ARRIVAL PERIOD EARHART USED VOICE ENTIRELY STATIC INTERFERENCE HEAVY AND ITASCA RECEPTION FRAGMENTARY IN EARLY HOURS. 1945

The *Itasca* was covering an area along the probable Earhart track when apparently reliable radio intercepts indicated that the Earhart plane was 281 miles north of Howland. The *Swan* was approaching that vicinity en route to Howland and was directed to conduct a coordinated search with the *Itasca*. The steamship *Moorby* also joined in the fruitless search of this area.

10. On 6 July, the Commandant, 14th Naval District, was directed to take charge of all naval forces engaged in the search. The *Itasca* was also directed by Coast Guard Headquarters to operate under the Commandant's authority. Accordingly, the Commanding Officer, U.S.S. *Colorado*, then approaching the area, was directed to take charge of all vessels in the area and conduct a coordinated search until the arrival of Commander, Destroyer Squadron Two, when the latter would assume command.

Weather station on Howland Island - 1937
Photo credit - National Archives Negative #80-CF-79868-4

Itascatown on Howland Island - 1937
Photo credit - National Archives Negative #80-CF-79868-5

11. The details of the search were left to the discretion of the Commanding Officer, U.S.S. *Colorado*. The decision to search the quadrant southeast from Howland and the Phoenix Islands still appeared to be sound. The search was conducted as shown in the Commanding Officer, U.S.S. *Colorado*, report. No evidence of the fliers or their plane was found. With the elimination of that quadrant, however, the Commander, *Lexington* Group, was later enabled to plan and execute an extensive sea search of the western semicircle from Howland.

12. In order to release the *Colorado* at the earliest practicable date, it was decided that she would complete the search of the Phoenix Islands and vicinity, then rendezvous with and transfer fuel to the *Lexington* Group destroyers. This was done on 12 July and the *Colorado* was released from further duty in connection with the search. The result of her operations was to establish that neither the plane nor its passengers were ashore in the Phoenix Group (sic) and, therefore, that they were neither on any known land within 450 miles of Howland nor afloat in the extensive area searched by pilots flying the three floatplanes. The duty was efficiently performed under conditions of considerable hazard, due to the inadequacy of surveys of the waters traversed. During the search Captain W. L. Friedell, the Commanding Officer of the *Colorado*, exercised sound judgment and effectively directed the units at his disposal.

13. While the *Lexington* Group was being fueled at Lahaina and Pearl Harbor, the Commandant held a conference with the Commander, Destroyer Squadron Two, the Commanding Officer of the *Lexington*, and senior commanders in the District. Information on the

flight, studies of the weather, and the probable location of the Earhart plane were made available to the *Lexington* Group. The daily search plan for the *Lexington* Group was submitted and accepted. (The details of the studies and assumptions are included in those set forth in Commander, *Lexington* Group report and are omitted from this book for the sake of brevity.)

USCG cutter *Taney* offloading supplies at Howland Island
Photo credit - National Archives Negative #80-CF-79868-2

14. Captain J. S. Dowell, Search Commander, Destroyer Squadron Two, took over command of all units in the search area on 11 July and put his search plan into effect. This plan was based on the information available up to that time and subject to certain limitations of fuel and

Landing tractor on Howland Island by barge being towed by launch from USCG cutter
Photo credit - National Archives Negative #80-CF-79868-3

endurance of the vessels in his command. The *Lexington* was required to complete the operation and return to the West Coast with the fuel on board. The *Itasca* and *Swan* could operate until 16 July and reach Honolulu without refueling. The destroyers could match the *Lexington's* time limit. There was thus an absolute maximum of nine successive days for destroyer operations in the search area. Prudence dictated a reduction of this time to seven days to provide a fuel reserve. To insure an efficient search despite some anticipated bad weather, the Commandant directed that the plan provide for no more than seven days of searching. Subsequently, he directed that it terminate on 18 July if good weather prevailed on 17 and 18 July and, if not, on 19 July. The Commander, Destroyer Squadron Two, accordingly laid out and executed his search.

15. The details of the plan and the reasons for its various provisions were sound and met with the full approval of the Commandant. The operation was well-conceived, skillfully executed, and reflected great credit on Captain J. S. Dowell and on the commanding officers, ship officers, and crews of the vessels and plane squadrons under his command.

Amelia Earhart twice failed (March and July 1937) to reach Howland Island, her announced destination. Ann Pellegreno, following "The Earhart Trail" located the illusive island in July 1967, 30 years later.
Photo credit - Ann Holtgren Pellegreno, © World Flight, The Earhart Trail

16. The performance of duty of the Commanding Officer of the Coast Guard Cutter *Itasca*, Commander W. K. Thompson, had been commended by letter to his immediate superior. His intelligent and zealous conduct of the initial phase of the search under the most trying conditions deserved especial commendation. His reports, together with the wholehearted cooperation of the Commander, Hawaiian Section, USCG, were of great assistance to the subsequent conduct of operations by the Navy. Throughout the flight and search, the performance of the *Itasca* crew was excellent in all respects. Careful study of all communications, other information pertaining to the flight, and the preparations indicate clearly that the *Itasca* crew left nothing on their parts undone to insure the safe completion of the Earhart flight.

17. The U.S.S. *Swan*, the smallest vessel engaged in the search, was the last to return to port. She was at sea for 37 days during which she steamed approximately 7,000 miles. Despite the onerous operating conditions involving shortages of provisions and supplies, she carried out all assigned duties in a manner reflecting great credit on the commanding officer, Lieutenant H. F. MacComsey, the officers, and the crew. Neither machinery failure nor a single sick day occurred during the entire cruise.

18. It is most gratifying that there was no serious injury to men or material in the very extensive and sometimes hazardous operations of ships and planes.

19. To summarize briefly: The initial phase of the search was based on Thompson's well-reasoned belief that the plane was north of and fairly near Howland. A rather complete search of this area was made on 2-3 July.

Ann Pellegreno in the 1937, Model 10, Lockheed Electra which, in June and July, 1967, she piloted around the world in commemoration of the 30th anniversary of Amelia Earhart's flight.
Photo credit - Champion Spark Plug

U.S.S. *Swan,* **aircraft tender, was first U.S. Navy ship to join the Earhart Search.**
Photo credit - National Archives

Then, on the strength of radio intercepts which appeared too reliable to be ignored, the search was shifted to the westward and then 281 miles to northward of Howland. Both areas were searched without success and upon subsequent analysis the radio intercepts on which this search was based were discredited.

The second phase of the search moved to the southeastern quadrant on the basis of intercepts, bearings, and other considerations which indicated the plane was on land and probably in the Phoenix Islands. With this assumption eliminated, the third phase was logically based on the assumption that the plane had landed in the water probably within 200 miles of Howland and that the wreckage or raft would have drifted well to the westward and northwestward in the 11-day interval prior to arrival of the *Lexington.*

The *Lexington* Group covered an area approximately 300 miles square to the west and northwest of Howland which included all probable positions of plane or passengers if afloat. As an additional, but unlikely, possibility the Gilbert Islands were searched. It is regrettably unreasonable to conclude other than that the unfortunate fliers were not above water upon conclusion of the search.

Miles steamed by vessels en route to	
and during the search:	48,000
Miles flown by planes:	149,000
Plane hours in air:	1,654

Square miles searched:	
By vessels	94,800
By aircraft	+167,281
TOTAL	262,081

20. Due to the geographic location of the search area and the composition of the force, certain features of the search were of outstanding interest:

The extensive weather and current data should prove a valuable contribution to the knowledge of the area.

It is believed that the plan used by the *Lexington* and her squadrons is unique, and was particularly well-designed for the management of widely-separated forces and for communications concerning the operation.

The experience in false messages, interference, and confusion on critical frequencies indicates the need for authoritative control of such frequencies in emergencies. Obviously, such realistic radio programs as the "March of Time" should not be broadcast when they may affect relief measures in progress.

If the Navy or Coast Guard are to be involved in future private transoceanic flights, the licensing authority for such flights should be prevailed upon to require from the fliers a specific minimum performance in giving to those concerned reliable information prior to and during the progress of the flight.

21. It may be assumed that the Navy will be called upon to attempt rescue of crew and passengers of a trans-Pacific clipper should one unfortunately be forced down at sea. Plans for coordinated rescue efforts in the Hawaiian Area have been under consideration for the last several months. They provide for joint action by local agencies of the Navy, Coast Guard, and Pan American Airways. The greater part of the trans-Pacific air route is beyond the effective radius of local forces. Therefore, it would appear desirable to provide tentative plans for such rescue efforts by units of the Fleet as may be anticipated.

(Signed) Rear Admiral Orin G. Murfin, USN

OFFICIAL VERSION OF THE
U.S.S. *COLORADO* SEARCH

At 0700 on the morning of 9 July in Latitude 3°54' South, Longitude 174°46' West, the *Colorado* launched her planes in the direction of McKean Island. Upon locating McKean and searching the vicinity, the planes continued to Gardner and then to Carondelet Reef before returning to the ship in Latitude 4°30' South, Longitude 174°24' West. After the vain search for reef and sandbanks and for Winslow Reef, it was to be expected

U.S.S. *Colorado* (BB-45) joined Earhart search from Hawaii on 7 July 1937. Note three Vought Corsair observation floatplanes on fantail/aft turret "C" catapults.
Photo credit - United States Naval Institute

that the other islands did not or might not exist. They were, however, all located by the pilots. Although not in their exact charted positions, they were seen from a considerable distance and the pilots had no difficulty in locating them.

McKean Island showed unmistakable signs of having at one time been inhabited. On the northwest side of the island there appeared buildings of the adobe type. No one was seen on either Gardner Island or McKean Island.

McKean Island was such that a plane could have made a safe crash landing either on the beach or in the center of the island. No dwellings or any other signs of habitation appeared on Gardner. A long, shallow lagoon extends the entire length of the island and through most of the width.

A seaplane could land in the lagoon and it is believed that a land plane could make a forced landing there and the occupants walk ashore. Coral reefs extend out from the shoreline for about 150 yards. At Gardner Island a 4,000-ton tramp steamer has piled up head-on and remains there with her back broken. Groves of coconut palms grow on the western end and the entire island is covered with tropical vegetation. Myriad birds cover both islands.

Carondelet Reef was underwater, but could be plainly seen from the planes at a distance of ten miles. This was of interest in regard to the possibility of Winslow Reef existing and the reef and sandbank to the northwestward of Winslow Reef. If the two existed, it is apparent from the way in which Carondelet Reef was seen, that they are many miles from their charted positions.

The *Colorado* continued on course 090° and at 1400 planes were launched in Latitude 4°33' South,

Longitude 173°45' West. The purpose of the flight in the afternoon was to search the water ahead of the ship to locate Hull Island and to search the island and the water in the vicinity for any signs of the Earhart plane.

As the planes approached Hull Island, natives were seen running out of their huts and waving at the plane. Lieutenant Lambrecht, the senior aviator in charge of the flight, landed for the purpose of asking if the inhabitants had seen or heard the Earhart plane. A European resident manager of the natives came out in a dugout canoe to meet the plane. He and his natives were astonished and excited in seeing the three planes. The resident manager asked where the planes were from and when informed Honolulu, nearly upset the canoe in his excitement. It was necessary to explain to him that the planes had not come direct but had arrived by the battleship, which was relatively close. The resident manager said that there was a radio on the island; however, he knew nothing of the Earhart flight and created doubt of his having ever heard of Miss Earhart herself. Neither he nor his natives had seen or heard a plane. The planes returned to the ship in Latitude 4°33' South, Longitude 173°8' West.

During the night the ship steamed north and then east arriving at Latitude 3°51' South, Longitude 172°15' West, at 0700 on 10 July.

The *Swan* had been directed upon arrival at Latitude 2° South, Longitude 170° West to proceed to rendezvous with the *Colorado* in Latitude 3°10' South, Longitude 172° West at 1100 and to search in the vicinity of Canton Island en route. The planes were launched at 0700 and proceeded to Sydney, Phoenix, Enderbury, and Birnie Islands in the order named. At 1015 in Latitude 3°22' South, Longitude 172°2' West they were recovered by the ship. Sydney was the only island which showed any signs of recent habitation and in appearance was much the same as Gardner Island. It had the usual shallow lagoon which in this case was large enough for a seaplane to make a safe landing. Phoenix and Birnie Islands had the appearance of a lagoon, but the latter island was very small. Enderbury had a lagoon, but it was very shallow.

When the planes were recovered, the *Swan* was taken alongside and refueled and provisioned. Upon completion of fueling, the *Swan* was directed to search in a northwest direction across the open water north of the Phoenix Group en route Latitude 2° South, Longitude 175° West.

At 1445 the *Colorado*, in Latitude 3°22' South, Longitude 175°45' West, launched planes for a search to and of Canton Island. This island was located and carefully searched by the planes. It was the largest of any of the islands searched. Its lagoon was deeper than those of the other islands but was crossed with coral reefs in such a manner that it would be dangerous to land except at two places, one at each end of the island. At the western end there remain the shacks and scaffolding erected by the recent eclipse expedition. When the planes were recovered, the course was set at 350° to take the *Colorado* to a rendezvous at 0700, 12 July, with the destroyers approaching the search area with the *Lexington* Group.

Upon refueling the destroyers, the *Colorado* was detached from the search group and directed to return to the West Coast in order to debark the Naval Reserve Officers Training Corps students and Naval Reserve officers. These students with the distinguished guests embarked for a month's cruise, which extended into a six-weeks' cruise that covered many more miles than was expected at the time of embarkation.

If it is considered that the search area began with the position where the *Colorado* fueled the *Itasca*, 0600, 7 July, and ended with the position where the *Colorado* fueled the destroyers of the *Lexington* Group, 12 July, it will be found that the *Colorado* steamed 1,240 miles, and that each of her planes was flown 21.2 hours and covered 1,980 miles. The *Colorado* with her planes covered within the radius of visibility, an area of 25,490 square miles. Adding this to mileage from Pearl Harbor to the Search Area and return, the *Colorado* steamed 3,980 miles and was on search duty 320 hours, much more than anticipated when the Naval Reserve Officers Training Corps cruise commenced.

(Signed) Captain W. L. Friedell, USN

THE *COLORADO* SEARCH, COVERT ASPECTS

Lt. John O. Lambrecht, USN, was one of the busiest men aboard the U.S.S. *Colorado* in early July 1937. Since crossing the equator at 174° West Latitude, he and two other pilots had flown their observation aircraft three flights a day in a sweep through the Phoenix Island area. As senior aviator, his aircraft was the first launched from a shipboard catapult, and, following flights of several hundred miles away from the 33,000-ton battleship, was the first to be brought back aboard.

Beginning 6 July, shipboard activity was centered around launching the aircraft on search missions, the goal of which was to locate Earhart, Noonan, the Lockheed, or possibly a raft if they had landed on the water. Both Winslow Reef and Carondelet Reef as well as the eight islands of the Phoenix Group were to be searched.

Lt. John O. Lambrecht, USN, senior aviator, U.S.S. *Colorado*, 1937. He landed his 03U-3 Corsair on Hull Island lagoon on 9 July 1937.
Photo credit - Mrs. J. O. Lambrecht

On 9 July, Lambrecht had just secured his three aircraft aboard the ship after the morning flight when Captain F. W. Friedell ordered him to the bridge where the aviator was directed to the navigator's cabin. There the captain and the navigator were consulting several charts and the sailing directions for the area. Friedell pointed to the ship's track through the Phoenix Group. As Lambrecht was well aware, the afternoon target was Hull Island, some 60 miles away. As he unrolled a large chart of Hull, the captain said that a secret meeting had been arranged with the white resident manager of the island. Lambrecht's planes were to fly there. Only Lambrecht was to land on the western end of the lagoon, whereupon the manager would come by boat and turn over a very important package which Lambrecht was to bring to the ship.

Lambrecht was dumbfounded. For several days the pilots had been searching miles of open ocean and uninhabited islands. Quickly he looked at the enlarged map of the island. It was not a United States Hydrographic Office chart but a British Admiralty chart which showed the lagoon full of protruding coral outcroppings. He told the captain that the lagoon appeared unsafe. The captain assured him that he had been informed that it was safe to land there. Apparently, someone with firsthand knowledge that the chart was in error and the surface clear of obstacles had informed the United States Navy of that fact.

Aerial view of extensive lagoon at Hull Island. This island is the second largest of the eight Phoenix Islands.
Photo credit - National Archives

As noted in the ship's log, pilots and observers (aviation cadets) on that afternoon flight were:
Floatplanes: O3Us

> Number 404
> Pilot: Lt. John O. Lambrecht
> Observer: James A. Wilson
> Number 405
> Pilot: Lt. (jg) L. O. Fox
> Observer: W. Jordan
> Number 406
> Pilot: Lt. (jg) William B. Short
> Observer: Lt. William A. Sullivan

Lambrecht must have had misgivings as he was launched that afternoon. No other island was inhabited. Why should this one be? What was in the package he was to obtain? What did it have to do with Earhart? Even if he landed safely, would he be able to take off? If a coral outcropping were within a foot of the surface, it would rip the bottom out of his float.

After flying about thirty minutes, the pilots saw Hull Island on the horizon. Descending from 1,000 feet to 450 feet, they circled the island, the unmuffled Wasp engines roaring. After the first circuit, about 40 natives rushed onto the beach showing great excitement at the unaccustomed sight of airplanes. Lambrecht flew lower for a closer look and saw many signs of habitation, including storage sheds, huts, and so forth. Next he flew slowly across the lagoon to inspect the surface. In the clear water he saw many coral heads, but could not judge how far below the surface they were and whether a safe landing could be made.

Comments by another pilot in the trio, Lt. Bill Short, are worth examining. He believed that Lambrecht made a spontaneous decision to land on the lagoon and that Lambrecht would not have "decided to land and ask the white resident manager if he had seen Amelia or her airplane." In the first place, how did Lambrecht know if the manager was white or spoke English? Many islands had native rulers. Second, it should have been obvious that the Navy had no intention of landing on any of the islands.

Western end of Hull Island, Phoenix Group (ca. 1939). Note settlement with large "copra shed" in foreground and wide expanse of sand on platform reef which surrounds the perimeter of the atoll.
Photo credit - National Archives

Hull Island taken in 1969 after evacuation of natives and subsequent disuse of atoll. Encroachment of tropical vegetation on sandy beach is evident due to unattended coconut palm plantation. Wrecked Korean fishing vessel in foreground.

Photo credit - United States Air Force

The *Colorado* had come up on Gardner Island, which was heavily foliaged, and no landing party had been sent ashore. The sovereignty of Hull Island was reputedly British, but still under dispute, and the U.S. State Department didn't want to alienate Britain at that time. Technically and territorially, the lagoon was part of Hull. Landing safely was one consideration. Taking off in a floatplane required ten times more distance than landing, in this case, with much more exposure to coral heads. Also, if the lagoon had a smooth-as-glass surface, the plane might not have been able to get "on the step" so as to break clear from the water. It was inadvisable to shut down the engine because a hand-cranked inertial starter was used to restart the engine. If the engine had balked, mechanics from the battleship would have to be brought to Hull Island. To Short, it seemed unlikely that a young lieutenant would have risked landing on an unknown lagoon without authorization. While Lambrecht might have radioed Friedell for approval, there is no evidence that he did so, and, therefore, the aviator must have received prior orders.

A few minutes after Lambrecht and his observer in the rear seat, Aviation Cadet James "Ash" Wilson, landed on the lagoon, the white manager left the western shore of the lagoon near the village in an outrigger canoe. Lacking paddles, three natives took more than half an hour to pole the canoe to the airplane.

According to newspaper accounts released by the Navy, Lambrecht asked the white resident manager if he had seen Amelia Earhart or her airplane and received a negative reply. Although the resident manager had a radio receiver, he said he hadn't been aware of her flight. When Lambrecht told him that the three floatplanes had come from Honolulu and that a U.S. battleship had transported them to within "60 miles" of the island, the

Naval aviator J. Ashley Wilson, Jr., flew as observer in the rear seat of Lambrecht's floatplane during the flight to Hull Island and the critical landing on the lagoon.

Photo credit - J. Ashley Wilson, Jr.

Aerial view of Sydney Island (looking south) located 60 miles east of Hull Island. When *Colorado* floatplanes flew above Sydney on 10 July 1937, native huts were seen, but 14 laborers on Sydney remained hidden in the huts during overflight in sharp contrast to the behavior of the natives on Hull Island.
Photo credit - National Archives of New Zealand

manager appeared surprised. The manager then left without telling Lambrecht his name. Lambrecht took off from the lagoon and, with the other two pilots who had been circling the atoll, returned to the ship.

That was the story given to the press and the same one given by Lambrecht in the unclassified semi-official report on the aviation phase of the activities of the *Colorado*. So far as is known, no one has challenged this story. Unfortunately so, because it was the crux of the entire naval search for Earhart and Noonan. As this story unfolds, it will be seen how false it really is and how the public was deceived under the guise of keeping the fate of Earhart away from the Japanese Navy.

Colorado observation plane on harbor surface.
Photo credit - San Diego Aerospace Museum

According to Lambrecht's observer, naval aviator J. A. Wilson, who later became a captain for Pan American Airways, and was at the time of this writing a retired lawyer, no package of any sort was given to him or Lambrecht during the visit to the lagoon on Hull Island.

The results of the *Colorado* search were that the fliers, in all probability, crashed in the ocean. Knowledge that Earhart failed to reach either Howland or Baker and was not in the Phoenix Group, left only the Gilbert Islands still farther to the west as the only remaining land in the region. The remoteness of the Gilberts meant that finding lost fliers there could be little less than a miracle. *Colorado* personnel not only scouted a vast area, but also directed operations of the *Itasca* and the Navy seaplane tender *Swan* pending the arrival of *Lexington* and Destroyer Squadron Two.

The most dramatic moment of the search, after the opening hours had elapsed, was afforded by the flight of the three floatplanes to Hull Island, apparently, at that time the only inhabited island in the group. Some 200 (*sic*) shouting natives, wearing nothing but loincloths, ran from their grass (*sic*) huts when the Vought Corsairs flew overhead, seemingly appearing out of nowhere.

U.S. Navy observation airplane, O3U-3 Vought "Corsair", being hoisted aboard assigned warship. They were called the "eyes of the fleet."
Photo credit - San Diego Aerospace Museum

Typical observation plane launch from United States Navy battleship stern catapult (circa 1937)
Photo credit - National Archives

Comments were also made in the newspaper published on the *Colorado* in an article titled: "Plane Search Halts Cruise," and further subtitled "*Colorado* Departs from Honolulu to Search Area at Equator" and "Three Planes Cover the Phoenix Group" appeared in one of the July issues. Parts of the text follow:

"A 3,980-mile cruise in search of Amelia Earhart Putnam and her navigator, Frederick Noonan, ended early Friday afternoon 16 July, when the *Colorado* arrived off Pearl Harbor.

"Return of the battleship to Oahu marked completion of the most important phase of the search for the two world fliers, last heard from July 2nd when nearing their Howland Island goal on the long hop from New Guinea.

"Despite popular attention focussed on the aircraft carrier *Lexington* because of the number of planes she carried, it was the *Colorado* which first put planes into the air in the search for Mrs. Putnam and her Lockheed plane.

"There is the further fact that it was the *Colorado* which conducted the swift but careful (*sic*) aerial search of the Phoenix group, regarded as the likeliest place to find the fliers.

"The search of the Phoenix group, disappointingly negative, nevertheless eliminated those islands from further consideration, and narrowed the field to be covered by the *Lexington* and Destroyer Squadron Two.

"In discharging her assignment with dispatch, the

Colorado and her planes scouted an area of 25,490 square miles, chiefly in the vital region lying to the southeast of Howland Island."

SEARCH ANALYSIS—RADIO MESSAGES
During the search, hundreds of radio messages were logged by personnel in the *Itasca* radio room. These "flimsies," as they were sometimes called, ranged from essential to trivial and from routine to irrelevant. In this volume, some selectivity is essential, but important messages relative to the Earhart disappearance cannot be discarded. Therefore, a limited number of significant radio messages logged by *Itasca* personnel are cited along with brief explanations.

Obviously, no two researchers would select the same group of messages. What might seem important to one would seem irrelevant to another. This compilation is based on the prior work of Commander Warren K. Thompson, USCG, and Captain Lawrence L. Safford, USN, plus deletions and additions deemed relevant by the author. This composite is a compromise regarding brevity, sufficiency, and comprehensiveness.

Rear Admiral Robert A. Theobald, USN, in *The Final Secret of Pearl Harbor* (1954), wrote that the government authorities used the tactical Japanese attack "to bury the true story under a mass of evidence that would preserve its secret" (pp.170-1). In other words, relevant facts were mixed with so much irrelevancy that the truth was difficult, if not impossible, to ascertain.

When Earhart's broadcast of "One half hour fuel" was reported to him, Thompson hurried the passengers through their breakfasts, had them gather their belongings, and at 0800 sent them ashore to serve as a supplementary shore party to assist Earhart upon her landing. At 0826, Thompson radioed Howland Island, recalling the regular shore party and telling them that he believed that Earhart was down. Frank Ciprianti was ordered to remain with the direction finder (D\F) on Howland and attempt to obtain bearings on the airplane. This order could not be carried out completely, because the gun-firing batteries borrowed from the *Itasca* to power the D\F had completely run down by 0900, and he spent the rest of 2 July and all of 3 July recharging them. He wrote in his log that the batteries were weak at 0745 on 2 July. Fortunately, living on Howland were two Hawaiian nationals, Yat Fai Lum and Ah Kin Leong, who were amateur radio operators. A battery-charger was available on Howland, so by midnight 3-4 July, the Howland D\F was operating again. This D\F was manned continuously for the following 13 days by Ciprianti and the two amateurs. During that period, only one bearing was obtained on 3105 kc.

FROM: HOWLAND ISLAND
TO: ITASCA
8005 AT 0035 HST OBTAINED BEARING ON A CONTINUOUS WAVE OF UNKNOWN ORIGIN INDICATING SOUTH SOUTHEAST OR NORTH NORTHWEST ON MAGNETIC COMPASS PERIOD UNABLE TO OBTAIN UNILATERAL BEARING DUE TO NIGHT EFFECT PERIOD NO CALL GIVEN PERIOD FREQUENCY IS SLIGHTLY ABOVE 3105 KC 0425.

Note: Ciprianti's log was one day in error as to dates and his watch was one hour fast as it was set to Hawaiian time. HST is Howland standard time.

According to the radio log of the *Itasca*, the official landing party returned to the ship from Howland Island at 0912. Meanwhile, Earhart's radio had ceased transmissions at 0847 and nothing more had been heard from her on any frequency since that time. In the *Itasca* log for 1045 HST is the notation, "Underway at 155 rpm on course 337° to search most probable area of landing to north and northeast of Howland." Allowing sufficient time to hoist the two boats, an hour and a quarter had been lost when the rescue of the fliers depended on finding them with a minimum of delay.

The *Itasca* steamed for about 50 miles along the line-of-position (LOP) signalled by Earhart, made a right-angle change of course, and then paralleled her track to Howland. Persons on the ship were certain that the Lockheed had splashed within 100 miles of the ship. Thompson had more faith in the theory that Howland and the ship's smoke had been missed in the glare of the rising sun than in Earhart's LOP which had only an implied origin. After running about 100 miles on course 67° magnetic, 76° true, the ship resumed its former course of 337° true. At 8:00 p.m. HST on 2 July, in accordance with orders from a higher authority, the *Itasca* headed for Howland to rendezvous with and refuel a Navy patrol plane (PBY) which was to be flown from Pearl Harbor to assist in the search. By daybreak on 3 July, the *Itasca* was back at Howland and the probability of finding Earhart and Noonan was estimated to be less than 1 percent.

In the text of the dispatches for 2 July is a relatively complete story of what occurred.

FROM: ITASCA
TO: COMHAWSEC
6002 SUGGEST NAVY CONTACT FOR SEA PLANE SEARCH PERIOD SIXTEEN HUNDRED GALLONS AVIATION GASOLINE NOW ON HOWLAND AND NINETY FIVE GALLONS LUBRICATING OIL 1018

More information came from San Francisco:

FROM: COM SF DIV
TO: ITASCA
8002 POSSIBILITY PLANE MAY ATTEMPT USE RADIO ON WATER AS RADIO SUPPLY WAS BATTERY AND ANTENNA COULD BE USED ON TOP OF WING (*SIC*) PUTNAM AND LOCKHEED STATE POSSIBILITY OF FLOATING CONSIDERABLE TIME EXCELLENT AND THAT EMERGENCY RUBBER RAFT AND PLENTY OF EMERGENCY RATIONS CARRIED ON PLANE 0910

Of the 24 long-range PBY-1s at Pearl Harbor in July 1937, only one was sent toward Howland Island during the Earhart search. Rear Admiral Murfin planned on sending three others, but Washington vetoed their use. As they were the only available vehicles for a timely and thorough search, this denial was either (1) gross negligence or (2) indicative that Earhart was not really "lost."
Photo credit - San Diego Aerospace Museum

Thompson wrote the following in his report:
"This information formed the basis of the *Itasca's* search at sea until the information was contradicted by Lockheed on or about 5 July. The *Itasca* assumed the plane would float nine hours or so. The *Itasca* kept listening on 6210 kc, 3105 kc, and 500 kc. The probability of the plane being able to use radio gave credence to the numerous amateur position messages. Arrival of the Navy plane on 3 July, it was hoped, would expand the search efforts. As long as radio use was possible, the search was not a hopeless affair. The *Itasca* steadily called the plane. (Entire sentence underlined by Thompson in the report.) The period 1733 to 1748 was occupied with commercial press requests and routine traffic pouring in during an emergency situation."

Another message was:

FROM: COM PAT SQD. PLANE 6F
TO: COM AIR FAB PEARL HARBOR
1002 PSP LIEUT HARVEY DEPARTED PEARL HARBOR FOR HOWLAND ISLAND 1923

Only one plane was sent, whereas Thompson had expected three and had hoped for more. There was an excellent reason for this: The 1,600 gallons of aviation gasoline on Howland would refuel one Navy patrol plane. But it pointed out a serious deficiency on the part of the Navy of tendering patrol airplanes at remote locations.

FROM: RDO TUTUILA
TO: ITASCA
1902 FOLLOWING RECEIVED FROM HMS ACHILLES AT 0730 GMT QUOTE UNKNOWN STATION HEARD TO MAKE QUOTE PLEASE GIVE US A FEW DASHES IF YOU GET US UNQUOTE HEARD GOOD STRENGTH BOTH ON 3105 KCS STOP FIRST STATION THEN MADE KHAQQ TWICE DISAPPEARED STOP NOTHING MORE HEARD OF EITHER AT 0620 GMT UNQUOTE ACHILLES POSITION AT 0700 GMT 10-00 SOUTH 160-50 WEST 2030

FROM: RDO TUTUILA
TO: COMHAWSEC
INF: ITASCA
1903 YOUR 8003 0925 REQUEST CONFIRMATION FROM HMS ACHILLES AND FOLLOWING RECEIVED QUOTE AT 0600 3 GMT A TELEPHONE TRANSMITTER WITH HARSH NOTE WAS HEARD TO MAKE PLEASE GIVE US A FEW DASHES IF YOU GET US PERIOD A SECOND TRANSMITTER WAS HEARD TO MAKE DASHES WITH NOTE MUSICAL STRENGTH GOOD PERIOD FIRST TRANSMITTER THEN MADE KHAQQ TWICE BEFORE FADING OUT PERIOD THE EVIDENCE EXISTS THAT EITHER TRANSMITTER WAS THE AIRPLANE ITSELF PERIOD WAVE FREQUENCY WAS 3105 KCS SIGNED COMMANDING OFFICER HMS ACHILLES UNQUOTE

The term "musical note" meant "modulated carrier wave" (MCW) not "carrier wave" (CW). If the *Itasca* had used CW for homing signal, it might have been heard by Earhart. The *Achilles* sent the first signal while the Lockheed was still airborne. Both Tutuila messages were included in Thompson's report, but neither of them evoked any comment by him. Incidentally, "Please give us a few dashes if you get us," was not recorded in any of the *Itasca* communication logs.

The *Swan*, as well as the other seaplane tenders at Pearl Harbor, carried 10,000 gallons of aviation gasoline. That ship should have been stationed at Howland, along with at least three of the patrol planes. Naval personnel knew, or would have known if anyone had given the matter any thought, that it would be called on for search and rescue if Earhart's plane came down at sea anywhere between Lae and Oakland. The precedent of the ill-fated Dole Race fliers in 1927 and Australian Charles T.P. Ulm was on the records if there were any

The H.M.S. *Achilles*, a British light cruiser, en route from American Samoa to Honolulu, Hawaii, picked up radio message from KHAQQ (Earhart's radio call letters) six hours after fuel exhaustion would have forced a landing. After arrival at Honolulu as a guest of the U.S. Navy, *Achilles* officers retracted radio intercept story.

Photo credit - Alexander Turnbull Library, New Zealand

doubters. The Secretary of the Navy had directed "Department desires full cooperation" but had designated nobody closer than Washington to coordinate the details and assume responsibility. What was everybody's business became nobody's business. Where the Department had given specific instructions, they were carried out to the letter. On the occasion of the Earhart loss, foresight, imagination, and initiative exercised by USN personnel were nonexistent. Concerning the Earhart search, it was the familiar story of "too little and too late" followed by "much too much" when it was too late to be of any use. The Navy risked lives of the crews of 64 planes aboard the *Lexington* on a hopeless search that was foredoomed to fail because of the elapsed time before the *Colorado* arrived on the scene and nine days before the *Lexington* was in position. If a flight of Navy patrol planes had taken off for Howland as soon as Earhart's "Running out of gas" message had been received, it could be presumed that the Lockheed could have been sighted while still afloat. Howland Island enjoyed unusually good weather on 2 and 3 July 1937. Not until 4 July did the customary local showers set in.

USN O3U-3 observation airplane details. Note step on main float to enable breaking surface of water during take-off. Airplane was powered by dependable WASP air-cooled engine.
Photo credit - San Diego Aerospace Museum

To continue with the story of 2 July 1937.

FROM: COMDT. 14TH NAV DISTR
TO: ITASCA
0002 BE AT HOWLAND ISLAND AT DAYLIGHT TOMORROW SATURDAY 3 JULY ONE PATROL SEA PLANE CALL LETTER 62 CAST FREQUENCIES 355 AND 4235 SERIES KILOCYCLES DEPARTED PEARL HARBOR FOR HOWLAND ISLAND 1927 PLUS TEN AND ONE HALF TIME COMMUNICATE DIRECTLY WITH PLANE AND PROVIDE TENDER SERVICES PLANE WILL MAKE HOURLY POSITION REPORTS ON THE HOUR USING ZONE TEN AND ONE HALF TIME KEEP PLANE ADVISED ON OUR POSITION AFTER PLANE WITHIN 500 MILES RADIUS HOWLAND ISLAND BE PREPARED FURNISH RADIO BEARINGS AND MAKE MO's AS REQUESTED 2050

Thompson wrote: "The above orders from the 14th naval district necessitated the *Itasca* discontinuing

scouting the area northwest of Howland and proceeding on a direct course for Howland in order to be at that point at daylight. These orders also necessitated recalibration of the T-10 radio in order to handle the Navy plane frequency. This work, combined with the plane guard, compelled the *Itasca* radio to limit its radio attempts to contact Earhart.

"The *Itasca* throughout the night, had no trouble in receiving the Navy plane reports direct. It is to be further noted that the plane laid a direct course for the *Swan* and made it in spite of very adverse weather."

The radio record for 2 July will be closed with the following:

2300 (HST) FROM: SAN FRANCISCO (NMC-KPH)
            TO: ITASCA
NMC DE KPH FOLLOWING FROM VKT VOICE HEARD FAIRLY STRONG SIGNS STRENGTH TO S3 0843 0854 GMT 48.31 METERS (i.e, 6210 kc) SPEECH NOT INTERPRETED OWING BAD MODULATION OR SPEAKER SHOUTING INTO MICROPHONE BUT VOICE SIMILAR TO THAT EMITTED FROM PLANE IN FLIGHT LAST NIGHT WITH EXCEPTION NO HUM OF PLANE IN BACKGROUND GMTX. PSE

This most important message, relayed from Nauru to the *Itasca*, produced no comment in Thompson's report.

With the following incoming message, 3 July 1937 began for the *Itasca*.

FROM: COMHAWSEC
TO: ITASCA
INF: COM SF DIV
8003 LAE NEW GUINEA REPORTS LAST CONTACT WITH EARHART PLANE BY LAE RADIO WAS AT 1720 FRIDAY GAVE HER POSITION AS 4.33 SOUTH 158.6 EAST WHICH IS ABOUT 795 MILES DIRECTLY ON HER ROUTE TO HOWLAND 0030

This information arrived about 30 hours too late. The next messages of any real importance are quoted below.

FROM: PLANE 62C
TO: FLEET AIR BASE, PEARL HARBOR; ITASCA
1003 WEATHER BECOMING UNFAVORABLE LOW BROKEN CLOUDS HIGH OVERCAST LIGHTENING (*SIC*) TO WEST SOUTHWEST AND TO SOUTHWARD 0445

FROM: PLANE 62C
TO: COMDR AIRCRAFT; FLEET AIR BASE, PEARL HARBOR
INF: SWAN, ITASCA
2003 APPROXIMATE POSITION LATITUDE 0635 LONGITUDE 7200 PERIOD LAST TWO HOURS IN EXTREMELY BAD WEATHER BETWEEN ALTITUDE 2000 AND 12,000 FEET SNOW SLEET RAIN ELECTRICAL STORMS PERIOD IN DAYLIGHT CONDITIONS LOOK EQUALLY BAD CLOUD TOPS APPEAR TO BE 18,000 FEET OR MORE PERIOD AM RETURNING TO PEARL HARBOR NOW HAVE 900 GALLONS FUEL ON BOARD 0710

Lt. Harvey's plane (62C) returned safely to Pearl Harbor.

FROM: ITASCA
TO: COMHAWSEC
6003 DRIFTING OFF HOWLAND COMPLIANCE COMDT 14TH NAVAL DIST DISPATCH 6002 2050 PERIOD WILL LOAD GAS PERIOD PLANE APPARENTLY RETURNING TO BASE PERIOD IMPERATIVE CONTINUE SEARCH TODAY TIME ELEMENT VITAL WEATHER CONDITIONS UNSETTLED FOR FLIGHT 0800

FROM: ITASCA
TO: FLEET AIR BASE, PEARL HARBOR; SWAN
6003 DRIFTING OFF HOWLAND SHALL WE LOAD GAS OR LEAVE FOR FUTURE PLANE OPERATIONS 0805

FROM: 14TH NAV DISTR
TO: ITASCA
0003 YOUR 6003 0805 RESUME SEARCH OPERATIONS PLANE RETURNING TO BASE 1138

FROM: COM SF DIV
TO: ITASCA
INF: COM24TH NAV DIS; COMHAWSEC
8004 UNCONFIRMED REPORTS FROM ROCK SPRINGS WYOMING STATE EARHART PLANE HEARD 1600 KCS PERIOD POSITION ON REEF SOUTHEAST OF HOWLAND ISLAND THIS INFORMATION MAY BE AUTHENTIC AS SIGNALS FROM MIDPACIFIC AND ORIENT OFTEN HEARD INLAND WHEN NOT AUDIBLE ON COAST VERIFICATION FOLLOWS 1510

Thompson later wrote, "This message started the Phoenix Island Reef theory. It was logical due to sun line and reciprocal bearings (from Howland D\F). When Pan American bearings came in later, the theory took a more definite form. The *Achilles*, *Monterey*, and *Mariposa* all passed near this area soon after Earhart was reported down. Being on a reef was safer than drifting at sea. One ship could not cover the entire possible area of more than 450,000 square miles. The *Colorado* later searched the islands with planes."

FROM: COMDESRON 2
TO: COM 14
INF: CINCUS; CNO; COLORADO, ITASCA
0004 CINCUS 0004 1050 LEXINGTON GROUP PROCEEDING ON DUTY ASSIGNED WILL FUEL LAHAINA ROADS

Thus ended 4 July 1937. On the following day, a new hoax appeared.

FROM: COMHAWSEC
TO: ITASCA
8005 FOLLOWING COPIED NAVY RADIO WAILUPE 1130 TO 1230 GCT QUOTE 281 NORTH HOWLAND CALL KHAQQ BEYOND NORTH DONT HOLD WITH US MUCH LONGER ABOVE WATER SHUT OFF UNQUOTE KEYED TRANSMISSION EXTREMELY POOR KEYING BEHIND CARRIER FRAGMENTARY PHRASES BUT COPIED BY THREE OPERATORS 0242

Thompson felt that this message, received by three Wailupe Navy operators on 3105, yet not received by *Itasca*, *Moorby*, and other listening agencies, was probably a faked message originating in the Hawaiian Islands. Howland operators, on the night of 4 July, did get a bearing on some signal. It was received in clearer form the next night at Oakland and was undoubtedly fraudulent. At the time of its receipt, *Itasca* was 30 miles west of Howland. The British freighter *Moorby* was within 100 miles of the position. The radio operator aboard that ship, listening on 3105, reported signals. *Itasca* operators had difficulty reaching *Moorby* because that vessel had a one-operator watch. The *Swan* was northeast of the position and was requested to move toward it. On 5 July at sunset, three searching vessels converged on the position 281 miles north of Howland.

Newspapers and radio commentators were giving prime coverage to the "distress signals" and the efforts of the searching vessels. Hopes of rescue were raised, only to be dashed to earth.

FROM: COM SF DIV
TO: ITASCA
INF: HQ; COMHAWSEC; COM 12; COM 14.
8005 FOLLOWING FROM SAN FRANCISCO DIVISION SPECIAL MONITOR STATION ITASCA HEARD MAKING FIRST TEST ON 3105 AT 2330 PST 4 JULY ON CW QUOTE NRUI CALLING KHAQQ UNQUOTE INTERFERENCE CAME THROUGH HERE THEN QUOTE PLEASE ANSWER NRUI UNQUOTE PERIOD SHORTLY AFTER THAT CARRIER WAS HEARD ON 3105 PERIOD CARRIERS WERE HEARD 3105 AT APPROXIMATELY 15 TO 20 MINUTES PAST EACH HOUR TO 0505 PST SEEMINGLY A PREARRANGED SCHEDULE PERIOD AT 0617 PST ON 3105 HEARD ON CW QUOTE NRUI CALLING KHAQQ MAKE FOUR LONG DASHES THEN YOUR POSITION NRUI UNQUOTE ALMOST IMMEDIATELY FOUR LONG DASHES OF APPROXIMATELY FOUR OR FIVE SECONDS DURATION IN SPACES SAME LENGTH ON FREQUENCY

Thompson further felt that, "The *Itasca* operators were never convinced that signals were received from Earhart or could have come from the Lockheed. The *Itasca* with two operators on watch, the *Swan*, Howland, and Baker were closest to the signals. None of these units heard the messages." Naval Operators at American Samoa, listening on 3105, did not hear them. Throughout the search, *Itasca* operators believed that if the plane were down, some of these units would receive the traffic, traffic consisting of useful information instead of just call signs or dashes. (Neither Earhart nor Noonan could use code.) Thompson theorized, "Why should a plane in distress waste time on repeated calls or on making special signals? If the plane were using battery, the carrier signals were all out of proportion to the length of time the battery could stand up."

FROM: COM SF DIV
TO: ITASCA; COMHAWSEC
INF: COLORADO; COMDESRON 2
8005 YOUR 8005 2010 PLANE CARRIED NO EMERGENCY RADIO EQUIPMENT EXCEPT ONE SPARE BATTERY IN CABIN PERIOD DYNAMOTORS ALL MOUNTED UNDER FUSELAGE WOULD POSITIVELY BE SUBMERGED IF PLANE WAS IN WATER PERIOD IN ABSENCE OF POSITIVE IDENTITY OF SIGNALS SUGGEST EVERY EFFORT BE MADE TO

OBTAIN DIRECTION FINDER BEARINGS HAVING IN MIND RECIPROCALS FROM HOWLAND PERIOD ROUGHNESS IN NOTE OF PLANE SIGNAL COULD BE CAUSED BY VIBRATION AND ALTHOUGH SET CRYSTAL CONTROLLED POSSIBLE SOME SLIGHT DEVIATION DUE TO POOR ADJUSTMENT OR FRACTURED CRYSTAL 0115

FROM: COM HAW SEC
TO: COM SF DIV
8005 ITASCA SIGHTED FLARES AND PROCEEDING TOWARD THEM AT 2216 2243

Thompson wrote that this message was apparently due to commercial or service stations monitoring *Itasca*, which, along with the *Moorby* and *Swan*, was converging on the 281-mile position. Suddenly, two lookouts and the officer of the deck saw a distinct flare to the northward. It came up from and settled down to the horizon. Hoping the plane or boat could be afloat, *Itasca* headed for the flare site and radioed, asking Earhart if she was sending up flares and, if so, to send up another one. A few seconds later another green light appeared bearing 75 degrees and was seen by 25 witnesses.

The *Moorby* operator heard *Itasca* calling Earhart. *Itasca* operators, on 500 kc, asked the *Moorby* operator if he had seen the flares. The reply was negative. Persons on Howland Island, 281 miles away, reported flares to the northeast and burned three drums of gasoline. The *Swan* reported lights and considered them meteors. The flares were undoubtedly a meteoric shower. The position, appearance, and timing, however, gave credence to flares.

When *Itasca* talked with the *Moorby*, commercial monitoring stations apparently picked up part of the traffic and released it to the press. The result was a deluge of commercial requests. Thus, 5 July ended with meteoric fireworks, which added to the man-made snafu.

On 6 July, Putnam got into the act again.

FROM: COM SF DIV
TO: COM HAW SEC, ITASCA, COM 14, COLORADO, SWAN, COM 12, CG HQ
8006 FOLLOWING FROM PUTNAM QUOTE PLEASE NOTE ALL RADIO BEARINGS THUS FAR OBTAINED ON EARHART PLANE APPROXIMATELY INTERSECT IN PHOENIX ISLAND REGIONS SOUTHEAST OF HOWLAND PERIOD FURTHER LINE OF POSITION GIVEN BY NOONAN IF BASED ON HOWLAND WHICH APPARENTLY REASONABLE ASSUMPTION ALSO PASS THROUGH ISLANDS PERIOD BELIEVED NAVIGATOR AFTER OBTAINING SUCH LINE NATURALLY WOULD FOLLOW IT TO NEAREST INDICATED LAND PERIOD ADDITIONALLY IS MESSAGE STATING POSITION 281 MILES NORTH OF HOWLAND ACTUALLY WAS QUOTE SOUTH UNQUOTE INSTEAD OF NORTH ALSO INDICATED SAME PERIOD WEATHER ANALYSIS INDICATED LIKELIHOOD HEADWINDS ALOFT MUCH STRONGER THAN NOONAN RECKONED WITH PROBABILITY NEVER GOT 100 MILES FROM HOWLAND AS THEY THOUGHT PERIOD LOCKHEED ENGINEERS STATE POSITIVELY PLANE COULD NOT OPERATE ITS RADIO UNLESS ON SHORE AND NO ISLANDS APPARENTLY EXIST NORTH OF HOWLAND THEREFORE SUGGEST THAT PLANES FROM COLORADO INVESTIGATE AREA AS PROMPTLY AS PRACTICABLE UNQUOTE 0201

This was logical reasoning, but the wrong answer. By this time the *Itasca* was using carrier wave on 3105, but it was too late.

FROM: FLEET AIR BASE, PEARL HARBOR
TO: ITASCA, SWAN, COLORADO
2505 FORECAST TONIGHT AND TOMORROW TUESDAY HOWLAND TO LATITUDE FIVE PARTLY CLOUDY GOOD VISIBILITY LIGHT SOUTHEAST EARLY

Canton Island had thousands of acres of flat landing surface and was Earhart's designated landing site in March 1937. She was not allowed to land there in July because facility was allocated to another airplane.

Photo credit - National Archives Negative #80-CF-79883-2

WINDS PERIOD LATITUDE FIVE TO LATITUDE TEN BROKEN CLOUDS WITH OCCASIONAL SQUALLS FAIR VISIBILITY VARIABLE WINDS MOSTLY EAST TEN TO FIFTEEN 1915

FROM: ITASCA
TO: COMFLEET AIR BASE AND SWAN
INF: COMINEBATFOR; COM 14
8005 REFERENCE COMDR AIRCRAFT F.A.B. PEARL HARBOR 1105 0632 SUGGEST YOU SWEEP WEST ON LATITUDE FIVE DEGREES THIRTY MINUTES NORTH 1035

FROM: HOWLAND ISLAND
TO: ITASCA
8005 AT 0035 HST OBTAINED BEARING ON A CONTINUOUS WAVE OF UNKNOWN ORIGIN INDICATING SOUTH SOUTHEAST OR NORTH NORTHWEST ON MAGNETIC COMPASS PERIOD UNABLE TO OBTAIN UNILATERAL BEARING DUE TO NIGHT EFFECT PERIOD NO CALL GIVEN PERIOD FREQUENCY IS SLIGHTLY ABOVE 3105 KCS 0425

FROM: COM SF DIV
TO: ITASCA
8005 LAE VERIFIES EARHART TOOK OFF WITH 1100 GALLONS GAS PERIOD ESTIMATED TIME FLIGHT 24 TO 30 HOURS 1419

Although Lae officials were somewhat slow in providing this information regarding time aloft, it was of some help in the search.

FROM: COM SF DIV
TO: COLORADO, ITASCA, COMHAWSEC, COMDT 14TH NAV DIST
8005 OPINION OF TECHNICAL AIDES HERE THAT EARHART PLANE WILL BE FOUND ON ORIGINAL LINE OF POSITION WHICH INDICATED POSITION THROUGH HOWLAND ISLAND AND PHOENIX GROUP PERIOD RADIO TECHNICIANS FAMILIAR WITH RADIO EQUIPMENT ON PLANE ALL STATE DEFINITELY THAT PLANE RADIO COULD NOT FUNCTION NOW IF IN WATER AND ONLY IF PLANE WAS ON LAND AND ABLE TO OPERATE RIGHT MOTOR FOR POWER PERIOD NO FEARS FELT FOR SAFETY OF PLANE ON WATER PROVIDED TANKS HOLD AS LOCKHEED ENGINEERS CALCULATE 5000 POUNDS POSITIVE BUOYANCY WITH PLANE WEIGHT 8000 1525

Thompson commented, "This message changed the whole search problem and virtually eliminated all intercepted radio traffic ideas (unless the plane was on land). The message arrived at a time when the three ships were checking the 281-mile report. Until this time, the *Itasca* had considered the plane had emergency radio capable of transmitting on water."

FROM: COM SF DIV
TO: COMDT 14TH NAVDIS, COLORADO, COMHAWSEC
8005 PAN AMERICAN AIRWAYS THROUGH COLONEL YOUNG REPORTS RADIO BEARING ON PLANE SIGNAL THIS MORNING FIFTH AS ONE FOUR FOUR DEGREES

FROM WAKE ISLAND AND ARE REASONABLY CERTAIN OF BEARING PERIOD POSSIBILITY INTERSECTION POSITION LINE GIVEN JUST BEFORE LAST PLANE TRANSMISSION AND LATITUDE LINE 281 MILES NORTH OF HOWLAND USING HOWLAND AS REFERENCE POINT MAY BE PLANES POSITION BEARING FROM WAKE ISLAND PLACES PLANE NEAR LINE OF POSITION AND INTERSECTIONS OF RADIO BEARINGS FROM WAKE AND HONOLULU GIVEN INDICATIONS OF POSITION IN PHOENIX GROUP PERIOD WHICH FURTHER SUBSTANTIATED BY TECHNICIANS WHO FEEL PLANES RADIO COULD FUNCTION ONLY IF ON SHORE 2135

Thompson commented, "Another indication of the Phoenix Island or reef theory. These messages led to Mr. Putnam's request to the *Colorado* to search the islands." At this point, two messages were sent.

FROM: CHIEF OF NAVAL OPERATIONS
TO: COLORADO
3806 ADVISE POSITION AND WHETHER SEARCHING WITH PLANES 0918

FROM: NAVY RADIO ARLINGTON (Washington, D.C.)
TO: COLORADO
COLORADO DIRECTED MAINTAIN CONTINUOUS WATCH ON 4235 KCS

This radiogram from Naval Headquarters in Washington, D.C., leaves little doubt as to who was actually directing the search. They were the Washington insiders; Commander-in-Chief F. Roosevelt through the Chief of Naval Operations. Top level interest in search of Phoenix Group signifies that they were focal point of entire navy search operation.

FROM: COLORADO
TO: SWAN, ITASCA
INF: CNO, COMDESRON 2, COMFRANDIV, COMHAWSEC, COM 14TH   NAVDIS
1006 EIGHT HUNDRED POSITION LAT 0738 LONG 17055 EXPECT BEGIN SEARCHING SOUTHEAST HOWLAND WEDNESDAY WILL INVESTIGATE ISLANDS PHOENIX GROUP ENROUTE WHAT IS LATEST DATE YOU REQUIRE FUEL 0520

FROM: COM SF DIV
TO: COMHAWSEC
INF: ITASCA, COMDT 14TH NAV DISTR.
6006 ON ACCOUNT OF PREPONDERANCE OF NAVAL CRAFT TO BE ENGAGED IN EARHART SEARCH AND NECESSITY FOR COORDINATION HEADQUARTERS HAS AUTHORIZED THAT ITASCA REPORT TO COMMANDANT FOURTEENTH NAVAL DISTRICT FOR DUTY PERIOD DIRECT ITASCA ACCORDINGLY 1445

Thompson wrote, "From this point on the search was under the Navy. Commanding Officer *Colorado* conferred with Commanding Officer *Itasca* (by sound power telephone) while Itasca was taking fuel from *Colorado* on 7th. Plans were outlined as shown in operational orders. Later *Lexington* relieved *Colorado*. With advent of Navy, *Itasca's* work consisted of complying with orders of senior vessels. Navy took over 3105 guard."

Military aerial camera in USN PBY. Used for aerial surveys and reconnaissance.
Photo credit - National Archives Negative #80-G-410153

This order came somewhat late. The *Itasca* had been complying with orders from the Navy since late in the evening of 2 July, and this had been done on Thompson's own initiative. This officer's performance of duty in connection with the search was in marked contrast to the way in which he had handled radio communications.

The Navy was fortunate in having two forceful and capable officers in charge of the search, Captain W. L. Friedell, USN, CO of the *Colorado* and, later, Captain J. S. Dowell, ComdesronTwo, aboard the *Lexington*. There can be no valid criticism of the search as conducted from 7 July onward, considering the information which was available to them and the information which was withheld. There were, however, several more 6 July messages important enough to go into the record.

FROM: COM SF DIV
TO: ITASCA, COLORADO
8006 ANALYSIS WEATHER CONDITIONS FROM LAE TO HOWLAND ON DATE OF EARHART FLIGHT ESPECIALLY AS REGARDS UPPER AIR PROBABILITIES APPARENTLY INDICATES IMPORTANT AREA OF IMMEDIATE SEARCH OF COLORADO PLANES IS SECTOR 320 TO 350 DEGREES RADIUS 250 MILES FROM HOWLAND STOP THIS BASED ON STUDY AEROLOGIST ESPECIALLY ACQUAINTED REGION STOP

FROM: COM SF DIV
TO: COLORADO, ITASCA
INF: COM 12, COM 14, COMDESRON 2
8006 HELD CONSULTATION THIS DATE WITH PERSONS FAMILIAR WITH NAVIGATION METHODS OF NOONAN AND THEY STATE HE WOULD FOLLOW COURSE CORRECTING COURSES BY INFREQUENT FIXES PLANNING TO TAKE FIX JUST BEFORE DAWN AND THEN CORRECTING COURSE FOR DESTINATION DETERMINING LINE OF POSITION WHEN NEAR END OF ESTIMATED RUN PERIOD THIS PROCEDURE WOULD ALLOW FLIGHT OF ABOUT 300 MILES DURING MORNING WITHOUT GOOD FIX AND PROBABLE ERROR SHOULD NOT BE GREAT HOWEVER IF SHORT OF GAS IT WAS STATED HE PROBABLY WOULD FOLLOW LINE OF POSITION TO NEAREST LAND 2352

Thompson wrote, "It also indicates that Earhart apparently depended on radio for her landfall and when radio failed she failed to make Howland. (Air sights are not accurate within 20 miles as a rule.)"

Beginning 7 July with the Navy officially in charge of operations in the vicinity of Howland, the search took on a different aspect and became less frantic. Friedell reasoned that there was no chance of finding Earhart and Noonan alive, unless they had come down on land or very near land. There was no land in the search-sectors recommended by San Francisco other than Eastern Siberia; the only other lay in the opposite direction—the Phoenix Islands. The distress signals if authentic, the radio-bearings if trustworthy, and Mr. Putnam's direct request all indicated the same thing. The *Itasca* was refueled from the *Colorado* on 7 July at a point about 150 miles eastnortheast of Howland and the *Swan* was refueled on 10 July in the vicinity of the Phoenix Islands. Both ships conducted independent searches, as directed by the *Colorado*. The *Ontario* had left her plane-guard station shortly after the flight was over on orders from Governor Milne, USN, and returned directly to Tutuila. The following signals are significant.

U.S.S. *Swan* off Canton Island. During Earhart search, a party from this ship landed on Canton Island on July 10, 1937 to remove aviation gasoline, equipment and personnel left by sister tender U.S.S. *Avocet* three weeks earlier.
Photo credit - National Archives Negative #80-CF-79883-1

FROM: COLORADO
TO: COM 14TH NAV DIS
INF: SEARCH GROUP
1007 YOUR 1007 1440 FORENOON COLORADO FUELED AND PROVISIONED ITASCA PERIOD SWAN CONDUCTED SEARCH TOWARD POINT LAT ZERO LONG ONE SEVEN FIVE WEST AFTER CALLED POINT AFIRM WILL CONTINUE THURSDAY PERIOD ITASCA PROCEEDING TO POINT LAT ZERO TWENTY SOUTH LONG ONE HUNDRED SEVENTY EIGHT WEST HEREAFTER CALLED POINT BAKER AND THURSDAY WILL CONTINUE SEARCHING AREA TO SOUTH AND EAST THIS POINT COLORADO SEARCHED WITH PLANES ON COURSE ONE NINE FIVE TOWARD REEF AND SAND BANKS NORTH OF WILSON REEF PERIOD REEF AND SAND BANK NOT FOUND PERIOD THURSDAY WILL CONTINUE SEARCH FOR THESE REEFS AND ISLANDS IN PHOENIX GROUP 1755

FROM: COM 14
TO: COLORADO, COMDESRON 2
INF: SEARCH GROUP
0011 COMDESRON TWO TAKE CHARGE ALL UNITS IN SEARCH AREA PERIOD SEARCH OF PHOENIX GROUP AREA CONSIDERED COMPLETED PERIOD UPON COMPLETION FUELING DESTROYERS COLORADO RELIEVED SEARCH DUTY AND PROCEED PREVIOUSLY ASSIGNED DUTIES FOLLOWING ITINERARY SUBMITTED COLORADO DISPATCH THE TENTH 0905

SUMMARY OF THE SEARCH

The Earhart search was as good as could be expected considering the ships and planes available, and the late arrivals of the *Colorado* and the *Lexington*. The Earhart search conducted by the Navy and Coast Guard, 2-18 July 1937 was summarized in the report dated 31 July 1937, of the Commandant, Fourteenth Naval district to the Chief of Naval Operations. (See pages 57 to 62.)

It is most gratifying that there occurred no serious injury to men or damage to material in the very extensive and sometimes hazardous operations of ships and planes.

The initial phase of the search was based on Commander Thompson's well-reasoned belief that the plane was northwest of and fairly near Howland. A reasonably complete search of this area was made on 2-3 July. Then, on the strength of radio intercepts, the search shifted westward and then 281 miles to the north of Howland, again without success. Subsequent analysis discredited the radio intercepts.

The second area searched was the southeastern quadrant because radio intercepts, radio bearings, and other considerations indicated the plane was probably on one of the Phoenix Islands. After nothing was found there (*sic*), the third phase began, logically based on the assumption that the plane had landed in the water probably within 200 miles of Howland and that the aircraft or life raft would have drifted westward and northwestward in the 11 days prior to the arrival of the *Lexington*.

The group covered an area approximately 300 miles square to the west and northwest of Howland which included all probable positions of airplane or passengers if still afloat. Additionally, the Gilbert Islands were searched.

MILITARY SEARCH ANALYSIS

The following significant points are evident from a careful study of the evidence surrounding the military search for Earhart conducted from 2-18 July 1937.

1. U.S.S. *Ontario*: By USN direction at CNO level, the *Ontario* did not participate in the search. It was under the command of U.S. Naval Station, Tutuila, American Samoa.

2. PBY search: Although the PBY was the only effective vehicle available to the USN to launch a timely, far-reaching, and meaningful search, after one aborted attempt this method was abandoned in favor of slow ineffective surface ships.

3. H.M.S. *Achilles*: Shortly after the 24-hour flight must have terminated due to fuel exhaustion, a message was received from KHAQQ on the 3105 kc aircraft frequency. The *Achilles* was below the equator and to the east of the Phoenix Islands en route to Honolulu. Except for confirmation of the message, no further follow-up was undertaken. A request was made by the USCG to the USN to ask the U.S. State Department to request that the British government assist by directing the *Achilles* to join in the search, but nothing was forthcoming. *Achilles* made public this message, but after the ship reached Honolulu, the message was negated (censored).

4. Nauru Island Intercepts on Aircraft Frequencies: The Coast Guard Headquarters at San Francisco received word through commercial radio that Nauru Island Radio had received intercepts. Nauru Island was a professional station and in the vicinity of the flight path. Any transmission on aircraft frequencies in this area would have been significant and yet no follow-up was attempted.

5. Northern Diversion, 281 miles north of Howland: This red herring was a deliberate attempt to divert the Imperial Japanese Navy ships believed to be engaged in the search to stay in their own waters north of the equator. It diverted the *Itasca*, *Swan*, and the M. V. *Moorby*, the only rescue ships in the central equatorial Pacific area at the crucial time, to a known phony area. It further revealed the presence of a U.S.S. submarine, whose personnel perpetrated the radio hoax, in waters north of Howland Island. This was a deliberate diversion of all available surface vessels for a critical four-day period.

6. Appearance of Public Relations Stunt: USN control of search. Every person who publicly expounded a theory or talked to the spirit world elicited a search response in some respect. Not all were practical, but "pacifying" the squeaking wheels and abating public criticism in this country by catering to loudmouthed persons, seems to have been the underlying objective. Keep the truth from the U.S. public by a public-relations response. Contain the Imperial Japanese Navy.

7. No landing on southern Phoenix Islands (except Hull Lagoon): In spite of the fact that Gardner Island, Hull Island, and Sydney Island were densely foliated, no landing was made on any of the southernmost islands in the Phoenix Group. Sydney Island in particular was overflown and circled several times at 450 feet and huts were observed. A Burns-Philp employee was on Hull. The *Colorado* received a message from the CNO at Arlington, Virginia. "Look, but don't find."

Canton Island, largest atoll in Phoenix Group, was visited by U.S. Navy sponsored scientific party to view the June 8, 1937 solar eclipse in May-June 1937. Aircraft tender U.S.S. *Avocet* left cache of aviation gasoline, equipment and supplies at this base camp site.

Photo credit - National Archives Negative #80-G-410143

8. Landing on Canton Island: Although it was never acknowledged, the U.S.S *Swan* landed a boat crew on Canton Island near the camp of the May-June Eclipse Expedition (U.S.S. *Avocet*).

        a. Trace of either U.S. or British party
        b. Recover gasoline cache

9. Command Set-up: The Earhart affair in the remote South Pacific was no tempest in a teapot. Involved were Japan, New Zealand, Great Britain, Gilbert and Ellice Island Colony, Australia, U.S. Coast Guard under the Treasury Department, Department of the Interior, U.S. Army, U.S. Air Corps, U.S. Navy, CNO, Commander 14th Naval District, Captain Dowell, USN, U.S. Naval Station Tutuila, American Samoa.

10. Overflight of Marshall Islands by *Lexington* aircraft did occur. *Smith's Weekly* reference.

11. Ocean Island snafu. After the fact. British High Commissioner, etc.

12. Failure to act on Captain John W. Jones' information. Pan American Adcock direction-finding information and Jones' acknowledgement led to only one conclusion: Pre-knowledge of island condition, lagoon, landing site and marker identification of prominent feature (red roof on copra shed). Pre-provisioning of supplies on Hull by *Achilles* after leaving U.S. Naval Station at American Samoa.

13. Putnam's request for search of Gilbert and Marshall Islands' beaches and areas.

MILITARY SEARCH-CONCLUSIONS

1. If Earhart had really been lost, the *Ontario* would have joined the search despite its limitations.

2. If Earhart had really been lost, the maximum number of PBYs (estimated to be three) which could have been accommodated at Howland Island would have been used after the freak storm abated.

3. If Earhart had really been lost, all three available ships would not have been diverted for four crucial days and the Imperial Japanese Navy would have been a welcome aid to the search.

4. If Earhart had really been lost, a serious effort, not a public relations charade, would have been conducted using "all the facilities at the U.S. Navy's disposal," as directed by the Naval Department overtly (but not covertly).

5. If Earhart had really been lost, landing parties from the *Colorado* would have been sent to all three of the southern Phoenix Islands instead of making overflights at 450 feet.

6. If Earhart had really been lost, the Gilbert Islands would not have been plumbed for Hydrographic Office information and the Marshall Island of Wotje overflown by search aircraft from the *Lexington*. Radio cooperation from the nearby Gilbert and Ellice Colony would have been solicited immediately after it had been ascertained that Earhart was lost.

NON-MILITARY SEARCHES

At the request of Putnam, a cutter from Suva was sent to investigate a non-existent reef to the east of the Gilberts where the islanders were accustomed to visit (according to a charismatic beachcomber) for the purpose of gathering imaginary eggs laid by mythological sea turtles.

The Japanese Navy offered assistance and sent the survey ship, *Koshu*, to search the waters around the Marshall Islands. The *Koshu* was just as unsuited for this task as the *Ontario*. Although the Japanese complained because they were given no information as to the probable location of the downed Electra, they conducted their search a day longer than the U.S. Navy. There is nothing in the record to suggest diplomatic correspondence between the United States and Japanese governments was not conducted with tact and politeness.

CIVILIAN SEARCHES

The United States Navy had no sooner concluded the 2-18 July 1937 Earhart Search than persons who had been closely associated with the woman pilot called for additional civilian search efforts. This followed after the furor about the alleged cost of 4,000,000 depression dollars used by the government and the official declaration that the search was both comprehensive and adequate.

Good and sufficient reasons existed for additional searching.

1. The brevity of the search by the government was inadequate to cover the area within the range of the aircraft.

2. The recognition that the services had not used many of the resources available to them.

3. Positive radio contacts, including the Pan American Airways Adcock D\F fixes were largely inadequately pursued.

Professional radio engineer/operator Paul Rafford, Jr., long-time Pan American Airways flight crew member whose employment began prior to World War II. Later he was on the United States team of radio experts for recovery of astronauts. He has traced the Earhart flight to Hull Island. His analysis is based on computer-aided radio propagation calculations and radio D\F fixes taken by the Pacific Pan American Airways radio operators during early July 1937.

Photo credit - Via Paul Rafford, Jr.

4. Search parties were not landed on any of the islands to adequately see what was actually hidden beneath the abundant foliage present on many of the islands.

5. Efforts to expand the search by on-site personnel were ignored by Washington.

6. Recommendations by searching personnel to investigate questioned sightings (like the "newly-constructed native huts" on Sydney Island) were vetoed by their superiors.

In short, the official explanation was too transparent for knowledgeable persons to believe. Personnel close to the flight and fliers were well aware that Earhart carried an adequate fuel reserve to reach adjacent island groups if unsuccessful in locating Howland or Baker Islands.

In addition to the search deficiencies, knowledgeable non-government parties gave little credence to the official story that Earhart ran out of gasoline and ditched the Lockheed in the waters adjacent to Howland Island. Obviously, this was a cover-up if an overflight of the Marshall Islands had occurred. When the revealing article in *Smith's Weekly* was published in October 1937, along with the international repercussions which followed, there was little doubt but that the overflight of the Japanese Mandates had occurred. This episode in 1937 was almost exactly parallel to the May 1960 overflight of Central Russia by Francis Gary Powers in a Lockheed U-2 photographic spy plane a generation later.

Despite the concern of numerous individuals and groups, very little civilian search activity was consummated in the pre-World War II years. In particular, Elmer Dimity tried for several successive years to launch a search from the West Coast but was repeatedly thwarted by non-cooperation by the West Coast maritime labor unions. Powerful forces in Washington, D.C., were blocking any effort of civilians to make their own searches.

Only two actual searches of the central Pacific islands area were made prior to the end of 1941 when hostilities began. Millionaire Vincent Astor made a search through the British Gilbert and Ellice Island groups in early 1938. Although he was seeking information for President Roosevelt about designated islands in the Japanese Marshalls, any relevant factors about the missing fliers would also have been determined.

In 1940, an abbreviated search by the world-girdling schooner *Yankee* was conducted by Captain Irving Johnson[1] through the same Ellice and Gilbert Island groups with negative results. Johnson launched this search from the Hawaiian Islands, thus bypassing the West Coast maritime unions. He served on U.S. Navy survey vessels during World War II and revisited many of these same islands. In 1945 he publicly stated that none of the persons on islands he had visited both before and during[2] the war had reported any trace of the missing fliers. Johnson's track was far to the westward of Howland/Baker, the Phoenix Islands, the Tokelau Islands, and the Samoas.

Because of the limited number of island groups actually surveyed by either Astor or Johnson, it is apparent that neither of these searches would be considered adequate in terms of drawing any meaningful conclusions from them.

---

1 Johnson, Captain Irving and Electra. "Westward Bound on the *Yankee*," *National Geographic*, January 1942.

2 Johnson, Captain Irving. "Adventures with the Survey Navy," *National Geographic*, July 1947.

Amelia Earhart's Final Flight

The Pan Am Direction Finding Network's Position Fix

During the night hours of July 4th and 5th, stations in the Pan Am direction finding network received very faint radio transmissions on 3105 khz., Earhart's night frequency. Finally, after considerable effort, they obtained the four bearings shown below. They fixed the position of the mysterious transmitter to within 200 miles of Hull Island. Considering that the average error of bearings taken with the long distance direction finders of those days was ± 5° at 500 miles, these bearings, taken from nearly 2,000 miles, appear remarkably accurate, particularly so because Pan Am's D\Fs were calibrated only for Pan Am frequencies, not 3105 khz. Ironically, during her pre-flight planning sessions, Earhart was offered the services of their direction finding network to track her plane across the Pacific if she would install a Pan Am frequency. For reasons best known to herself, she rejected the offer immediately without further discussion.

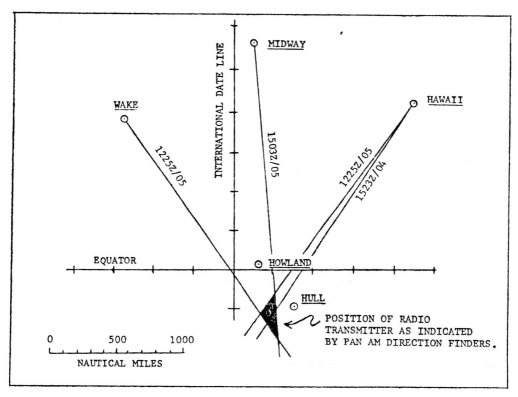

Station	Time/Date	Distance*	Calculated Bearing*	Observed Bearing	Error
Hawaii	1523z/04	1,760 mi.	210°	213°	+3°
	1225z/05	1,760 mi.	210°	215°	+5°
Wake	1225z/05	1,900 mi.	136.6°	144°	+7.4°
Midway	1503z/05	1,986 mi.	170.8°	175°	+4.2°

*Based on the assumption that the signals originated on Hull Island.

Pan American Airways' Radio Direction Finder Fixes
Paul Rafford, Jr.

Part Three

The Odyssey

U.S.S. *Ontario* (AT-13)
This station ship at American Samoa was so deeply involved in the Earhart disappearance that it did not participate in the search. Although strategically located to render aid if Earhart was really lost, the ship was recalled to Pago Pago on "imperative" local business. The definition of what that duty was is a key factor in the disappearance of Earhart.
Photo credit - National Archives

THE ODYSSEY

In the previous sections of this book, the research technique used was to start with the most reliable information available, use what was acceptable, and add an extrapolation or expansion where necessary. These same sources, documents and mission/search personnel are available to any serious researcher. In this section, new ground is broken. From information in "The Searches," an obvious and logical projection of the forces set in motion were used to trace the Earhart odyssey. In so doing, the reasons for one of the greatest cover-ups in United States history and the reasons why the truth was withheld became known.

To anyone not ideologically biased, the fact that certain elements in the Roosevelt administration (later identified as the "War Cabinet") were behind the Earhart flight subterfuge is evident. Of greatest concern was not the Japanese threat to the United States in 1937, which was minimal, but the threat to the Communist forces in northern China and, to a lesser extent, Siberia. Thus, the Japanese invasion of the Chinese mainland in July 1937 was a threat. With Roosevelt in this ideological camp and running the armed forces, Army and Navy personnel had to become fellow travelers or "be transferred to Guam" as required by his dictum issued prior to World War II. Of course, Guam would not be defended in the event a war began, and military personnel stationed there would become prisoners of war if they survived the invasion of the island.

When Earhart transmitted the names of the mandated islands she overflew, starting with Jaluit, these messages were picked up by *Itasca* radio operators. Once the cover for the "overflight" of Japanese mandated territory had been blown, the alternate Hull Island became her destination. She may not have wanted to go there initially, but after getting instructions using the U.S. Navy-supplied receiver aboard the Electra on a designated (secret) frequency and upon the coercion of Noonan, she decided to make what amends she could for her misconduct.

Adequate documentary evidence exists to support the initial leg of what happened after Earhart landed on Hull. She and Noonan were taken by Captain John W. Jones (1901-1965) in his small motorized sailboat from Hull Island to Sydney Island, a distance of 60 miles. Jones was a master mariner with papers in both sail and steam. July weather in the Phoenix Islands was generally tranquil and he could communicate with Naval Radio Tutuila (Pago Pago) and could receive weather forecasts from both there and Apia, Western Samoa. He knew, however, that a floatplane from the *Colorado* was likely to be landed on the lagoon at Hull because he had told the Navy that it was feasible. The solution was to transport Earhart and Noonan to Sydney Island and instruct the natives to keep themselves and their "guests" hidden when the pilots flying floatplanes from the *Colorado* searched the Phoenix Islands.

Except for personal possessions, a Samoan female companion for Earhart because only male natives were on Sydney, and a small supply of food, the only other cargo was the film magazine from the aerial camera, the reason for the entire Earhart flight and "disappearance." It could have caused an international

incident and an early outbreak of hostilities. The primary reason for the PBY-1 flight from Pearl Harbor was to retrieve the film. Apparently, that aircraft had been turned back by weather. Did Lt. Lambrecht, flying a floatplane from the *Colorado* and landing on the lagoon at Hull on 9 July 1937, retrieve the film? Lambrecht's observer, Jim "Ash" Wilson, said no film was picked up at that time. This author believes him.

British resident manager at Hull Island and Sydney Island, Captain John William Jones, Royal Navy Reserve, was key individual in Earhart disappearance.
Photo credit - Via Heather Jones

The search phase of the Earhart mission ended with the fliers on Sydney Island along with the woman traveling companion for Earhart. The Electra was off the reef on the northwest corner of Hull Island. Now the Odyssey begins. This analyst is entering virgin territory. With careful research and analysis, however, answers are forthcoming.

The Earhart Electra had been flown its last mile when it landed wheels-up on the sandy portion of the fringing reef of Hull Island during the morning of 2 July 1937. Earhart might have thought differently and been promised otherwise. After all, her airplane had been brought back from Hawaii in a basket, the damaged parts replaced, and the bill paid by parties unknown, but suspected. Once the Earhart Electra had been hidden from the *Colorado* aviators (and, so far as is known, anyone since), in deep water off the platform reef, the aeronautical phase of the Earhart flight was terminated. From Hull Island to Sydney Island, the sphere of operations becomes geographical, nautical, and political in nature. Although documentary records of this phase are few, they are sufficient, with the proper interpretation, to make a "most-likely" judgment as to the outcome of the disappearance episode.

Of major interest is the Howland Island-Tutuila Island axis in the defensive and offensive strategy of the United States in the Pacific in 1937. Not only was knowledge of naval/maritime activity in the Phoenix Islands essential, but after July 1937 this must be extended to Samoa, both American and Western, 600 miles to the south. Thus, it is obvious that Sydney Island was only a temporary stopping place for Earhart and Noonan. Ultimately they had to be transported to the vicinity of the main island of Tutuila in American Samoa.

The first task was to transport the Earhart party from Sydney to Aunu'u Island in the vicinity of Tutuila. Jones' small motorized sailboat could not be used for this comparatively long and risky trip, nor could the *Ontario* because it was ruled out in favor of another ship. No aircraft were based there, and a PBY-1 from Pearl Harbor was stretching its range and the risk was high. The only local copra ship, the M.V. *Makoa*, had been wrecked at Hull Island on 24 May 1937, and the New Zealand naval ships were en route to other destinations. The choices of

chartered vessels were few. Preferably, the vessel should fly the flag of the United States and be available when needed at either Pago Pago, American Samoa, or Apia, Western Samoa. An inter-island boat, the M.V. *Tutuila,* which was used mainly for the Apia-to-Pago Pago shuttle and was available for charter, was considered and ultimately rejected.

Obviously, Earhart and Noonan could not remain on Sydney for an extended period. Documentary evidence of their destination and how they were taken there exists. Just 600 miles south of Sydney Island was the United States naval station at Pago Pago on Tutuila Island, a logical nearby sanctuary for the fliers if their government wanted to keep them in seclusion.

Pertinent documents are two United States Navy radio messages concerning the U.S.S. *Ontario*, the Samoa naval station ship, which was the guard ship stationed half way between Lae and Howland Island. On the night of 2 July 1937, a few minutes after Earhart was scheduled to have passed over his ship, Lt. Horace Blakeslee left his station and headed for base, believing his assignment complete. Being 1,300 miles distant, he was unable to communicate with NPU and he remained on a homeward course throughout the day, apparently unaware that Earhart was lost. During the day Captain M. Milne, USN and Governor of American Samoa, sent the following message to Arlington Radio, "Imperative that *Ontario* return to home station!" Several hours later came

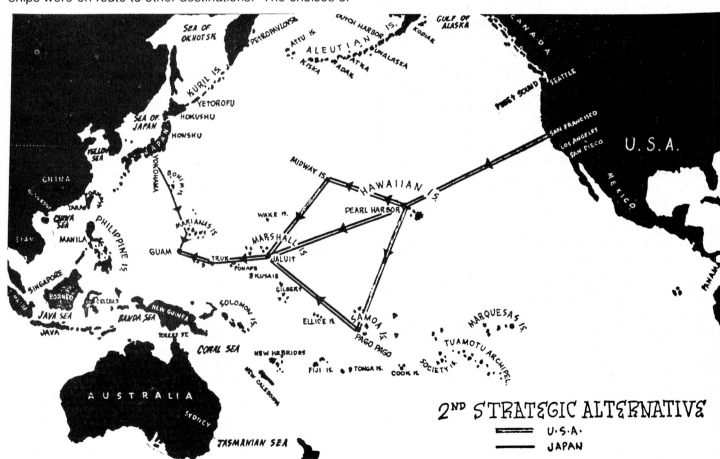

U.S. "Orange" War Plan - 1937
United States war plan against "Orange" (Japan) called for initial conquest of Marshall Islands. Direct frontal attack was to be supported with flank attacks from Wake Island and American Samoa. Plan was followed in 1943-1944.

the reply from Washington, "Permission granted for *Ontario* to return to home base," signed by Admiral J. O. Richardson, USN, Assistant Chief of Naval Operations.

During more recent interviews with Blakeslee, he stated that not being required to participate in the search was the reason he took his ship back to port. Also, he was short of coal (fuel), water, and supplies and, with only short-range low-frequency radio equipment, could do little to assist in the search.

Ship captains, civilian and military, are obligated by international law to render aid and comfort to personnel of ships and aircraft in distress. Even in wartime, naval ships are not exempted from international maritime law. Although not criticized, Blakeslee was backed up by both his local commander, Captain Milne, and the CNO in Washington. Further questions are raised when these messages are examined. The first concerns Milne's. What was so "imperative" that the *Ontario* was needed back at Tutuila immediately? Blakeslee had no answer for this and couldn't think of anything done that was other than ordinary duty. According to the *Ontario* log, the engine was torn down for dockside repair and only routine duties were undertaken the remainder of that year. This duty was "imperative?" Further, normal assignment and relief of station ships like the coal-burning *Ontario* ordinarily do not come to the attention of the CNO. Usually an officer of far lesser rank handled the lighter traffic. In this instance, however, a senior United States Naval Officer was personally involved in releasing this coal-burning rust bucket from duty. Why? The context of the radiograms makes no sense on casual perusal. No imperative duty existed for the *Ontario* immediately upon its arrival there on 9 July 1937. Obviously, some shift in planning had occurred in Washington. At the time Milne had sent the 2 July radiogram, a mission did exist. By the time the *Ontario* returned to Tutuila 7 days later, however, the requirement for the ship had been superseded. Some other ship had been given the assignment originally intended for the *Ontario*. Personnel at both Naval Operations (OPNAV), Washington, D.C., and the naval station (NAVSTA) at Pago Pago, Tutuila, American Samoa, knew what this mission was. The reason for the exchange of "flimsies" was to inform 14th Naval District (Hawaii) Commandant Admiral Orin Murfin and Earhart Search Task Force Commander Captain Dowell to keep hands off the *Ontario* as it was not to be used in the Earhart search. The "imperative" task for *Ontario* didn't develop until early September, and was not as originally planned because of several unforeseen events and requirements which were:

1. Retrieval of film canister from the Earhart Electra required a fast return to the West Coast under guard.

2. Acquired knowledge of Earhart's dysentery required a drastic change of plans.

3. Medical supplies and a Navy tropical disease medic had to be sent from the West Coast via a fast ship.

4. Suitable medical facilities had to be prepared at the quarantine station on Aunu'u Island just off the southeast coast of Tutuila.

5. Selection of a destroyer, from the West Coast, was required so that no interference with scheduled fleet operations would occur.

6. Selection of a naval specialist in tropical diseases had to be made and that person transported to the West Coast and on to Samoa via a destroyer, with the latest medicine.

RETRIEVING THE FILM CANISTER

The first attempt to retrieve the film canister was made by the pilot of a PBY-1 sent from PatWing2 in Hawaii. He was forced to turn back because of severe weather. Admiral Murfin's original intention had been that three of these aircraft, with Howland as an operations base with the *Itasca*, *Colorado*, and the *Swan* as tenders, would provide a superior method for a quick initial search of the Howland Island area. No other PBYs were sent on orders from Washington. An aircraft tender, the U.S.S. *Swan*, was at Howland as a support ship with 10,000 gallons of gas for an expedient search for Amelia Earhart. The 4-5 July diversion of all available surface ships to a point 281 miles north of Howland was wasted effort. Men from the *Swan* recovered the fuel cache on Canton which had been initially left for Earhart.

The second attempt to recover the film was Lt. Lambrecht's "spontaneous" landing on the lagoon at Hull Island.

Existing charts (available on the *Colorado*) showed numerous coral outcroppings in the lagoon, and it is difficult to believe that Lambrecht would have taken the initiative to land there. Captain Friedell was in direct contact with Radio Arlington and would have cleared the landing with Washington. The real reason Lambrecht landed on the lagoon was to retrieve the film from the Electra. Noonan was supposed to have given it to Captain Jones, the British resident manager on Hull Island, who was to give it to the USN as represented by Lambrecht. James "Ash" Wilson, Jr., his back seat observer, would have carried the film canister on his lap on the return flight to the *Colorado*. During a lengthy interview, Wilson stated that no transfer of film occurred. His four years in naval aviation (1936-1940) were a bitter experience, and he resigned in 1940 to fly for Pan American Airways where he had a most distinguished career.

Captain Jones on his second wedding day in April 1936 following his return to Apia, Western Samoa, from Hull Island service, 1937 to 1940.
Photo credit - Via Heather Jones

Most probably, Commander Fred Noonan, USN, didn't turn over the film to Jones because he was a foreigner (British) and Noonan only had his word that he was connected with the United States Navy. Equally important, he realized that Earhart had blown the covert mission and even their wheels-down alternate of Canton had been denied them for reasons unknown. The landing at Hull Island, the third alternate, wiped out the airplane and made them dependent upon outside rescue. At Hull there was radio contact with Samoa and rescue. When their proposed move to Sydney Island was discussed, Noonan realized that he was being shanghaied for Earhart's transgression. The film was his only bargaining power. Jones could have used force to take it, but this would complicate his relationship with the U.S. Navy. Noonan would agree to go to Sydney Island only if he kept the film, thus insuring that the promise to take him and Earhart to United States territory was kept. That territory, however, was nearby American Samoa.

Twice, Roosevelt's insiders and the United States Navy had failed to recover the film canister. Because the naval air arm had failed twice, the surface navy was given the task. The *Ontario* was ruled out because it could only return the film to the naval station at Samoa. No other navy ships were closer than Hawaii or the West Coast. Armed couriers could go north on a passenger liner which went to Hawaii once a month. A fast, long-range destroyer could go to Samoa and the Phoenix Group from the West Coast and transport a needed medical officer to provide treatment for the fliers.

Some persons might consider a south sea isle like Aunu'u Island at American Samoa an earthly paradise, especially those running from civilization, the law, or past ties. It was no paradise, however, for either Earhart or Noonan. Jones, a former merchant mariner, had his home brew on Hull Island which he shared with Noonan. With no entertainment except imbibing, Noonan quickly resumed his alcoholism addiction. His demise in early 1938 could well have been from acute alcoholic poisoning which was inevitable, even predictable, under the circumstances.

When the news of Noonan's demise reached Washington, consideration was given to move Earhart closer to Oahu, Hawaiian Islands, where she could obtain prompt medical attention. The only place near there which afforded sufficient isolation was Niihau Island, a small, privately-owned island 20 miles southwest of Kauai Island and 160 miles from Oahu. Rumors have surfaced that Earhart did spend several years on Niihau, but confirmation is lacking.

In early 1938, Earhart not only required medical attention but she also needed psychological counseling, something the Navy medics could not provide. Many times she had stated that she could not tolerate confinement of any kind, even in a "gilded cage." She had lost her traveling companion; the Samoan food was unbearable to her sensitive stomach; and her last connection to the past, Fred Noonan, was gone. Unlike criminals in the United States who have a defined sentence before incarceration, hers was indeterminate. Her end was again both obvious and predictable. What is incomprehensible was that this gross mistreatment of two United States citizens was kept secret for 50 years to protect the "image" of some sacred cows.

RELEASE OF DOCUMENTARY EVIDENCE

Since the enactment of the Freedom of Information Act (FOIA) in 1967, a large amount of official documentation relating to Earhart has been released by seven government agencies, both civilian and military. Previously, personnel of these agencies had categorically denied that any information on Earhart existed in their files. The records regarding the Earhart flights and the military and civilian searches were, for the most part, unclassified and had been in the public domain. For 50 years, through successive government administrations, the official contention has remained that, because of faulty navigation, Earhart and Noonan failed to locate Howland Island, their announced destination, ran out of gasoline, and ditched (or crashed) at sea. Fifty years of evidence has since been accumulated and made this viewpoint untenable.

Official records which have been released since 1968, contain facts about the Earhart/Noonan last flight and the military/civilian searches which may be used to dispel much of the mystery of those episodes. Little evidence of the disappearance of Earhart, Noonan, or the Lockheed has surfaced in half a century. Although known to exist, those records are still classified.

Archival records which do exist are supported by contemporary records from five countries in the South Seas (the area in which the fliers disappeared) and are sufficient to solve the mystery of Earhart's disappearance. Supporting documentary evidence (official archival and local printed sources) along with on-site surveys and first-person interviews have been important in supplying the missing links. Historical research and reporting is a three-phase effort. First is the collection of facts from the best sources available; second is the interpretation of data in a coherent and logical way; and third is to present the findings in a clear and concise manner to the intended audience.

The crux of the disappearance revolves around the United States Navy and the search of the Phoenix Island Group by personnel aboard the U.S.S. *Colorado* in early July 1937. The result of that four-day search was a naval declaration that nothing of consequence had been found (after a comprehensive effort). The conclusion presented to the public was that the fliers and the Lockheed were not in that area. Upon receiving the report of the *Colorado/Swan* search of the Phoenix Group and adjacent areas below the equator, Admiral Orin Murfin, Hawaiian search commander, stated publicly that the odds of finding the fliers were practically zero. It is now known that the U.S. Navy did, in fact, solve the disappearance during the search of the Phoenix Islands, but on orders from the Washington administration, concealed the truth from the public. Official archival records of the search of the Phoenix Islands as conducted by crew members aboard the *Colorado* and items in the cruise report of the United States Coast Guard cutter *Taney* reflect the official cover-up of these findings. While perhaps justified in classifying these findings in 1937 and before the commencement of hostilities in the Pacific four years later, little apparent justification exists for 50 years of concealment. Only government reluctance is now served by keeping the facts from the public.

From: Senior Aviator, U.S.S. *Colorado*
To: The Chief of the Bureau of Aeronautics
Subject: Weekly Newsletter: Aircraft Search for
        Earhart Plane on 9 July 1937

"From McKean the planes proceeded to Gardner Island (sighting the ship to starboard en route) and made an aerial search of this island which proved to be one of the biggest in the group. Gardner is a typical example of your south sea atoll . . . a narrow circular strip of land (about as wide as Coronado's Silver Strand) surrounding a large lagoon. Most of this island is covered with tropical vegetation with, here and there, a grove of coconut palms. Here signs of recent habitation were clearly visible, but repeated circling and zooming failed to elicit any answering wave from possible inhabitants, and it was finally taken for granted that none were there.

"The lagoon at Gardner looked sufficiently deep and certainly large enough so that a seaplane or even an airboat could have landed or taken off in any direction with little if any difficulty. Given a chance, it is believed that Earhart could have landed her plane in this lagoon and swam or waded ashore. In fact, on any of these islands, it is not hard to believe that a forced landing could have been accomplished with no more damage than a good barrier crash or a good wetting.

"At 1430 that afternoon, planes were again catapulted and flown some 70 miles to the eastward to Hull Island. In appearance, Hull is much the same as Gardner, somewhat smaller perhaps, nevertheless, similar in shape and formation, the same lagoon, with the same vegetation and identical groves of coconut palms. The one difference . . . Hull was inhabited.

"As the planes approached the island toward its southern end, natives could be seen clustered around a large shack erected on high stilts and otherwise fabricated in what appeared to be the conventional native fashion. When the planes zoomed the beach, the natives, dressed in their traditional loin cloths, turned out en masse to wave and yell and to wonder at such strange birds. After a circle of the island, during which other (and smaller) native shacks were noted, the "village" was again zoomed. This time as many of the natives as possible were on the roof of their "civic" center and all of them entirely naked waving their loin cloths! It is not known whether this is their especial form of welcome for oceanic fliers, but it was later learned that none of them had ever seen an airplane.

"Although the lagoon was spotted with coral reefs that looked from the air to be near or on the surface, an examination disclosed a safe landing area at the southern end closest to the village. The senior aviator then decided upon landing his plane for the express purpose of making inquiries, and after a preliminary "dragging," the plane sat down on the calm waters of the lagoon. Almost immediately after the landing an outrigger canoe was pushed off from the beach carrying what later proved to be three native boys and the white resident manager.

"It took the natives exactly forty-five minutes to paddle three-quarters of a mile! But the wait supplied the senior aviator and his Cadet observer with sufficient time to take stock of their surroundings.

"It was noted that the reefs which from the air appeared to be close to the surface were, in reality, at least four to six feet or more deep. A little sailing afforded a chance to pass over several of these and it was finally

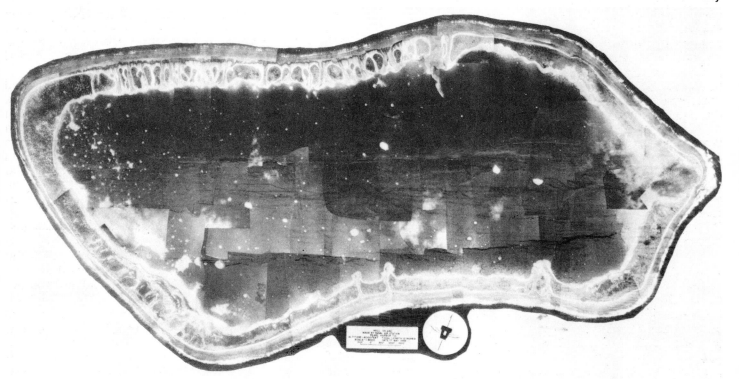

Aerial mosaic of Hull Island and lagoon. Coral outcropping visible throughout lagoon surface. Lt. Lambrecht, U.S.S. *Colorado* Senior Aviator, would not have landed there without *a priori* information from ground-level observer that a safe landing was possible.

Photo credit - National Archives Negative #80-G-451054

Captain John Jones was master mariner with papers in both sail and steam. He brought this personal boat to Hull Island in May 1937. A former lifeboat, it had both sail and auxiliary engine for deep-water interisland passages between Hull, Sydney, and Gardner Islands in the Phoenix Group.

decided to turn and taxi downwind, closer to the beach, and to the approaching canoe. This we did and then settled down to wait.

"As the canoe came nearer, the reason for its breathtaking speed was readily apparent . . . the natives were using small round poles as paddles! When within hailing distance, we received a hearty wave and a cordial "Cheerio" from the resident manager. He was a man of about medium height, deeply tanned, and dressed as may have been expected, in white duck trousers, white shirt, and a straw hat, which he removed to wave at us. His appearance led one to believe that his nationality was German, due, no doubt, to his closely-cropped hair and rotund face, but his accent proclaimed him British.

"We told him we were searching for a plane which we believed may have been forced down somewhere in the Phoenix Islands, that the plane had left Lae, New Guinea, for Howland Island a week past and had not been heard of since, and we wondered whether he'd seen or heard of it. He replied that he hadn't and added that he possessed a radio receiver but had heard nothing on it. He was ignorant of the flight but evidenced quizzical surprise when told it was being made by Amelia Earhart. He then asked where we had come from and was considerably startled when we told him, "Honolulu." We hastily explained, however, that our ship was some 50 or 60 miles to the westward awaiting our return.

"After informing him that we expected to search the rest of the islands, we took off, rendezvoused with the other planes, and returned to the ship."

10 July 1937

"On the following morning (Saturday) the unit was ordered to search four of the five remaining islands. Heading southeast from the ship, we soon picked up Sydney but upon dropping down for an inspection of that island could discover nothing which indicated that the missing fliers had landed there. The lagoon was sufficiently large to warrant a safe landing but several circles of the island disclosed no signs of life and a landing would have been useless. There were signs of recent habitation and small shacks could be seen among the groves of coconut palms, but repeated zooms failed to arouse any answering wave and the planes headed northeast for Phoenix Island."

CRUISE OF THE USCG CUTTER *TANEY*

In September 1937 the United States Coast Guard cutter *Taney* went to the equatorial Line Islands, Samoa, and other islands of the South Pacific. The following are excerpts from the Confidential Cruise Report 601-64 dated 11 November 1937 from the captain of the *Taney* to the Commandant, U.S. Coast Guard.

United States Coast Guard cutter *Taney* made south seas cruise in September and October 1937. When it stopped at Hull Island, the resident manager, Captain Jones, R.N.R., came aboard.

Photo credit - United States Coast Guard

Item Number 15

"At 0811 13 November came up along the southwest shore of Hull Island and stopped off at the village at the northwest point, where the Union Jack was flying from a staff near a long shed. A small skiff came out to the ship with two native paddlers and a white man, who proved to be Mr. Jones, the Deputy Commissioner for the Phoenix Group. He stated that he was alone on the island, except for 39 Tokelau natives; that he had a radio transmitter and receiver with which he could work Australia; that he had a small sailing vessel in which it was his custom to visit other islands of the group; also that he expected to raise about 90 tons of copra a year on Hull Island, which would be handled through Burns-Philp, Ltd., of Apia. He stated that he would be glad to have a party come ashore at Hull Island, but that there was not enough water on the reef to admit the passage of one of our boats. When he heard that we were going past Sydney, he requested that we take his skiff on board and leave it there, as the natives there had no boat of any kind. This was done, Mr. Jones going ashore in an outrigger canoe, and at 1105 *Taney* proceeded on course for Sydney."

Item Number 16.

"At 1555 13 November, anchored on the shelf of the reef off Sydney Island, in 20 fathoms of water, with 90 fathoms on the port chain; the wind being from east northeast, force 2. Lowered motor surfboat and Lieutenant Kenner and the commanding officer went in to take a look at the landing place marked on the chart. A few natives appeared on the beach to watch us and indicated the landing spot by arm signals. Decided that it would be too risky to try and effect a landing with the ship's boats, so motor surfboat returned to the *Taney* and towed to the beach the small skiff brought from Hull Island, with three Hawaiian boys as paddlers. The small skiff negotiated a landing successfully, the three boys swimming back through the surf to the motor boat, which

Captain Jones aboard United States Coast Guard Cutter *Taney* off Hull Island, October 1937. *Taney* cruise report contains details of interview with Jones and leaves little doubt as to his involvement in Earhart disappearance.

Photo credit - Via Kenneth Lum King, Hawaii

returned to the ship and was hoisted. During the evening, natives on the island paddled out to the ship with a large sea turtle as a present. The turtle was found to weigh 261 pounds, and the meat formed a welcome addition to the officers' mess."

THE ROLE OF THE U.S.S. ONTARIO

Three radio messages between the Chief of Naval Operations, Washington, D.C. (OPNAV), and the commanding officer of the naval station at Pago Pago (NAVSTA), Tutuila, American Samoa, are of importance regarding the part played by the Ontario in the Earhart flight scenario.

16 June 1937
FROM: OPNAV, WASH DC
TO: COMFOURTEENTH, NAVSTA TUTUILA, SAMOA
CLASSIFICATION: PRIORITY
EARHART EXPECTS ARRIVE AT LAE NEW GUINEA 23 JUNE AND HOWLAND ON 25 JUNE PERIOD DESIRE ONTARIO TO BE ON STATION 25 JUNE AND OTHER ASSISTANCE FURNISHED AS PREVIOUSLY PLANNED

2 JULY 1937
FROM: NAVSTA TUTUILA SAMOA
TO: OPNAV WASH DC
CLASSIFICATION: PRIORITY
IMPERATIVE ONTARIO LEAVE EARHART FLIGHT STATION FOR TUTUILA NOT LATER THAN 1800 SATURDAY 3 JULY ZONE MINUS ELEVEN

3 JULY 1937
FROM: CHIEF OF NAVAL OPERATIONS
TO: NAVSTA TUTUILA SAMOA, U.S.S. ONTARIO,
CLASSIFICATION: RESTRICTED
ONTARIO RELEASED FROM PLANE GUARD DUTY PROCEED TO TUTUILA

Indicated by a careful study of the last flight, the search and its aftermath, along with information released by the United States government, is that the initial post-mission focal point was Hull Island. Not only was it set up to (under certain conditions) succor the fliers, but a considerable amount of effort was made to conceal its true role. Obvious now is that the presence of Jones and his high-powered radio was a contributing factor to the secrecy. Just as obvious is that much more was involved than Jones and his transgression. United States government personnel could have protested to the British (New Zealand) authorities about suspected bogus use of that transmitter in conjunction with the Earhart disappearance, but this was not done.

Photographs from the Office of Naval Intelligence files establish that the Earhart Electra passed Gardner Island and approached Hull Island, her destination and landing place after Howland and Canton were denied her. She arrived at Hull on the morning of 2 July 1937. In all probability, after a wheels-up landing on the sand of the platform reef, she was able to send a limited number of radio messages until her two batteries were exhausted. At sea level, however, the range was limited. With the proper ionospheric skip, however, Karl Pierson's claim of hearing her voice on 3 July 1937, long after her fuel was exhausted, is credible.

Professional radio engineer/operator Karl Pierson heard Earhart radio transmissions for several days after the fuel aboard the Electra would have been exhausted. Officials in Washington, D.C., discounted this evidence because it repudiated their contention.
Photo credit - Via Karl Pierson

ONTARIO SKIPPER BLAKESLEE'S TESTIMONY

Lt. (now Captain) Horace W. Blakeslee, USN, has been interviewed by a number of persons. His standard answer for the Ontario not participating in the search was a shortage of fuel (coal), water, and supplies. Noted in the Ontario log was that upon leaving the naval station at Pago Pago on 16 June 1937, 512 tons of coal were aboard. Upon her return on 9 July 1937, 181 tons were "on hand." This was not exactly depleted of fuel! Further, noted in the then current issue of the Hydrographic Office Sailing Directions was that coal and supplies were available at Ocean Island, which was only a few miles off the course the ship would have taken to the area of the Earhart search. Thus, this report of shortages is not a valid excuse any more than the lack of adequate communication equipment. In an emergency situation, messages can be relayed from one station to another. Clearly, officials and naval personnel in the United States had another role for the Ontario.

Apparent now is that the initial "imperative" requirement failed to materialize due to a change in requirements in the week that Blakeslee needed to bring the Ontario back to its home port. Once there, the ship was inactive until 14 September, when she was used for an official visit to a very prominent outrider island, which every mariner would see during the approach to Tutuila, the main island of American Samoa. Aunu'u Island is approximately a mile in diameter and has a peculiar structure due to the two-humped cone of its truncated volcano. On 14 September 1937, Governor Milne and an "official party" made a half day trip to Aunu'u Island for unstated reasons. This was in connection with a covert role which had developed, making this visit necessary. Because the purpose of the visit wasn't stated, the assumption is that it was covert. If the group had been composed only of local officers, it would have been called the governor's party in the ship log. The word "official" implies that someone had arrived from Washington for an official investigation. The reason why Milne wanted the ship away from the island was because the party was not going to the village on the western end, but around the southern shore to an isolated compound. The Samoan Islands had been plagued with epidemics in 1936 as had other South Central Pacific areas. American Samoa had needed an isolation area away from the main island where persons with contagious diseases could be quarantined. When fiscal money became available in 1937, a small facility was constructed on the south central shore some distance from the village. Successive aerial photographs over a three-decade period, shown in the accompanying vertical views of Aunu'u Island, depict the progressive expansion of this government compound from an almost inconspicuous site to an area covering many acres.

The official party was, therefore, apparently medical in nature with the prime "visitor" from the staff of Admiral Edward R. Stitt, Surgeon General of the United States Navy, who was an authority on tropical diseases. This particular medical officer was a specialist in dysentery and had the latest medicine and techniques for treating patients with that ailment. In peacetime ship logs, the reason for trips of this type are generally stated and the log forwarded monthly to Washington. The major exception is that classified activity is covered in a separate report. The log of the *Ontario* for 14 September 1937 is shown on the next page. While the activities may seem inconsequential, much more is evident than the words convey.

A log of a United States naval ship is more than an itinerary of that vessel. Universal guidelines are used in preparation. After a few years practice, the entire 14 September operation would appear suspect to a trained researcher. The way the ship log was consistently prepared over Blakeslee's signature is important. Also, contemporary events in American Samoa and nearby areas are a decided help. The key words are "official party." As this party was ashore for only two hours, a rapid inspection of a government activity ashore occurred. The brief time rules out a normal annual inspection of an outriding island or the usual lengthy Kava ceremony/banquet. The fact that Blakeslee first anchored his ship and then pulled up the anchor indicated that the governor did not want prying eyes seeing where the party went on the island. With no protection from the ship there may well have been members of the Fita Fita guard with the party to offer protection. To place this visit in perspective, the original covert role of the *Ontario* in early July 1937 must be examined. The two applicable radiograms between NAVSTA Tutuila and the Chief of Naval Operations in Washington are worth studying. Governor Milne's message to the CNO was: "Imperative that *Ontario* return to Tutuila not later than 9 July." The reply from Washington, routed through Pearl Harbor so that Admiral Murfin's staff would see it, removed the ship from search duties, ostensibly for more imperative duties at its home station. According to the *Ontario's* log, however, the ship remained at the naval station dock until 14 September except for an exchange visit to nearby Apia, Western Samoa. This rather obvious contradiction is a further cover-up for what actually happened and stresses the importance of American Samoa, the closest United States territory to Howland Island.

RADIO TRAFFIC ANALYSIS
Of importance in the Earhart "disappearance" was

the continuation of radio messages after the fuel was exhausted and the airplane went down. Both the location of the transmitter and the person who sent the messages have been identified. United States naval personnel also located the sender and knew about his high-powered radio. They covered up this fact, a covert act that is proof of a cover-up and that Jones was either working with or for them in keeping the Earhart search alive.

The 1937 aerial photograph of Hull Island was taken with a civilian, not a military, camera in the Earhart Lockheed and is proof of her arrival there. This photograph may be found on page 51. A landing into the prevailing wind would have been made on the sand of the flat fringing reef on the northwest corner of that island. The fact that the airplane, which had arrived at Hull Island on the morning of 2 July 1937, had disappeared by 9 July, when Lt. Lambrecht landed a floatplane on the lagoon, meant that Jones, with the help of Tokelan natives, pushed the empty Electra across the reef to the water. Using his small motorized sailboat, which he had brought from Apia, Western Samoa, aboard the *Makoa*, the Lockheed was hauled into some 14 fathoms of water offshore before it was sunk. What has happened to the airplane in the ensuing 50 years? This author believes it is still there.

The timetable of the radio signals heard during the period 2-5 July 1937 is indicative that the messages initially came from KHAQQ, the downed Earhart Lockheed. After approximately two hours of transmitter operation, the two onboard batteries were discharged and later messages were sent from Captain John Jones' high-powered radio station on Hull Island. KHAQQ could only transmit in the vicinity of Hull Island, but Jones' transmitter could reach the entire Pacific basin. In the list that follows, the hour and day are given first. The times are all GCT. The last reported reception from the Lockheed in flight was at 2015 on 2 July.

0831-0834/3 VKT Nauru Radio: Unintelligible voice signals on 6210 kc. "Voice similar to that heard from plane during flight, except no hum of plane in the background."

0900-0920/3 Karl Pierson, et al: Heard a faint carrier, then code poorly transmitted, "SOS SOS SOS KHAQQ" repeated for about 5 minutes. Then followed by unreadable code from which "179" and "1_6" were distinguished.

1330/3 Pierson: Woman's voice (which Pierson recognized as that of Miss Earhart), "KHAQQ calling SOS" repeated.

0833/4 Pan American Airways station KNBF, Mokapuu Point, Oahu: "Faint carrier on 3105" immediately following broadcast of appeal from KGU (broadcast station in Hawaii) to Earhart to respond with 4 long dashes. These signals were also reported by San Francisco Coast Guard Station and the naval station at Wailupe, Hawaii.

1215/4 PAA station KNBI, Wake Island: "Intermittent phone of rather wobbly characteristics" on 3105 kc.

1437/4 PAA station KNBH, Midway Island: "Weak, wobbly signal which sounded like a phone" on 3105 kc.

1523-1530/4 PAA station KNBF, Mokapuu: Made a bearing of 213 on "Carrier again heard."

ZONE DESCRIPTION _plus_11_   REMARKS.

0 to 4: Moored starboard side to U.S. Naval Station Wharf Tutuila, American Samoa. Boilers secured receiving power and water from dock. 0200 Lighted fires under #1 and #2 boilers.

                                        E. H. McCauley
                                        E.H. McCAULEY, GM1c., USN.

4 to 8: 0700 Held quarters for muster; no absentees.

                                        E. H. McCauley
                                        E.H. McCAULEY, GM1c., USN.

8 to 12: 1130 Made all preparations for getting under way. 1148 Governor and Official party came on board.

                                        E. H. McCauley
                                        E.H. McCAULEY, GM1c., USN.

12 to 16: 1200 Underway way in in accordance with movement order #23-37, Commandant U.S. Naval Station, steering various courses to conform with channel, standard speed 9.5 knots, 89.0 RPM. 1213 Passed Breaker point light abeam to port, distance 400 yards. 1210 Set course 088° T, 077° PSC. 077° PSTGC. 1245 Steering various courses approaching Aunu'u Island. 1314 Anchored in 31 Fathoms of water with 55 fathoms of chain to starboard anchor. 1316 Governor and Official party left ship. 1335 Underway cruising on various courses and at various speeds off Aunu'u Island. Ave. steam 195. Ave. RPM 49.0.

                                        E. H. McCauley
                                        E.H. McCAULEY, GM1c., USN.

16 to 18: Steaming as before on various courses and at various speeds approaching Aunu'u Island. 1604 Stopped to embark Governor and Official party. 1611 Ahead on various speeds and courses conforming to the southern coast of Tutuila Island, standard speed 10.0 knots, 94.0 RPM. 1652 Passed Breaker point abeam to starboard distance 400 yds., steering various courses and at various speeds conforming to channel of Pago Pago Harbor. 1710 Moored starboard side to U.S. Naval Station Wharf. 1711 Secured main engines and boilers. Receiving water and power from dock. 1712 Governor and Official party left ship. Ave. steam 195. Ave. RPM. 75

                                        B. Hiddenga
                                        B. HIDDENGA, CWT., USN.

18 to 20: No remarks.

                                        B. Hiddenga
                                        B. HIDDENGA, CWT., USN.

20 to 24: No remarks.

                                        B. Hiddenga
                                        B. HIDDENGA, CWT., USN.

Approved: H.W. Blakeslee   Examined:
          H.W. BLAKESLEE,
          Lieutenant, U.S. Navy,
          Navigator and Commanding.   U. S. N., Navigator.

0630-0640/5 Broadcast station KGMB appeals to Earhart to "Respond with four long dashes if you hear us." Immediately four long dashes were heard by the San Fransicso Coast Guard station, Wailupe naval station, PAA station KNBF at Mokapuu, PAA station KNBH at Midway Island, (which took a bearing of 201 degrees), Baker and Howland Islands, and the U.S.S. *Colorado*.

0730-1035/5 Operators on Baker and Howland hear weak carrier, "NRUI (*Itasca*) from KHAQQ." Signal too weak to be confused with signal from *Itasca*.

1130-1230/5 Navy Radio at Wailupe and M.V. *Moorby*: Received, "281 . . . north . . . KHAQQ . . . be on . . . north . . . don't hold . . . with us . . . much longer . . . above water . . . shut" on voice on 3105 kc.

1225/5 PAA station KNBI, Wake Island: Took bearing of 144 on "very unsteady voice modulated carrier" on 3105 kc. KNBF, Mokapuu, took bearing of 215 on the same signal at that time.

1330/5 Howland D\F station: Took bearing of SSE-NNW on "weak carrier " that had previously been heard calling NRUI from KHAQQ on NNW-SSE (157°-337°)

1503-2350/5 Howland D\F station and PAA station KNBH, Midway Island: Took bearings of 157-337 and 175 respectively on "strong unmodulated carrier" slightly off 3105 kc. These bearings intersect in the same place, near the Phoenix Group, that the previously-taken bearings on the "weak, wobbly" carrier had converged.

H.M.S. *ACHILLES* RADIO INTERCEPT

Both New Zealand ships, the *Achilles* and *Wellington*, were at Pago Pago on 26 June 1937 where 220 tons of fuel were transferred from the *Achilles* to the *Wellington*. Considering that the capacity of the latter ship was 250 tons, she was almost dry. The *Wellington* left American Samoa the same day. Earhart was originally scheduled to leave Lae, New Guinea, on this date, but all those short overnight stops (St. Louis to Dakar, etc.) put her days behind her original schedule. The week in Java was also a long delay.

When the *Wellington* and the *Achilles* left Pago Pago, they were asked to monitor the aviation frequencies (3105 kc and 6210 kc) after 1 July. Normally surface ships ignore these frequencies and have their own assigned bands. The radio operators on the *Achilles* were supposed to call U.S. Naval Radio Tutuila, American Samoa, if any pertinent messages were heard.

After the radio operator aboard the *Achilles* picked up the intercept, Rear Admiral Drummond, R.N., the Commodore Commanding New Zealand Navy, who was aboard the *Achilles*, decided to share his "good news" with the world, so he sent the message intercept to the press in Honolulu, (knowing that the British Consulate would receive the message and pass it along) *without* clearing the message with the U.S.Navy. This, of course, blew the cover of the entire alleged disappearance act! When the *Achilles* arrived at Honolulu, at the request of the U.S. Navy, Captain Drummond belatedly retracted the message and denied that any such message from Earhart and Noonan had been received by anyone aboard the ship. Censorship, 1937 style!

All of this information is in the public domain.

What isn't, is why the Royal Navy, through the British High Commissioner of the Western Pacific Islands (at Suva, Fiji Islands), would agree to the use of a light cruiser, the *Achilles*, and a warship like the escort ship *Wellington* in the support of the Earhart stunt flight. Obviously, the answer is that they wouldn't unless they themselves had a considerable stake in the flight or appendages thereof. If the British had an airplane in the air which was supposed to land at Canton Island, then the use of the *Wellington* in the Phoenix Group and the *Achilles* standing by to the eastward would be justified. Drummond released the "good news" to the press because he interpreted it to mean that Earhart and Noonan were talking to the RAF team which had landed safely on Canton Island. He wanted the world at large to share in the good news. Obviously, the RAF airplane did not arrive at Canton for a wheels-down landing, refuel from the aviation gas cache left by the U.S.S. *Avocet* in June 1937 (solar eclipse expedition), and then fly on to the Fiji Islands. To whom was John W. Jones, using the call sign KHAQQ, talking?

It now appears that Captain Jones was calling Canton Island. It is known that KHAQQ was used (on 3105) because Jones didn't want the message to get out. By using the 50-watt rig (at sea level), it was, for all intents and purposes, a localized area call. As noted, the radio operator on the *Achilles* picked it up "by accident" by being in the right place at the right time. The operator on Nauru Island might also have picked up this message by ship. Why a radio station on Canton Island is suspected is due to several covert documents classified SECRET from the New Zealand National Archives and several others better known.

ANALYSIS

The seaplane tender U.S.S. *Avocet* brought the U.S. solar eclipse party of civilians to Canton on 22 May 1937. The eclipse was on 8 June. The *Avocet* left for Pearl Harbor on 10 June after breaking up camp on the island and loading the gear. The H.M.S. *Wellington* which had brought the New Zealand scientists from Suva, Fiji Islands, had arrived at Canton on 31 May and departed on the evening of 8 June as that party had only a limited amount of gear to load.

Well known is the fact that Earhart was supposed to have been in those waters on 25 June, or two weeks later. All of the ships being used for her flight support had been required to be "on station" by 25 June although Earhart, after a large number of detours, half-day flights, and other delays caused by "unsuitable weather," was behind her original schedule.

COVERT INFORMATION

In the file on the Canton Island expedition in the New Zealand National Archives at Wellington, are two SECRET documents which contain the following information.

1. Mitchell, U.S. chief scientist said, "We had decided to pass on this event (Solar Eclipse), but the USN insisted that we must go and paid all the bills from the East Coast to Hawaii and provided a ship for the last 2,000 miles. Total expedition miles were 15,000. With many tons of scientific telescopes and other heavy gear, the cost must have been in the tens of thousands of dollars for the 12-man party." The U.S. Navy really wanted an excuse to look over Canton Island.

2. After the H.M.S. *Wellington* left Canton on 8 June in the late afternoon after the gear had been loaded,

the CO of that ship sent a SECRET/Priority Radiogram to the British High Commissioner for the Western Pacific Islands at Suva, Fiji Islands, which said, in effect: Something is "fishy and smells bad." The Yanks are dug in and it looks as if they plan to stay. Suggest southern return trip of H.M.S. *Achilles* be altered for stops at Canton and Hull to see what the Yanks are up to. This is exactly what the British did. They changed their cruise schedule so that the ships went through the Phoenix Islands.

Before this ship arrived, however, the U.S.S. *Swan*, another airplane tender attached to PatWing2 at Pearl Harbor (as was the *Avocet*), arrived. The naval claim that no landing party from the *Swan* went ashore on Canton on 10 July is false. All of the newspapers carried the story, Honolulu, London, Wellington, New Zealand, etc. The news was blacked out in the United States. The question is, "What did the *Avocet* leave behind on 10 June that the *Swan* had to pick up on 10 July, exactly one month later?"

A cache of aviation fuel was needed in the event Earhart landed wheels down on Canton and required fuel to proceed further. This appears quite rational because both ships were seaplane tenders and carried 10,000 gallons of aviation gas to tender their assigned aircraft when at an advanced base. This happened even though Earhart was ordered to land elsewhere (wheels up) and the British airplane never arrived at Canton, having ditched off Mili Atoll in the Marshalls.

The question is, what did the British see concerning the U.S. camp on Canton that "spooked" them? For one thing 24 barrels (55 gallons each) or more than 1,000 gallons of aviation gasoline were there. The motor-generator for the radio equipment was the only thing that burned gasoline, and this amount of fuel would have kept it operating for six months. Was picking up all of the aviation gasoline that urgent or important? High-test automobile gasoline retailed for 18 cents per gallon, including taxes, in 1937. The military bought gasoline at bulk prices, below wholesale, and paid no tax on it. The most that aviation gasoline would have cost the Navy in 1937 was 15 cents per gallon. This $150 worth of aviation fuel on Canton was insignificant. In fact, if the cache on Canton was deemed important enough to remove, the fuel would have been dumped on the sand and the empty barrels taken back to the ship. Bringing barrels in through the surf with the tide is easy, but the reverse is not. In fact, during World War II, gasoline taken ashore was considered expendable and never brought back to the ship.

It would seem that the *Avocet* had left much more on Canton that the Navy did have to recover after Earhart's mission was completed. Now evident is the fact that the Navy left the radio gear they had taken ashore on the island along with two or more navy ratings, a radio operator and aviation specialist to help with refueling or work on the Lockheed and perhaps a rifleman or two for protection.

In late 1937 and in 1938, three articles about the solar eclipse expedition on Canton Island appeared in the *National Geographic*. Also, a broadcast by an NBC newscaster was made from the island during the 8:00 p.m. solar eclipse and phone patches were made nightly to the states for the entertainment of the scientists. There were no 60-foot palm trees on the island, only a few dwarfs about 20 feet tall, and therefore

useless as substitute antenna masts. What the British observed was a "first-class" radio installation on the island. The messages were relayed to the West Coast through Navy radio Oahu. But even to transmit 2,000 miles required a moderate amount of power and a suitable antenna, in this case one supported by radio towers. With this type of semi-permanent installation and 24 barrels of gasoline in the fuel dump, the British would have reason for concern about Yank occupancy of the island which they claimed as British. Also, with ratings ashore and radio gear to recover, there was reason indeed to send a landing party ashore at Canton on 10 July, the first opportunity to do so.

Indicated in available documentary evidence is that Jones was calling the radio station on Canton (USN radio gear and ratings) to see if he could raise them, very likely at the request of the Navy Radio Tutuila.

When the Commodore commanding the New Zealand Navy, who was aboard the *Achilles* for the trip to Honolulu, learned about this radio intercept, he undoubtedly, having been told that there were two "birds" in the air (one of them British), interpreted the exchange to mean that both parties were down and safe and hastened to spread the "good news" to all concerned. One must be aware of how this security system operates. Drummond, the Royal Navy Rear Admiral aboard the *Achilles*, had been told to monitor the aviation frequencies after he left Tutuila, but had *not been told what to do if he heard anything*! So, he ad-libbed. Admiral Murfin in Honolulu must have cringed when the British released this good news to the press. Of course, Drummond had to rectify his honest mistake upon arrival at Honolulu a few days later to keep up the "lost at sea" propaganda.

In preceding sections, evidence has been reviewed that places the Earhart Lockheed in the Phoenix Island Group at the termination of the "last flight." This was the consensus of all professionals at that time and for the years prior to the attack on Pearl Harbor. The government search, while deemed satisfactory by the searchers "under the existing circumstances," was repeatedly challenged as inadequate by a number of interested parties whose combined efforts in launching Pacific searches were thwarted. Since World War II, search participants, including senior officers, have likewise expressed doubts that the search was adequate, and for good and sufficient reasons. The following general conclusions can be drawn using a comprehensive overview of actual conditions both above and below the equator in 1937, official documentation, and contemporary records.

1. The naval search was staged for the benefit of the Imperial Japanese Navy with the general public being duped in the process.

2. The search was directed by the insiders of the Roosevelt administration with the prearranged outcome that nothing of significance would be found.

3. Anything positive that was uncovered would be promptly negated and kept from foreign and public view using any diversion necessary.

4. Government spokesmen have kept this 1937 "finding" unchanged during the ensuing 50 years.

5. A conspiracy of silence was enforced to hide the actual events when they occurred, subsequent to when they occurred, and for half a century.

6. Documents pertaining to the alleged civilian

flight were classified, begrudgingly declassified after the passage of the Freedom of Information Act (FOIA), and partially released after careful scrutiny.

7. Secrecy has been maintained for decades after any legitimate reason for classification exists other than to cover up the wrongdoing of the parties involved.

8. The truth should be revealed if for no other reason than to help prevent the recurrence of presidential-military service collusion of this type.

In the history of the Earhart episode, the initial naval search effort was in the Phoenix Islands, by United States naval personnel who concentrated in that area. Not until 1943, when the fictionalized motion picture titled *Flight for Freedom* came out, did the Imperial Japanese Navy become the villain. At least a dozen variations of how they shot her down, murdered her, held her prisoner in the Emperor's palace or a fisherman's hut have emerged. Natives from a dozen different locations in the Marshalls, Carolines, Marianas, and even the Admiralty Islands and New Guinea have reported having seen her. Needless to say, these tales have no semblance of truth to them, in spite of the reported desecration of at least a half dozen assorted graveyards on Saipan and elsewhere.

As a matter of documented fact, the search by USN personnel in July 1937, deemed "adequate" by their account, has been shown to be far less than that. Their statements that nothing of account was found were lies and a cover-up. Less than four months after Earhart's disappearance, the United States Coast Guard cutter *Taney* stopped at Hull Island and learned that Jones had been on the island since May 1937 and had a high-powered transmitter and a motorized sailing vessel. Just as Jones' statements had been classified on 9 July 1937, this later disclosure was also classified for 30 years by the United States Coast Guard. Both of these government agencies had good reason to conceal the fact that Jones had such a radio because he had transmitted bogus radio messages which kept the search alive. Instead of censoring him and either shutting down his radio station, on which he illegally transmitted distress messages (against international law), the USN and USCG covered up his illegal activities, proving that collusion was involved.

At the start of the Marshall Island overflight mission, Howland ceased to be Earhart's prime destination. Instead, Canton Island became prime with Hull Island as an alternate. Both Canton and Hull were set up and provisioned as landing sites by the United States government (directly in the case of Canton Island and through intermediaries in the case of Hull Island). In the event that the Japanese became aware of the overflight, Earhart was directed to bypass Howland Island and land on the sand of the fringing reef at Hull. According to two different radio operators on the West Coast who were monitoring Earhart flight frequencies and the USCG radio traffic from the *Itasca* to San Francisco Coast Guard headquarters, that is what occurred.

What may be surprising is that most of this information has been known for years by many persons both in and outside of the government. The trouble is that too many "sacred cows" are involved and the pieces are scattered among dozens of individuals, each of whom has a small bit of the whole. Thus, no one put the obvious together, and the ones qualified to write the epic have not, and the ones not qualified have. This accounts for the past failures to present the truth.

The best approach for proving the Hull Island theory is to find the airplane, recover it, and let United States government officials explain how it got there. That way, no "sacred cows" are upset by presenting another concept that biased citizens won't accept because they don't want to hear the truth. Once the physical *prima facie* evidence is discovered, then, after half a century of conjecture, the truth must be revealed!

Based on all available evidence, a landing into the prevailing wind on the extensive sand of the fringing reef on the northwest corner of Hull Island occurred. The reef is flat and has a wide sandy beach essentially straight for several hundred yards, and oriented into the prevailing westerly wind. When retracted, the wheels of the Lockheed Model 10E protrude about 12 inches from the engine nacelles, so that the airplane is supported by the wheels even when they are retracted. Using planks under these main wheels and lifting the tail, the airplane could be pushed to the sea by the 24 adult natives, towed by Jones' motorized boat into deep water, and sunk. This explains why the airplane disappeared between 2 July 1937 and 9 July when pilots in floatplanes from the *Colorado* overflew Hull, with one being landed on the lagoon.

Burns-Philp (South Seas) Company, Ltd., officials must have had a tacit agreement regarding reimbursement with the British High Commissioner of the Western Pacific Islands at Suva, Fiji Islands. The Phoenix Island Group had been annexed by the British Gilbert and Ellice Colony before Jones' occupancy. Food and supplies were transported to Hull Island in late June 1937 as reported by the Commodore of the New Zealand Navy, and he wouldn't have lied about that.

The evidence is overwhelming and consists of documentary, pictorial, first-person (including four of the six pilots from the *Colorado*), and cartographic in nature.

To clarify Jones' radio transmissions from Hull Island in mid-1937, the following two explanations are evident. First, unless the supernatural is part of the scenario, Jones had to be the source of the bogus radio transmissions simply because he was the only person in the Phoenix Island Group known to have a radio station with a high-powered transmitter. If he was not being protected by United States governmental agencies, he would have been questioned as a leading suspect because of his violation of international maritime law in sending out false distress signals. As members of a U.S. government agency designated to uphold these laws, personnel aboard the USCG cutter *Taney* were particularly negligent in ignoring Captain Jones' role in the Earhart disappearance episode. Evidently the USN was well aware of Jones and his activities both prior to and during the Earhart search. Second, not only did Jones have the high-powered radio transmitter he had brought from Apia aboard the *Makao*, but he also had the radio equipment from that ship. According to the Maritime Court of Review (held in Suva, Fiji Islands) on the sinking of that ship, it struck an off-shore reef in the early morning, could not be disengaged, was stove in on one side, and began taking on water. By noon the engine compartment was flooded, thus stopping the engine and the pumps. During the day, equipment, supplies, and personnel were evacuated from the ship to Hull by using lifeboats and Jones' motorized sailboat, which had been brought to Hull Island on the vessel. By late afternoon the *Makoa*, awash in heavy swell, broke in two. Obviously the radio equipment would have been salvaged and taken ashore although there is some question as to whether the electrical generator, which was powered by the engine, was salvaged. Jones had brought a motor-generating power plant with him for lighting purposes and for operating his radio equipment. Thus, he had a complete standby radio transmitter (code) and receiver from the *Makoa*. When the crew from the Makoa was picked up by the Royal Mail Ship (R.M.S.) *Niagara*, when it made a distress stop at Hull on 21 June 1937 on its regular passenger run from Honolulu to Suva, a skiff from the *Makoa* and most of the salvaged items, including the radio gear, were left behind. Only the crew members, their personal luggage, and the ship's papers were taken aboard. The assignment given a Royal Mail Ship is to carry the mail with dispatch and, in the process, cater to paying passengers, maintain schedules, and last, to pick up shipwrecked sailors. While a modest amount of point-to-point cargo might be carried aboard such a ship, the mail was the main subsidy. Also, transferring bulk cargo at sea outside a harbor was not in the best interests of the carrier.

Another topic in the Earhart disappearance episode is the use of a "tidal flat beach" as a take-off/landing site. In the jet age of runways more than two miles in length, the use of a beach for operations may seem impractical. This was not the case in the 1920s and 1930s when propeller-driven aircraft had to be operated from runways which were 2,000 to 3,000 feet in length. For long-distance flights, takeoffs and landings on hard, flat, and lengthy beaches were commonplace. For example, Kingsford-Smith took off twice from a tidal flat airstrip during his 1928 trans-Pacific crossing, first at Barking Sands, Kauai, Territory of Hawaii, and second from a long stretch of beach near Suva, Fiji Islands. His Fokker tri-motor had fixed gear. With its heavy load of gasoline, a hard sand surface was required for takeoff.

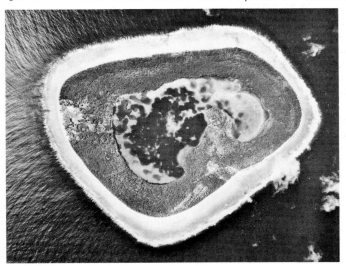

Swains Island, northernmost outrider of American Samoa, was 400 miles south of Hull and Sydney Islands. This could have been a hiding place for the fliers. Wallace Jennings, fourth generation owner of Swains Island, has stated that he was there in 1937 and Amelia Earhart and Fred Noonan were not.
Photo credit - National Archives

Landing on soft sand was dangerous with fixed gear, but relatively safe with retractable gear. Also, the friction of the sand would limit the landing slide of the aircraft. Unlike landing on a hard surface, a landing on soft sand greatly lessened the danger of a gasoline or oil fire as sparks would have been absent. Thus, landing on the sand at Hull Island would have been less dangerous than Earhart's ground loop on the concrete runway at Luke Field on 20 March 1937. The airplane would have sustained less damage as a result of a beach landing on Hull unless pilot fatigue after 24 hours in the air was a contributing factor. No special procedures were required for a wheels-up landing on the sand. On Earhart's Electra, the fuselage nose section had been structurally strengthened by the installation of a steel "I beam" keel impact member to protect the airplane in the event of a wheels-up landing. Additionally, landing on the sand would allow radio transmissions to continue until the primary and emergency storage batteries ran down. Of course, there was no way to recharge them because the engines could not be run. At sea level, the ground wave from the 50-watt radio-phone transmitter was restricted to about 200 miles at best by ground wave and somewhat farther by sky (skip) wave. Radio transmissions from the reef (by voice) were attempted, but were read only by operators aboard the *Achilles*, which was the only vessel within range. The Commodore Commanding New Zealand Navy who was aboard the *Achilles* at nearby Danger Island (en route to Honolulu) released the initial Earhart radio contact which circulated to the press. The Commodore received a "cease and desist" notice from the United States Navy at Oahu and, upon arrival at Honolulu, issued a denial that the message was authentic, thus ending further public disclosure. After the batteries in the Electra were depleted, radio transmissions from the reef at Hull ceased. Then Jones began his daily and nightly bogus transmissions from his high-powered transmitter. These were the radio signals heard throughout the Pacific Basin. They were sent to keep the search alive and to justify sending the *Colorado* and *Lexington* to the South Pacific for the specific purpose of convincing the Japanese that Earhart, Noonan, and the film were lost.

With the false writeoff of the Phoenix Group, it becomes obvious that the entire Saipan episode is a hoax perpetrated by the United States Navy to divert attention away from its own involvement. Mrs. Josephine Blanco Akiyama, the originator of the hoax, was an acknowledged former employee of the United States Navy on Saipan. After World War II, she migrated to the United States and decided to "tell her story" in 1960. Fred Goerner, author of *The Search for Amelia Earhart* (1966) was a member of the United States Navy Seabees before becoming a journalist at CBS radio (and later on television). He has done very well promulgating this theory. Untold millions of taxpayers' money are spent annually by the military services to promote a favorable image and minimize the impact of adverse events.

This author has attempted to find the truth by using all available avenues of research. For instance, the *Achilles* log was in the New Zealand National Archives in Wellington. The log of the *Wellington* was at the Public Record Office in Kew, England. The author interviewed more than 100 key individuals who had either direct or indirect involvement in the "last flight" and subsequent search. All evidence seems connected to direct involvement of the United States government from the purchase of the aircraft to the final burials of the fliers if their bodies were recovered. The United States Navy and six other government agencies were directly involved. Earhart's flight, as it occurred, could have led to war with Japan in 1937 except for Japanese commitment of Army and Navy forces to the invasion of mainland China in July 1937. They knew about Earhart's overflight in the southern Marshalls. They didn't know about the perfection of aerial nighttime photography and couldn't understand what was to be accomplished by sending amateurs like Earhart and Noonan over the islands at night. This also held true for Dr. Richard Archbold's night overflight of Truk (in the Caroline Islands) a few months later in Guba II, a civilian version of the Navy Consolidated PBY patrol airplane.

Civilian model of Consolidated PBY patrol airplane was sold to Dr. Richard Archbold's expedition in 1937-38 for use in New Guinea. It was called GUBA II by Archbold.
Photo credit - San Diego Aerospace Museum

Archbold in cabin of Consolidated PBY GUBA II in 1938. On delivery flight from San Diego to Hollandria, New Guinea, Archbold stopped at Pearl Harbor and Wake Island en route. On the final leg from Wake, Archbold flew over Truk lagoon in the Japanese mandates during the night. Photoflash bomb photography enabled aerial reconnaissance at night during this strategic period.
Photo credit - San Diego Aerospace Museum

The photograph shown on page 51 of Hull Island was taken in 1937 with a civilian camera of the Kodak 616 type and was inadvertently included in an Office of Naval Intelligence report. This particular photograph and a similar one of Gardner Island has been evaluated in relationship to every known airplane and ship, military and commercial, which could have carried a camera and gone through the Phoenix Island Group in 1937. The only one that fits is the Earhart Electra. It is concluded with 95 percent certainty that Noonan took the photographs with a personal camera on the flyby of Gardner Island and the landing approach to Hull Island. The conclusion was reached that the landing was made on the northwest corner of Hull after cartographic analysis, information in the U.S. Navy Sailing Directions, consultations with pilots, and viewing more than a dozen different maps of Hull dating back more than 100 years. This viewpoint is consistent with the overall Earhart scenario.

In discussions with Eugene Vidal and William Miller, government coordinator of the flight, Earhart had discussed the possibility of finding a "nice stretch of beach" for an emergency landing if Howland was not located. Even Miller realized that a wheels-up landing on the sand was preferable to a ditching at sea. In the 1930s, the prevailing wind was an important factor in laying out airfields, and the main runway was usually oriented into it. The year-round prevailing winds at Hull were the trade winds which blew from the east. The extra wide stretch of sand on the essentially flat fringing reef of the northwest corner of Hull was several thousand feet long and oriented into the prevailing wind. Additionally, it was close to the settled part of the island. Two prominent markers were located there, the large copra shed with its red roof on the western point and a 19-foot tower on the curve at the northwest corner. With the approach of the *Colorado*, the airplane had to disappear between the morning of 2 July 1937 and the afternoon of 9 July. Thus, this landing site fits into the scenario of the actual "last flight."

THE *COLORADO* SEARCH OF THE PHOENIX ISLANDS

Far from being a comprehensive operation, as claimed by representatives of the United States government, the search by crew members of the *Colorado* was deficient in most aspects. The search was controlled from Washington and its main function was to conceal the true situation. In the first place, no one from that ship set foot on any of the islands in the Phoenix Group, the lagoon landing at Hull Island notwithstanding. As the three southernmost islands were densely covered with tropical growth of all types, including coconut palms 60 to 80 feet tall, the airplane could have been hidden in the dense brush surrounding the rim of the atolls and from 450 feet aloft would not have been seen. On all of these coconut islands, pilots from the ship saw native huts. Yet neither Sydney nor Gardner Islands was investigated for possible residents. Lambrecht's unclassified report, which eventually became part of the public domain records, is quite incredible. According to it and news releases given to the public, Lambrecht never bothered to obtain the name of the white resident manager even though he spoke English. The high-powered radio transmitter the manager acknowledged having became a "radio receiver" in the news release. Far from not knowing where Earhart actually was, Jones had moved them to Sydney Island in his motorized sailboat.

Phoenix Isles Possible Earhart Haven

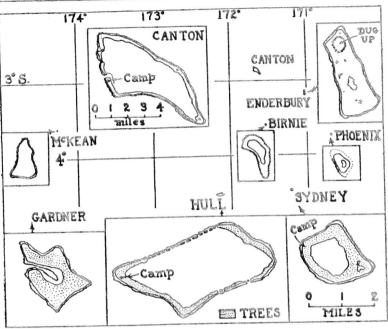

Might be able to land plane - Map of the Phoenix Group with detail sketch maps of the eight islands where the search for Amelia Earhart now centers. All of these except Canton are drawn to the same scale, which is indicated in the lower right hand corner. Canton is drawn to half this scale. The stippled areas are covered with trees of coconut palms.

Colorado aviator William Short suggested to senior aviator Lambrecht that the native huts on Sydney should be searched. When this was suggested to Captain Friedell, the idea was quickly vetoed. He was under orders to let no one set foot on any of the islands in the group. He was told not to take punitive action against the resident manager on Hull even when it became obvious that he was the one sending the fraudulent distress transmissions on aircraft frequencies. All of this information is documented and supported by first-person interviews of naval officers who were on board the *Colorado*. Five of the *Colorado* fliers who went to Hull Island have been interviewed or their official accounts read. Captain William A. Sullivan, USN, who flew rear seat (observer) to aviator William Short, has testified that it was well known aboard ship that Jones had a high-powered radio transmitter. That fact was covered up. Lt. Short's hunch that the natives on Sydney might be hiding in their huts was most certainly correct, but nothing was done about it. In the contemporary records at the Fiji National Archives at Suva are facts that support Jones hiring 40 natives from the Tokelau group, all from the southernmost island of Fakaofo. Of these, 14 who did not bring their wives or children were placed on Sydney Island and 14 others with 9 wives and 10 children were put to work on Hull. One doesn't need to be a cultural anthropologist to predict that the 14 natives on Sydney Island would have reacted the same as the ones on Hull Island when the airplanes flew overhead. Obviously, the natives on Sydney had been ordered to stay hidden in their huts and to keep their "guests" concealed with them when

South shore of Sydney Island showing native huts. Lt. Lambrecht, USN, senior aviator, reported seeing native huts on overflight, but natives working copra on island remained hidden. As the Hull Island and Sydney natives all came from the same home island in the Tokelaus, their diametrically opposed behavior during airplane overflights would be of considerable interest to cultural anthropologists.
Photo credit - National Archives

Sydney Island in Phoenix Group was 60 miles east of Hull Island. On Sydney Island in July 1937 were 14 native laborers who were harvesting copra. Jones had hired them from the Tokelau Group to the south. They remained hidden in their huts when floatplanes from the *Colorado* flew over the atoll on 10 July 1937. Why did they do this?

Photo credit - National Archives

SYDNEY ISLAND
ANCHORAGE

Natural Scale 1:7,229

Boat landing on western rim of Sydney Island. Captain Jones commuted between Hull and Sydney, 60 miles, in his boat to direct native laborers.
Graphic credit - National Archives Negative #80-G-410898

the floatplanes overflew the island. Short's account of the aerial portion of the Earhart search appeared in the November 1986 issue of *Shipmates*, published by the United States Naval Academy Alumnus Society.

The only way the 14 natives could have gotten word was by Jones traveling from Hull to Sydney in his boat along with two other white persons recently arrived by air at Hull. It is no coincidence that the bogus radio traffic from the Phoenix Group stopped after 5 July 1937. Jones was no longer on Hull where his transmitter was located. He had more important business 60 miles to the east at Sydney.

As the *Colorado* pilots were finishing their aerial search of the Phoenix Group, the U.S.S. *Swan*, a seaplane tender from Patrol Wing Two at Pearl Harbor, was off the northwest corner of Canton Island. Although representatives of the United States government and Navy won't acknowledge that a landing party from the *Swan* went ashore at Canton, it was an "open secret" that it occurred. Even the *London Times* had that story, and, by that landing on Canton, the Roosevelt administration had broken the pledge to the British government that neither country should further occupy islands in the Phoenix Group until the issue of sovereignty had been resolved. The reason the *Swan* party visited the solar eclipse camp established in June 1937 was not to look for the lost fliers but to recover an aviation gas cache left by the U.S.S. *Avocet* in early June 1937 and reclaim radio equipment and operating personnel left there the previous month.

AMERICAN SAMOA IN THE 1930s

American Samoa consists of seven islands totaling 76.2 square miles in area which had a population of about 72,000 persons in 1935. All of these islands, except Swains, are part of the Samoan archipelago which lies approximately 2,300 miles southwest of Hawaii. The remaining islands of the Samoan group, four of which are inhabited, constitute Western Samoa, a New Zealand mandate from the 1920s until 1962 when it became an independent nation of approximately 130,000 inhabitants.

97

Panoramic aerial view taken in 1938 of naval station in American Samoa. Pago Pago Harbor was considered to be one of the best in the South Seas area.
Photo credit - National Archives Negative #80-G-410050

In spite of European-American involvement, political factors, population size, and economic organization, the status of the Samoan archipelago has been maintained at a fairly high level of cultural homogeneity and social integration. To some extent, participation in traditional events and kin-related ceremonies and crises transcends political boundaries.

The seven islands and their populations were: Tutuila (24,548); Manu'a group: Ofu (412); Ta'o (1,320); and Olosega (380); Aunu'u (425); Swains Island (74); and Rose Atoll (uninhabited). The four inhabited islands of Western Samoa are Upolo, Savaii, Apolima, and Manono, where there was a medical isolation station (leper colony).

United States administration of American Samoa was under the control of the Department of the Navy from 1900 until 1951. Used as a coaling station in the earlier years of this century, it was heavily manned during World War II. In 1951, the administration was transferred to the Department of the Interior. United States attention to American Samoa, in the form of aid, had gradually been increased during the decades of this century.

Although Western Samoa gained its independence in 1962, American Samoa has retained its status as an unincorporated territory with little demand for either independence or unification with Western Samoa.

Regardless of the long association and political impositions of European-American powers in Samoa, and despite visits to and temporary residence in Hawaii and in the contiguous United States by many Samoans, Samoan village life remains distinctive.

MEDICAL PROVISIONS FOR AMERICAN SAMOA

The introduction of government supported health care services took place in the early 1900s. At that time, a naval physician began to hold regular clinics, primarily on his own initiative. A few years later, he began to receive some budgetary support for supplies and the establishment of a dispensary. In 1912, a hospital was built and the dispensary service was enlarged. Two years after the opening of the hospital, a nursing school was dedicated.

The public health nurses who graduated from the school were sent to the villages to dispense a limited assortment of medical supplies, e.g., castor oil, iodine,

Aerial view of United States Naval Station, Tutuila, American Samoa, on Pago Pago Bay in 1938. Note radio towers in center of photograph and deep water dock close by naval station grounds.

Photo credit - National Archives Negative #80-G-410051

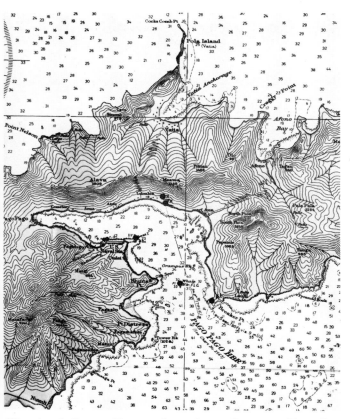

Chart of Pago Pago, American Samoa, Tutuila Island, showing the location of the United States Naval Station there.

Graphic credit - National Archives Negative #80-G-410881

Communications building at the United States Naval Station, Tutuila, American Samoa, in 1938. This was the United States Navy listening post in the South Seas area and the network hub for Earhart's communications.

Photo credit - National Archives Negative #80-CF-7991-1

and alcohol rubs. While yaws was still a problem, there were also some clinics held periodically for the administration of Salvarsan to treat diseases caused by spirochete organisms, i.e., syphilis and trench mouth. Other public health projects were undertaken such as the building of reservoirs to provide a supply of unpolluted water. By the 1920s, the use of Samoan treatment for

Customs dock, Pago Pago Harbor, United States Naval Station, American Samoa.
U.S.S. *Avocet*, aircraft tender, alongside (circa 1938).
Photo credit - National Archives Negative #80-CF-7991-3

conjunctivitis was being displaced by the use of treatment from the dispensaries.

In marked contrast to the limited nature of organized medical services available from the Department of the Navy in earlier times, is the scope and centralization of present-day government-supported medical services which have improved significantly. For example, the 1972 budget of the Department of Medical Services was approximately 3.5 million dollars for support of direct medical services, public health programs, and training. In addition to the recently constructed hospital, the L.B.J. Tropical Medical Center, dispensaries are available in almost every village, with two or more of the larger ones having clinics.

THE AMERICAN SAMOAN NATIVE FITA FITA GUARD DETACHMENT

The native guards, or Fita Fitas, were part of a unique organization organized about 1910 or shortly after Samoa came under American naval administration. Members received regular Navy pay as well as all allowances and retirement privileges. This was out of proportion to other standards of native wages and made a Fita a very respected person in his village, and, quite frequently, a chief. A marine first sergeant acted as commanding officer of the Fitas. Duties were parading

United States Navy Fita Fita, native Samoan guard unit, at United States Naval Station American Samoa. They are working as ship handlers on naval station dock in Pago Pago Harbor.
Photo credit - National Archives Negative #80-Cf-7991-2

Fita Fita native Samoan guard detachment. Called the barefoot sailors of Samoa, the impressive unit had 70 members trained in the manual of arms and had a United States Marine "top kick" as administrative officer.
Photo credit - United States Marine Corps

ring ceremonial visits and performing orderly, essenger, and guard duties at the naval station at Pago go, elsewhere in American Samoa, and on board the tion ship and other naval vessels. The men enlisted in the Navy for duty only in Samoa. In the 1930s, they tered as apprentice seamen. The senior men became atswains mates second class or one of two coxswains. ere were about 70 men, including 18 men in the band to played for colors every morning and participated ce a week in a sunset parade. A chief bandmaster nducted excellent concerts of standard band music.

Fita Fita uniforms were a regulation undershirt and white lava-lava (wrap-around skirt worn by all Samoans). stead of hats, they wore a red headband. Red sashes mpleted the outfits. Like all Samoans of that period, ey went barefoot. As insignia, a Fita Fita had two, three, four blue stripes around the bottom of his lava-lava. A tty officer wore a large chevron above the stripes.

These "barefoot sailors" were colorful and in eping with the trappings of other nearby colonial and lf-administered islands with their royalty and court endants.

CAPTAIN MILNE, UNITED STATES NAVY

Appointed by the Chief of Naval Operations NO) to be Governor of American Samoa (with oosevelt's endorsement), Captain MacGillivray Milne, 5N, was no stranger to the Office of Naval Intelligence NI) and the Japanese Mandated Islands problem. His rm as governor was extended six months beyond the stomary two-year period, or from January 1936 to June 38. This, of course, covered the entire period of nelia Earhart's presence in the Central Pacific. Since 33, he had been sending intelligence reports to the

Fita Fita native guard protecting his post at naval station, American Samoa. Their multi-faceted duty included preserving the peace on Navy-administered islands.
Photo credit - National Archives Negative #80-CF-7991-2

ONI regarding Japanese fortifications of their mandated islands.

Headquarters building at United States Naval Station, Tutuila, American Samoa. Governor Milne, Captain, U.S. Navy, served here from early 1936 to the middle of 1938, a duty of two and a half years. The normal two-year tour was extended six months in Milne's case.
Photo credit - National Archives Negative #80-G-410148

Milne's prior understanding of this sensitive problem may have had something to do with his posting to American Samoa following an earlier posting at Guam (see Dorwardt, 1983). These were the two United States Naval Stations closest to the Japanese Mandated Islands. To illustrate Milne's clout in Washington, it was he who requested the release of the *Ontario*, his station ship, on the phony plea that it was "imperative" to operations at Pago Pago. A detailed check of the *Ontario* log for the 18 months following its return to Pago Pago (9 July 1937 to 31 December 1938) shows nothing other than routine duties, except for an "official" visit to Aunu'u Island. Certainly there was nothing which could legitimately be classified as "imperative." When a ship or aircraft is in distress, international law of the sea requires that any ship in a position to render assistance in a reasonable period of time must abandon its normal pursuits and do so. Milne violated that old rule of the sea. His selfish pursuits at Pago Pago and catering to the native population appeared to be more important than searching for Earhart and Noonan.

Or so it would appear from the overt facts released to the public. There is good reason to believe that Milne knew a good deal more about Earhart's whereabouts on 2 July 1937 and during the remainder of his governorship. More realistically, it may be noted that he knew about her presence on a day-by-day basis from 2 July 1937 until shortly before the end of his extended term as governor.

Being acquainted with the actual situation in his sphere of jurisdiction, it is obvious why he prevailed upon the brass in Washington to have the *Ontario* withdrawn from the "search" on his recommendation. The "essential" requirement, i.e., transporting the fliers from the Phoenix Islands to his jurisdiction, did not materialize because of the requirement to return the film to the United States as soon as possible and the state of Earhart's health, which required immediate attention.

Milne's corollary duty was recruiting Captain Jones, his Apia neighbor who was well known to the naval fraternity at Pago Pago because of his radio "fist" and visits to the naval station. In 1936 Jones became prominent in the Samoas during the maritime inquiry into the sinking of the *Tiafau*, an inter-island vessel which floundered in January 1936. Because of his nautical background as a master mariner, he was selected to establish the circumstances of the loss of the vessel during the initial court of inquiry. [1]

Providing an inter-country water taxi had been a problem for decades even when the German governor of Western Samoa (1914) and the naval governor of American Samoa had found it necessary to license the vessels in the interest of public safety. The principal function of the inter-island service was transporting passengers to and from Pago Pago for connection with the steamers S.S. *Mariposa* and the S.S. *Monterey*. Therefore, Milne had an understandable interest in the safety and continuation of that service.

Milne's earlier contacts with the ONI relative to fortification of the Japanese mandates made him aware of the value of recruiting knowledgeable civilians as intelligence agents. When the call went out from Intelligence Chief Holmes at the ONI, word was circulating about Jones going to Hull Island in the Phoenix Group for Burns-Philp. A retail outlet for this company had been in Pago Pago since 1932, and it was one of the few businesses allowed on the island. While the actual details of how the recruiting occurred and by whom in the United States naval community is unknown, Milne obviously endorsed it. Prior to Jones' departure from Apia for Hull aboard the M.V. *Makoa* on 14 May 1937, he had been informed about frequencies to be used, coding, reporting requirements, and his remuneration. While documentary evidence does not exist due to its probable verbal nature, Jones' blood daughters have testified that he was working for both British intelligence and United States naval intelligence before World War II at Hull. Documentary proof of his British Connection is available. Because of Roosevelt's penchant for secrecy, Jones' American Connection is not documented by the written word, but by his actions. Someone in the Phoenix Islands was in radio contact with Naval Radio Tutuila in mid-1937 after Jones activated his radio station on Hull. Perhaps the best evidence of this is what occurred during the search of the Phoenix Islands conducted by the crew of the *Colorado* in July 1937.

1. Someone provided information as to the suitability for landing on the northwest corner of Hull Island on the sand of the fringing reef.

2. Lambrecht knew in advance that it was safe to land on the lagoon at Hull. His mission was to pick up the film cannister.

3. Someone told Jones to move Earhart and Noonan to nearby Sydney Island and keep them hidden in the native shacks when the floatplanes from the *Colorado* were above that island.

4. Someone instructed Jones to sink the Electra off the platform reef at Hull.

---

[1] *Pacific Islands Monthly,* March 1936, Page 45

5. Jones coordinated the transfer of Earhart and Noonan from Sydney to a United States naval destroyer for transport to American Samoa.

6. Communication with American Samoa regarding details of the flight and while the fliers were on the islands of Hull and Sydney was ongoing.

7. Jones provided Earhart and Noonan with supplies brought to Hull by the H.M.S. *Achilles.* These included food, sundries, toilet articles, etc. not available at Hull.

8. Jones notified the United States Navy of Earhart's problem with dysentery and her need for medical treatment.

CAPTAIN MILNE'S TENURE AS GOVERNOR OF AMERICAN SAMOA
(20 January 1936 to 3 June 1938)

The long-established tenure for a naval officer assigned by the Navy Department to the billet as military governor of American Samoa was two years. Additional military officers held most of the subordinate offices which ran the administration of the island group. Through the use of the 70-man Fita Fita native guard detachment, for all intents and purposes, American Samoa was under Martial Law. During the 50-year tenure of the U.S. Navy Department, few abuses of this control were reported. Also worth noting is that a high-ranking naval medical officer oversaw the health of the natives through a network of Navy-constructed medical facilities on various islands. In a few rare occasions, the medical officer assigned outranked the governor. Administrative control of American Samoa was shifted from the U.S. Navy to the Department of the Interior in 1951.

The assignment of the naval governor had the approval of the Navy Department, Secretary of the Navy, and the President of the United States as Commander in Chief of the military forces. During the two peacetime decades between the World Wars, the two-year duty assignment remained quite constant. (See the historical record on the accompanying chart.) Captain Milne's tenure was an obvious exception to the established peacetime precedent. His term was extended six months beyond the established two-year term without any official reason being given for the extension. After Milne's assignment of two and a half years, successive governors' tenures reverted to the established two-year period.

Panoramic aerial view of Tutuila Island, American Samoa, with Pago Pago Bay in center and Aunu'u Island, an outrider, off the southeast corner of Tutuila. Aunu'u Island played a major role in fliers' disappearance.

Photo credit - National Archives Negative #80-G-81886

Naval Governors of American Samoa (WWI through WWII)

Commander John M. Poyer	Mar. 1, 1915 - Jun. 10, 1919
Commander Warren J. Terhune	Jun 19, 1919 - Nov. 3, 1920
Captain Waldo Evans	Nov. 11, 1920 - Mar. 1, 1922
Captain Edwin T. Pollock	Mar. 1, 1922 - Sept. 4, 1923
Captain Edward S. Kellogg	Sep. 4, 1923 - Mar. 17, 1925
Captain Henry F. Bryan	Mar. 17, 1925 - Sep. 9, 1927
Captain Stephen V. Graham	Sep. 9, 1927 - Aug. 2, 1929
Captain Gatewood S. Lincoln	Aug. 2, 1929 - Apr. 3, 1931
Commander James S. Spore	Apr. 4, 1931 - Apr. 22, 1931
Lt. Cmdr. Arthur T. Emerson (Acting)	Apr. 23, 1931 - Jul. 17, 1931
Captain Gatewood S. Lincoln	Jul. 18, 1931 - Jul. 8, 1932
Captain George B. Landengerber	Jul. 8, 1932 - Apr. 10, 1934
Lt. Cmdr. Thomas C. Latimore (Acting)	Apr. 11, 1934 - Apr. 13, 1934
Captain Otto Dowling	Apr. 14, 1934 - Jan. 15, 1936
Lt. Cmdr. Thomas B. Fitzpatrick (Acting)	Jan. 15, 1936 - Jan. 20, 1936
Captain MacGillvray Milne	Jan. 20, 1936 - Jun. 3, 1938
Captain Edward W. Hanson	Jun. 6, 1938 - Jul. 30, 1940
Lt. Cmdr. Jesse R. Wallace (Acting)	Jul. 31, 1940 - Aug. 8, 1940
Captain Lawrence Wild	Aug. 9, 1940 - Jun. 5. 1942
Captain John G. Moyer	Jun. 5, 1942 - Feb. 8, 1944
Captain Allen Hobbs	Feb. 8, 1944 - Jan. 27, 1945
Captain Ralph W. Hungerford	Jan. 27 1945 - Sep. 3, 1945
Commandr Samuel W. Cana (Acting)	Sep. 3, 1945 - Sep. 10, 1945
Captain Harold A. Houser	Sep. 10, 1945 - Apr. 22, 1947

Briefly, without going into excessive detail, because of the often controversial method of assigning naval officers to billets in peacetime, these duty tours bordered on a fixed contract (or covenant) due to the vital morale factors involved. Particularly in peacetime it was usually inviolable unless there was some significant overriding reason which would cause an extended period of service. Many promising young naval officers resigned their commissions due to abuse of the tenure period.

Lt. Horace Blakeslee, USN, the skipper of the American Samoa station ship, the U.S.S. *Ontario*, and a member of Captain Milne's administrative staff, has given personal testimony concerning Milne's character and behavior as governor. Their tours of duty at Samoa were concurrent except that Blakeslee did not serve an extended tour. According to Blakeslee, Captain Milne was a senior officer near retirement and didn't particularly like this overseas assignment. In particular Milne disliked traveling in the station ship *Ontario* and would do so only if required by established policy. He detested the annual visits to the outriding possessions and the trip through the surf onto these islands which had no harbors, docks, or other naval attributes. For these reasons, he never went aboard the *Ontario* unless it was unavoidable and the duty couldn't be assigned to some subordinate officer. The very significant "official visit" to Aunu'u Island in September 1937 was one of the unavoidable trips that Milne would have liked to steer clear of.

As there was no discernible overt reason for Milne's unprecedented peacetime extension, there most certainly must have been a covert one. When the extension to June 1938 is coupled to the evidence of the Morgenthau Transcript (which is covered elsewhere in this section, Part Three), there is a solid covert rationale for holding this officer over and not bringing a new man on the scene. With some serious unfinished business within his jurisdiction, Milne must stay on station until the "problem" was resolved. In the Morgenthau Transcript

evidence, it is stated that as far as the U.S. Government was concerned, the problematical Earhart episode was "all over" by May 1938. If Earhart and Noonan were being sequestered within Governor Milne's jurisdiction, there would be reason indeed to hold Milne over for an additional period until the troublesome problem was resolved.

AUNU'U ISLAND, AMERICAN SAMOA

American Samoa is a group of seven islands, five volcanic ones and two coral atolls. The five volcanic islands are also the major inhabited ones. Tutuila, the largest and principal island, is the center of government and business. Aunu'u, a satellite, lies one mile off the southeast coast of Tutuila. The three islands of Ofu, Olosega, and Ta'u, collectively referred to as the Manu's Islands, lie 66 miles east of Tutuila. The two remaining islands of American Samoa are Rose and Swains, both of which are coral atolls. Rose Island, about 125 miles north of Tutuila, is the only uninhabited island because there is not enough water to support life. Swains Island, about 200 miles north of Tutuila, is the northernmost island of the territory and is privately owned by the descendents of a New England whaling captain.

Aunu'u is elliptically shaped and measures one mile east to west and 3,400 feet north to south. The land area is about 380 acres and consists of a volcanic tuff cone on the eastern half and a saucer-shaped plain containing a few marshy areas in the western half. The village of Aunu'u is located along the western shore of the island. The highest point on the island is Fogatia Hill, which is located on the south rim of the volcanic cone about 310 feet above sea level. The 29 acres of Famulivai Marsh are located within the crater, which also contains a fresh-water pool called Red Lake (with quicksand). Water from the marsh and pond drains into Maamaa Cove, located on the eastern end of the island. The interior part of the island on the western side is only about one to two feet above sea level. The oceanward rim around the lowland rises to elevations between eight and ten feet above sea level. A narrow fringing coral and beachrock reef 200 to 300 feet wide protects the shore around the lowland on the western half of the island. Steep tuff cliffs rise from deep water around the eastern side of Fogatia Hill.

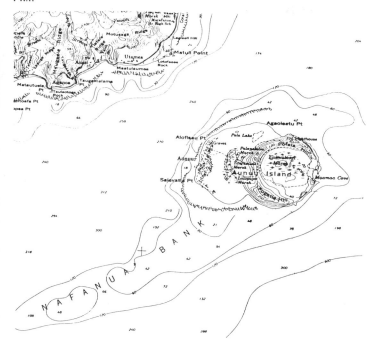

American Samoa's Aunu'u Island where U.S. Naval Administration established medical isolation facility in 1937.

Rainfall quickly runs into the ocean and is not captured in significant amounts except in the volcanic crater. The domestic water supply is obtained from shallow wells which tap a basal groundwater-bearing stratum located near the village on the western coast.

The environment is nearly pristine. Agriculture, fishing, and handcrafts are native pursuits. Most families on this island are engaged in subsistence farming. The small population is concentrated in the village where traditional Samoan lifestyle prevails. Cooking, agricultural and refuse fires, and dust are the most significant sources of water pollution. Noise levels are low due to the absence of motorized vehicles and industrial activity, and to limited construction. Emergency power generators and motorboats are the only significant sources of noise.

The isolated outlying villages, such as the one on Aunu'u remain essentially pristine and consist of "fales," the traditional Samoan dwelling. These structures are usually oval and are made of poles supporting a thatched roof over a foundation traditionally built of loose stones or coral raised to a height of one to two feet above the ground. The only village on Aunu'u consisted of about 75 homes varying from the traditional "fales" to Western style wood-frame dwellings. Communication was primarily by word of mouth except for radio communication between governmental agencies. Electrical power is obtained from Tutuila through an underwater cable. There are no roads or harbors on the island. The successive governments in American Samoa have been relatively successful in maintaining much of the territory's pristine environment by controlling urban development and its attendant environmental problems.

Aerial view of Aunu'u Island off the southeast tip of Tutuila Island. A channel one mile wide separated the islands. Peculiar structure of outrider with its truncated volcano was well-known to South Seas mariners.

Photo credit - National Archives Negative #80-G-81882

Sea-level view of Aunu'u Island from Tutuila Island. Two- humped cone of extinct volcano and flat plain on western end distinguish island.

Photo credit - United States Corps of Engineers, Fort Shafter, Hawaii

The climate is tropical with annual mean temperatures ranging from 70 to 90 degrees Fahrenheit and humidities ranging from 80 to 85 percent. Moderate southeast trade winds blow from May to November with an average velocity of about eight knots. The winds are variable the remaining months. The average rainfall at Pago Pago Airport is 130 inches per year.

A fringing reef approximately 200 to 300 feet wide protects the entire shoreline around the lowland area of the island. The reef narrows to 50 feet in width at Salevatia Point, where the United States Navy improved a natural channel in 1963 by blasting and excavation. Islanders use the channel to launch and recover boats and canoes. Subsistence fishing occurs in deeper water from canoes, and others fish from the land areas with both hook and line and spears.

TESTING DISAPPEARANCE HYPOTHESES

Unfortunately, all Earhart disappearance theories advanced in the past half century are based on conjecture and are lacking in hard evidence. Locating the Earhart airplane, verified skeletal remains, or one honest sailor coming forward to say, "I was there, and this is what really happened," have not occurred. Hard evidence in the form of SECRET documentary evidence, although known to exist, has not been released because "sacred cows" who would be the most damaged, control the documents. Needless to say, numerous theories have been promulgated. Typically, some highly unqualified individual with minimum research experience and capability was parlaying a gut feeling into a full-blown explanation without any legitimate evidence at all. A few interviews are conducted which are slanted to fit his position, thus building on past inaccuracies and ignoring all evidence to the contrary. The Saipan hoax is perhaps the best example of this approach. A dozen parties have twisted some very tenuous evidence about a Caucasian appearing couple who were forced down in the Japanese Marshall Islands before the war and had to be Earhart and Noonan. The only proof is by association. It must have been them; therefore, it had to be them. After questioning several score of illiterate natives who would shake their heads at anything asked of them, the "investigators" rest their cases. After collectively desecrating most of the graveyards on Saipan and finding

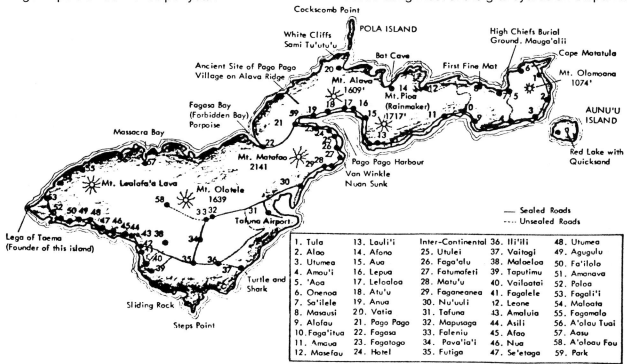

Map of American Samoa showing main island of Tutuila with Aunu'u Island off the southeast corner.

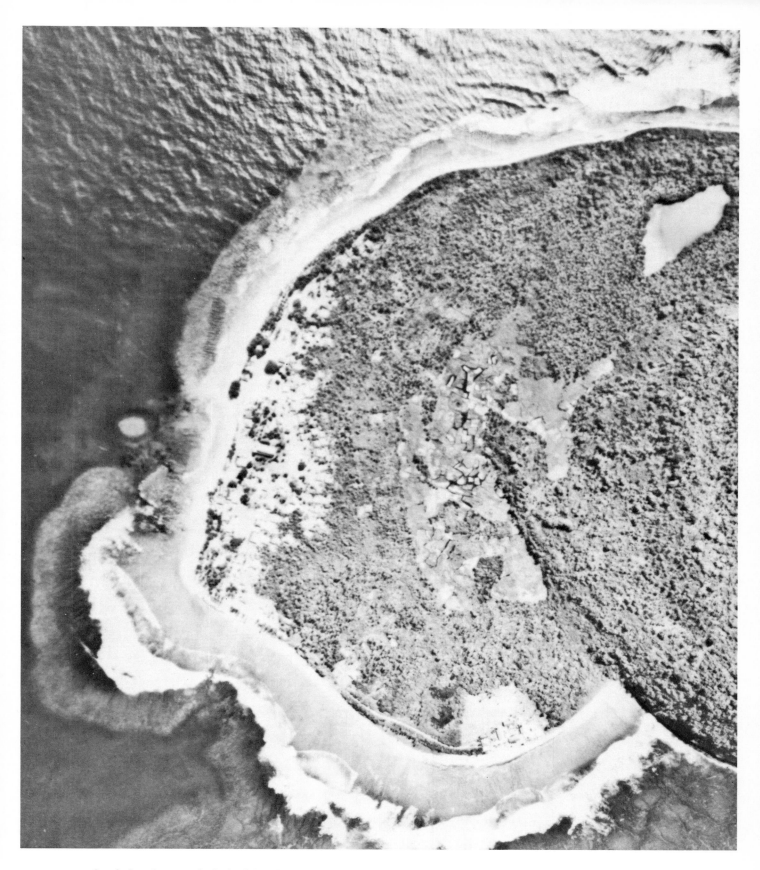

Aerial view of inhabited area of Aunu'u Island (circa 1974). Note large government installations on south (bottom) shore away from native village at left of photograph. Visible path connects isolated areas with village and boat landing site there.

Photo credit - United States Corps of Engineers,
Fort Shafter, Hawaii

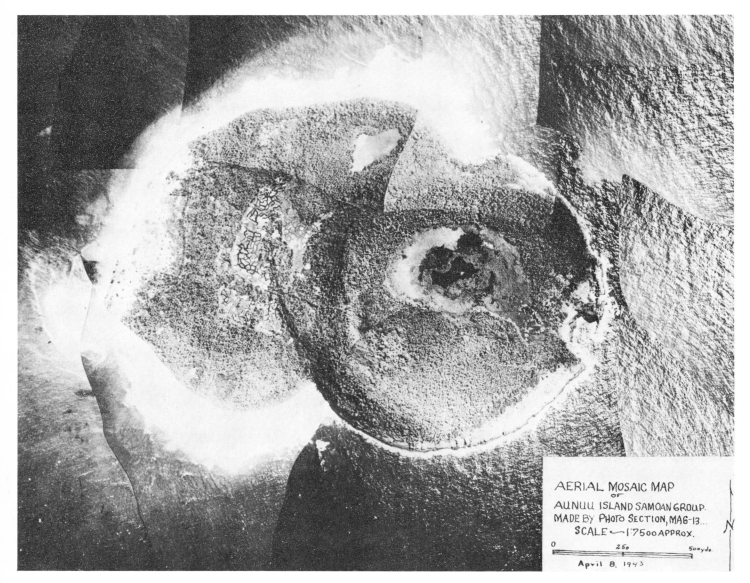

Aerial mosaic map (1943) shows Red Lake in extinct volcano crater. Note two clearings on southern shore where foliage has been removed in isolated area away from Aunu'u village on western end. Medical isolation facility was maintained here in 1936-38.

Photo credit - National Archives Negative #80-G-75144

nothing, the hypothesis that the government agents had gotten there before them and taken the bones away to be buried forever in some vault in Washington or elsewhere was given as the reason no bodies were found. It should be evident to all except the perpetrators that this form of research is little more than nonsense.

What is needed is some yardstick or measure of merit to test these specious theories to see how they measure up to several criteria which have surfaced in the past half century.

THE THREE CRITERIA

Over the past five decades, three divergent criteria have become available which can be applied to evaluating the relative merits of Earhart disappearance theories. These are the Chester Nimitz (military), the so-called Morgenthau Transcript (governmental), and the 1937-1942 scenario preparation for the 1943 motion picture *Flight For Freedom* (civilian). *Flight for Freedom*

was a parody on the Earhart around-the-world flight attempt. There are other highly technical criteria such as computer-aided radio propagation evaluation, traffic analysis, and radio direction finder (D\F) fixes which are equally valid, but will not be presented here.

Credence must be given to anything said by or credited to five-star Fleet Admiral Chester V. Nimitz, USN. He was the supreme naval officer in the Pacific from 1942 to 1946 and had served in the Pacific during the 1920s and 1930s. Although he probably had no connection with the Earhart last flight and subsequent naval search, his permanent naval status as a Fleet Admiral kept him on de facto active status after retiring.

Source: Fred Goerner, *The Search for Amelia Earhart*, 1966, p. 265.

"Admiral (Chester) Nimitz wants you to continue and says you're on to something that will stagger your imagination," was told to Goerner by Nimitz' naval aide, John Pilsbury, after his retirement from active duty.

The gist of the Nimitz criteria concerns the implied meaning of the phrase "stagger your imagination." By 1965, various pundits had suggested almost every imaginable bizarre fate for the fliers. Therefore, what Nimitz was referring to must be "mind boggling" or sensational in nature. In the context in which it was used, however, and considering the many close contacts between Admiral Nimitz and Earhart "search" author Fred Goerner, the phrase very likely has a much broader and complex meaning. In his effort to have the author continue his search activity, Nimitz was subtly trying to overtly pass information on what to look for. Of course, Nimitz himself had gotten the word by briefings from those who knew and/or SECRET documentary evidence spelling out the naval role in the flight, search, and subsequent disappearance. Most likely he was trying to spur Goerner's efforts by giving him a broad clue within the limits of the classification then in force.

MORGENTHAU TRANSCRIPT

The Morgenthau Transcript is by far the best evidence which depicts the almost total involvement of the Roosevelt administration in the last flight, naval search, detention, and subsequent death of Earhart while in protective custody.

The obvious knowledge of these secret details of many covert aspects of the Earhart episode puts the blame on the Roosevelt administration and not the Japanese.

The Morgenthau Transcript is unimpeachable because it is deposited with the Morgenthau collection of papers at the F.D.R. Library in Hyde Park, New York, which is a branch of the U.S. National Archives. Earhart researcher Charles N. Hill, a former Coast Guard veteran who was interested in the activities of that agency during the Earhart episode, discovered this vital documentary evidence.

EVALUATION OF THE MORGENTHAU TRANSCRIPT

The Morgenthau Transcript is a report of a telephone conversation occurring on 13 May 1938 between Secretary of the Treasury Henry Morgenthau, Jr., and Malvina Thompson (later Schneider) who was Eleanor Roosevelt's personal secretary. It was recorded during Morgenthau's morning staff conference. Although only Morgenthau's words are transcribed, they were the important ones which unequivocally tie the Roosevelt administration covert connection with the Earhart episode. This leak by the morning conference transcriber went unnoticed at the time and became part of the "Morgenthau Diaries" which were subsequently deposited in the U.S. National Archives.

HIGHLIGHTS, MORGENTHAU TRANSCRIPT

1. "I know how Amelia Earhart completely disobeyed orders. She had completely disregarded orders . . ."
2. "Because of this, they would be forced to smear her reputation."
3. "Can't release complete story to one individual without subsequently releasing it to others."
4. "Something would have to be done about all those messages received before anyone saw it."
5. "The anguish of those last 30 minutes which he would never be able to make public."
6. "The Earhart episode was 'all over' as of Friday, 13 May 1938."

EVALUATION OF THE MORGENTHAU TRANSCRIPT MATERIAL

1. "I know how Amelia Earhart completely disobeyed orders. She had completely disregarded orders . . ."

Since when do American civilians disobey, disregard all orders? And whose orders was she really under?

This statement gives credence to the claim that just prior to her departure Earhart had a military physical and was given the rank of Major in the Army Air Corps Reserve. The orders she completely disregarded were through channels from the Commander in Chief.

2. "Because of this, they would be forced to smear her reputation."

Actually the government report released to the public not only smeared Earhart's reputation as a competent pilot, but also impugned Noonan's reputation as well by blaming him for being such a poor navigator that they became lost. When Earhart spun in or botched the ditching of her airplane in the ocean, they were either killed on impact or the airplane sank before they were able to launch their life raft according to the Roosevelt administration.

3. "Can't release complete story to one indivual without subsequently releasing it to others."

An abbreviated, laundered, and desensitized report, including one version (of three) was subsequently released to Paul Mantz, Mrs. Bea Noonan, and an Oakland newspaperman.

4. "Something would have to be done about all those messages received before anyone saw it."

Here he is referring to all the Marshall Island overflight messages which, very likely, blew the cover of the operation. These messages are known to exist because Karl Pierson's radio-monitoring group picked them up as did Robert H. Myers of Oakland, California. Additionally, the radio contact while approaching Nauru Island clearly was disobeying orders because it verified a detour in the Lae-to-Howland great circle course to the northeast in the direction of the Marshall Islands.

5. "The anguish of those last 30 minutes which he would never be able to make public."

Morgenthau didn't make it public, nor did anyone else in the past 50 years. When, in the past century, have any public officials revealed self-incriminating misdeeds to the public? Unique here is the fact that the episode became a non-partisan issue and every administration during the past half century has refused to release details. The possibility of a foreign country (or countries) being involved could also be a factor for the tight control of pertinent details.

Morgenthau referred to the terrible thing that happened to her in the last few minutes and stated that it should never be released to the public because it isn't a very nice story. This administrative disclosure relates closely with the military (Admiral Nimitz) statement that the true Earhart story was "mind-boggling" in scope. Earhart didn't crash into the ocean. Because of what happened to her in a few minutes, dysentery can be ruled out as a direct cause, but not as an indirect one. What remains is a suicide or her demise at the hands of others.

6. "The Earhart episode was 'all over' as of Friday, 13 May 1938."

Here is the final evidence of the Roosevelt administration's reluctance to make the true details public obviously because of the repercussions such a disclosure would make.

Although this material is brief in detail, it is comprehensive in substance. It is an obvious indictment of the Roosevelt administration, but Earhart and Noonan paid the price.

The Earhart episode would not be complete without a brief discussion of the well-known motion picture of 1943 entitled *Flight for Freedom*. This movie is a flagrant copy of Earhart's last flight and, if it were entirely Hollywood-inspired, could be disregarded. The scenario, however, was not typical. The original script, a 60-page brief format, was written by radio engineer Karl Pierson, a member of the Amelia Earhart amateur radio network on the West Coast on both the 1935 and 1937 Earhart flights. He knew Earhart from these episodes and had talked her into Oakland in 1935 when she became disoriented after arriving at the California coast. During her last flight, Pierson, along with Walter McMenamy and others, picked up her voice messages from the Phoenix Islands several times after the Lockheed had landed. This group also copied the radio traffic between the *Itasca* and the United States Coast Guard Regional Headquarters in San Francisco. This traffic was on maritime frequencies in high-speed Morse and was initially sent in the clear. The Marshall Island overflight messages were picked up and copied when relayed in the clear to San Francisco. Later, all sensitive traffic was security coded on orders from Coast Guard Headquarters in Washington, D.C. The Pierson/McMenamy group never revealed these messages because they felt they would be embarrassing to the administration.

Pierson submitted the 60-page draft through an agent to RKO Studio. Employees there had to sound out officials in Washington, D.C., for approval and assistance in motion picture preparation. Pierson had to agree to relinquish his authorship in favor of Horace McCoy who was an establishment writer, a typical dodge in Hollywood. The Roosevelt administration vetoed the project in any shape or form in 1937 and the United States Navy wouldn't loan airplanes, pilots, battleships, or other movie props for publicity value in 1937 and 1938.

After being put on hold until 1942, when the war in the Pacific had begun, Office of War Information propagandists decided the script could be slanted as a propaganda piece, particularly, to lure young women into the military services. Thus, after a lapse of five years, an administrative green light and cooperation from the United States Navy allowed RKO to proceed, with Washington's approval, to revise Pierson's piece as propaganda. The Imperial Japanese Navy became the villain, Tonie (Amelia) the heroine, and Randy (Fred) the hero for the war effort. Although distorted and in an obvious propaganda format, it was rescripted by knowledgeable persons in the military intelligence offices who had access to classified material on the Earhart flight. The party who accomplished this infusion of fact and information was Leonard "Len" Hammond, who was a close friend and associate of Karl Pierson. Hammond had close contact with military intelligence and was himself an intelligence officer in World War II with the rank of major. For his efforts, Hammond received 25 percent of the $35,000 fee RKO paid for the script. (See contract.) Eventually, a screen play script was written by contract writers for RKO and a companion narrative story appeared in *The Woman's Home Companion* in January 1943, after the film had been released. This article was credited to Horace McCoy, who had very little to do with the project from the beginning to the end and admitted this fact many times in later years.

Although that story, patterned after Earhart's *Last Flight*, has limited credibility, by screening out its obvious distortions, some interesting facts can be noted. First, is the propaganda: the Japanese bogey, flag waving, heroine gives life for country, etc. Second, is the usual stereotyped, unlikely romantic development, with its Cinderella-like atmosphere, usual happy ending circumvented by wartime sacrifice for God, president, and country, etc. That leaves the following significant highlights of the version instigated in Washington, D.C., and they are worth considering.

```
The Goldstone Agency                          CRestview
9121 Sunset Boulevard                          6-1071
Hollywood
Calif.


To   MR. CARL PIERSON


                                April 30, 1942


Sale of story STAND BY TO DIE to
RKO Radio Pictures Inc.              $35000.00

commission - Nat Goldstone - 3500
             Frank Vincent - 1750
                                      5250.00
                                    $29750.00
Lee Kaplan - legal fee                 150.00
                                    $29600.00
to Mr. McCoy - - - - - 5450.00
to Mr. McNemey - - - - 5450.00
to Mr. Hammond - - - - 5450.00      16350.00
                                    $13250.00
to George Putnam                     6300.00
                                    $ 6950.00
repay Nat Goldstone for story
advance                              1500.00
to Mr. Pierson                      $ 5450.00
```

RKO Studio Contract for *Flight for Freedom* motion picture scenario.
Via Karl Pierson

FLIGHT FOR FREEDOM ANALYSIS
(Listed in approximate chronological order)
1.   Special Mission for Government/Military
FFF: We want you to undertake a mission, one of the most vital in the history of our country.
2.   Will provide competent navigator.
FFF: We'll furnish a navigator for you, the finest navigating mind in the entire navy.
ACTUAL: Fred Noonan was a last-inning relief player on Earhart's team. Navy papers refer to him as Lt. Commander Noonan, USNR. On the Honolulu flight, Manning was the radio operator and little else.
3.   Fly reverse direction west to east.

FFF: "You will fly around the world again, but this time you will reverse your direction.

You will start from Florida and go to Africa, India, Australia, and hop for the Hawaiian Islands from down below instead of up above."

ACTUAL: No comment needed. This is exactly what Earhart did.

4. Covert Flight Destination.

FFF: "Do I actually come down? . . . Yes, we will make the arrangements . . . this is Gull Island."

ACTUAL: I rest my case on G(H)ull Island being her actual destination. Somebody in the Office of War Information (OWI) who worked on this propaganda film had some inside information.

5. Destination well provisioned.

FFF: " . . . it will be provisioned and stocked for you."

ACTUAL: The H.M.S. *Achilles* made an unscheduled detour from its planned itinerary en route from Pago Pago to Honolulu to leave supplies for the "shipwrecked mariners" at Hull Island. *Achilles* left the U.S. Naval Station at Pago Pago on 28 June 1937 and arrived at Hull Island on 30 June 1937 (two days before Earhart left Lae, New Guinea.)

6. Location of sanctuary.

FFF: "They were skimming from ship to shore unloading supplies, enough to last three or four years . . . It was all stocked in a hastily-built house in the middle of the island."

ACTUAL: The hastily-built house was a medical quarantine infirmary located on the middle of the south shore of Aunu'u Island which is an outrider of Tutuila, the main island of American Samoa.

7. Provide special provisioning ship.

FFF: "The *Gilba*, the cutter out of Pearl Harbor, was moored just off Gull Island while that picked crew worked at top speed to get their job done unloading supplies."

ACTUAL: As previously noted, the H.M.S. *Achilles* was the Special Provisioning Ship which was on the way to Honolulu via the U.S. Naval Station Tutuila (American Samoa) for a "Good Will" visit to the Hawaiian Islands as a guest of the U.S. Navy.

8. FFF: " . . . there you will stay until the Navy comes and takes you off. That may be a week, a year . . . "

ACTUAL: This is the crux of the AE/FN disappearance. The fake disappearance, the sanctuary, the "protective custody," the indeterminate confinement, and perhaps someday a return to normal life again. We know from the Morgenthau Transcript that this was not to be. In nine months both Earhart and Noonan were dead. The propaganda of *Flight for Freedom* is that two American citizens gave their lives for their country in 1937-38, long before hostilities actually started in the Pacific.

9. Purpose of search.

FFF: "We shall look for you with photographic planes. It will enable us to accomplish our purpose; that is, a great and wide search for you somewhere in the ocean."

ACTUAL: Right on. The U.S.S *Lexington* (CV-2) steamed from San Diego in early July 1937 with 62 two-place observation aircraft from three carriers as follows:

Squadron VT-2	(*Lexington*)
Squadron VS-2	(*Lexington*)
Squadron VS-3	(*Saratoga*)
Squadron VS-41	(*Ranger*)
Squadron VS-42	(*Ranger*)
Squadron VB-4	(*Ranger*)

All of these two-place aircraft could have carried cameras, limited only by the number of aerial cameras available, which was probably fewer than 30, on the West Coast and at Pearl Harbor. The U.S. Navy was filming the Aleutians and the Alaska Coast and much photographic gear was being used there.

10. Photographing many uninhabited islands.

FFF: "A funny way to rescue somebody—photographing a lot of uninhabited islands. I hope those guys down in Washington know what they're doing."

ACTUAL: *Lexington* obtained permission about mid-July for an overflight of the Gilbert Islands to "look for Amelia." Actually, the reason was to obtain vertical shots of the islands for the USN Hydrographic Office to supplement the *Itasca* and *Swan* surface hydrographic data collection. Little photography was accomplished because the *Lexington* was short of provisions and fuel and had to return to the barn. Very likely one or two long-range two-place bomber aircraft from VB-4 with "slipper" long-range auxiliary fuel tanks made dawn flights (no photoflash bombs available on CV-2) over Wotje Atoll to pick up the shots lost by the RAF crew which was ditched south of Mili Atoll.

11. Personal mission objectives.

FFF: "The important thing in this job is not being found, it's being lost . . . Not a bad ending. Getting lost to save American lives . . . We'll pull this off right . . ."

ACTUAL: Sad, but correct, with a full measure of Elmer Davis (OWI) propaganda and "God Bless America" in the background.

12. Repatriation of Earhart to states after commencement of hostilities in the Pacific.

FFF: "All she had to do to disguise herself was to put on a dress. Whenever she became fed up with the extravagant curiosity of the world and the intrusions of the autograph hunters, she simply slipped into a dress, arranged her bobbed hair so that it didn't look bobbed any more and then she was just an ordinary citizen."

ACTUAL: This is the typical Cinderella/Hollywood "Happy Ending" syndrome. This didn't happen. Many still believe in the Bolam myth. The monster Gervais created will never die!

Little doubt exists but that Earhart and Noonan did survive the flight, landed safely on Hull Island, and were placed in governmental custody for an indefinite period. American Samoa was under the jurisdiction and control of the United States Navy and was the closest place where safety and security could be provided for an indeterminate time. Therefore, it would logically be given prime consideration by the group of "insiders" in Washington. With the fliers on Sydney Island, a survey of available ships, United States Navy or charter, was made. The U.S.S. *Preston* (DD-379), then accountable to the CNO, was available at its home base in San Diego, California. This ship had completed a shake-down cruise to American Samoa earlier in the year and the crew was familiar with these South Seas waters. Further, in conversations with *Preston* officers, the fact was

U.S.S. *Preston* (DD-379), a fast, long-range destroyer of *Mahan* class, played major role in Earhart disappearance. According to "blue suits" aboard her in 1937, she left San Diego for the Phoenix Islands in July 1937 and transported two V.I.P.s from Sydney Island to American Samoa.
Photo credit - National Archives

confirmed that various units of DesRon4 were involved in the Earhart mission.

Four officers who were aboard the *Preston* from its commissioning in 1936 until the end of 1939 were interviewed for this project. In this group were both skippers (now deceased), Captain Charles Swain, who placed the *Preston* in service and his replacement, Lt. Commander H. L. Grosskopf, USN, who took over in 1938. The two officers who still survive, as of 1987, will not be mentioned by name. Three of these former officers implied that the *Preston* was used for covert activities during 1937 and 1938. The senior officer of this group, who retired a vice admiral, told the author that the *Preston* was involved in the Earhart search although it was never made public. What is essential is that first person interviews with these officers verified that the *Preston* was involved in the Earhart disappearance.

All of the new high-speed, long-range destroyers based at San Diego were scheduled to leave on 2 August 1937 for the traditional summer cruise to San Francisco.

Except for two destroyers, all active ships were scheduled for this. The *Perkins* had a blown high-speed turbine and was due at Mare Island for repairs, and the *Preston* was undergoing an extensive engineering evaluation which would keep her occupied until 1939. Many problems had occurred with this class of ship and the newer DDs. The "fixes" had to be determined for the large number of "follow-on" destroyers still to be built. The rest of the fleet departed San Diego on Monday, 29 August, 1937.

In March 1937, the *Preston* had undergone a shake-down cruise to the South Seas. In July it was tied up at its assigned buoy in San Diego Bay, receiving supplies from local sources and making an occasional brief foray outside the harbor. Actually, the *Preston* was ready for sea and could perform tests while underway. Her absence was covered by painting over one number on the destroyer *Smith* (378 to 379) and no one would be the wiser. The *Preston*, the only long-range high-speed destroyer available in July, could make a trip to the Phoenix Islands and American Samoa and return in three weeks at a speed of 18 knots. Preparation for sea at San Diego to Sydney Island (seven days), to Aunu'u Island (three days), vicinity of that island (no refueling, two days), and return to San Diego (nine days).

A survey of incarceration locales was completed and on-site investigations were made to find the best possible place for detention. Aunu'u Island in American Samoa met the criteria for isolation, security, and accessibility, all of which would have been considered necessary and desirable.

Despite the attributes of the site, a notable lack of consideration on the part of the USN for the "human factor" is reflected and that is what ultimately led to Earhart's demise. It was no secret that both Earhart and Noonan had weak points to their characters. Noonan was an alcoholic. Earhart could not stand confinement of any sort, even in a "gilded cage." She was a finicky eater and normal or conventional fare had little appeal for her. In addition, both cherished their friends above all else. Each

had activities scheduled after the flight was completed. Noonan had just married a beautiful woman and had new business connections with bright prospects for the future. All of this was ruined by the stubborn misconduct of his flying companion. His motivation to escape detention was overwhelming and any possibility was worth considering. Using a raft to cross a one-mile channel seemed like a reasonable risk. In his stupor and impaired state of reasoning, brought on by intoxicating brews like "coconut toddies," he miscalculated and drowned in the cross-channel escape attempt.

Following Noonan's demise, tighter security would have been provided for Earhart, and further restrictions added. With this last human link with her former life and world gone, her despair must have been accelerated. Sleeplessness, lack of appetite, resistance to the coarse diet, the futility of serving an indeterminate sentence, and finally the basic lack of the will to live were all factors in her ultimate demise.

Captain John W. Jones, RNR, was hired as a civilian by Burns-Philip (South Seas) in May 1937 to manage their copra plantations at Hull and Sydney Islands. In early August 1937, Fiji archive records show that Capt. Jones was appointed Deputy High Commissioner for the British Western Pacific Islands and Resident Manager of the Phoenix Island Group (with no prior colonial office experience). Clearly, Capt. Jones had sponsorship in very high places by one or more interested governments.

Photo credit - James Donahue

Part Four

The British Connection

British freighter M.V. *Moorby* which participated in Earhart search didn't just happen to be east of the Japanese Marshall Islands on 2 July 1937. *Moorby* was on naval charter and served as a picket ship.
Photo credit - Courtesy of The Mariners Museum, Newport News, Virginia

THE BRITISH CONNECTION

Considering the evidence of a Caucasian couple in the Japanese Mandated Islands in 1937, it now seems evident that the Royal Navy (RN) and/or Royal Air Force (RAF) or combined British intelligence decided to expand Earhart's Italian Eritrea overflight with an extension of their mission in the Central Pacific. United States Navy personnel were ready to have anyone and everyone join in the flight activity: civilian, paramilitary, United States Air Corps, and other foreign nations. Why not the Royal Navy?

Overwhelming evidence exists that Earhart went down below the equator. Who went down above the equator? She couldn't be both places. When military air operations are contemplated, several questions must be answered. Are there strategic or tactical needs? Are the operations feasible? What are the risks? Are they worth taking as well as affordable? Can anything worthwhile be learned? Will future capability be enhanced?

Certainly, most of the above could be answered affirmatively. Time, however, was the limiting factor. An existing airfield and an available airplane, easily convertible, must be used. A look-alike "Electra" and a look-alike couple must be found.

Under time and cost constraints, the precedent of Charles T.P. Ulm's Pacific crossing attempt was the first consideration by the planners. Fanning Island, Canton Island, a twin-engine Airspeed Envoy, and a pilot and copilot/navigator were all obtainable in a reasonable period of time.

Some rationales for this British flight can be listed:
1. Accountability for Caucasian couple reported in the Marshalls who were fliers.
2. Aggregate of fifty years of continuing research.
3. Significant New Zealand Navy participation (H.M.S. *Achilles* and H.M.S. *Wellington*).
4. Shift of Earhart's planned alternate landing site from Canton Island to Hull Island to accommodate additional airplane.
5. H.M.S. *Achilles* release on 2 July 1937 of radio intercept from KHAQQ.
6. Separate, diverse targets in Marshalls considered tactical advantage.
7. Technology transfer period between the U.S. and the U.K. prior to World War II.
8. Three-month delay of Earhart flight from March to June 1937.
9. Lengthening Earhart's en route itinerary an extra week to synchronize takeoffs.
10. Radio Nauru signals on 6210 kc confirm *Achilles* KHAQQ intercept. Reference: Rafford analysis in Part I.
11. Four 55-gallon drums of 100-octane aviation gasoline on Howland Island. Far in excess of Earhart's requirements.

THE BRITISH EQUATORIAL FLIGHT

The precedent for the British participation in the 1937 equatorial flight is found in the Sir Charles Kingsford-Smith and Charles Ulm flights of 1928 and 1934, which were to promote an All-British airline around the world. In 1928, these two men flew a tri-motor Fokker from Oakland, California, to Brisbane, Australia via Hawaii,

and Suva in the Fiji Islands. In 1934 Kingsford-Smith successfully flew a Lockheed Altair named *The Lady Southern Cross* from Brisbane, via Suva and Hawaii, to Oakland. On 6 December 1934, Ulm attempted an east-to-southwest crossing planned from Oakland via Oahu, Fanning Island, Suva, and on to Auckland and Sydney. He and his two crew members were lost on the first leg.

Just as the laying of the final stretch of the British cable in 1904 was the most difficult of the "All-Red Cable System," so was the most difficulty encountered in starting the final link of the "All-Red" trans-Pacific air line from British Columbia to Australia. Details of Kingsford-Smith's trans-Pacific flight of 1934 are recorded in considerable detail by his copilot and navigator, Sir C. B. Taylor. The flight was covered by newspaper accounts and, along with a short biography of Ulm, will suffice for the discussion here.

Charles Ulm had originally intended to take off from Vancouver, but bad weather forced him to fly south and depart from Oakland. On 6 December 1934 Amelia Earhart flew from Burbank on a commercial airliner to wish him well, contributing little to the flight except that her photograph in the newspapers made his departure more newsworthy. His project attracted little attention until he failed to reach Hawaii after 24 hours had passed and he was known to be in the ocean. Having a radio, he had notified Hawaiian authorities of his ditching, but could give them no position because he was hopelessly lost. Further, through a reckless show of bravado, he had stated that he had not carried a life raft because he wouldn't get his "feet wet." A lengthy search in adjacent waters by ships and aircraft, military and civilian, including a special cruise of the *Itasca* to Johnston Island, was carried out, without success. The next legs of Ulm's flight were to have been from Hawaii to a tidal flat airstrip at Fanning Island, and on to Suva in the Fiji Islands.

That part of Ulm's proposed flight plan is worth study. On both of Kingsford-Smith's successful Pacific crossings, 1928 and 1934, he flew from Suva to Hawaii nonstop, a distance of 3,120 miles. For a stunt, this was permissible, but for commercial air service of that era, an intermediary landing field was needed. Several islands became candidates, some for seaplane bases or land plane airfields and also a few which might, with development, serve both needs. The search for and development of air bases in the Central Pacific Ocean was a prime objective of several governments, in this period, several air lines, and covertly, several navies. This involvement of diverse interests was to play a pronounced part in Earhart's intrusion in this hotly-contested arena. During the years 1934 to 1937, Fanning, Canton, and Hull Islands were of considerable interest. Canton Island, by far the best known, became the principal air base in the Equatorial Pacific from 1939 to 1961, when it was finally made obsolete by jet transportation. In 1934, an extraordinary secondary airfield was located on the south rim of Fanning Atoll about 1,000 miles south of Hawaii. Fanning Island was the site of the British cable station between Vancouver and Suva.

In the early years of aviation, airplane landing sites were often pastures in the interior of various countries and tidal flats along many sea coasts. Most long-range

Sir Charles Kingsford-Smith and his ocean-hopping *Southern Cross,* which he flew across 7,000 miles of Pacific Ocean in 1928. He completed a world record circuit near the equator in successive flights in 1929 and 1930. The *Southern Cross* may be seen at Brisbane, Australia, while "Smithy's" memory is perpetuated at Kingsford-Smith International Airport at Sydney, Australia.
Photo credit - Smithsonian Institution's National Air & Space Museum

In the *Southern Cross,* Kingsford-Smith completed a crossing of the Tasman Sea (circa 1933)
Photo credit - Smithsonian Institution's National Air & Space Museum

flights in the Pacific during the 1920s and 1930s were dependent upon finding suitable tidal flats for the necessary two-mile runway length needed for heavily loaded aircraft to take off. "Barking Sands" at Kauai, Hawaii, was one such tidal flat which was used by Kingsford-Smith. He also knew of a tidal flat on the lagoon side of the south rim of Fanning Island. With a minimum amount of manpower this essentially flat area, which stretched for almost two miles in an east-west direction into the prevailing winds, could be used as an airfield. Charles T.P. Ulm has worked with cable company personnel in mid-1934 to smooth the surface of the tidal flat so that it could be used for airplane takeoffs and landings. Aviation fuel was shipped by boat from Honolulu to the airstrip to be available in November and December 1934. Inasmuch as most of the cable station employees were Australian, they were glad to help. The Gilbert Islands, 200 miles south of the Marshall Islands, as well as Ocean and Nauru Islands with their valuable phosphate deposits, were also given consideration. Certainly, if Australians were interested in what was happening in the Marshall Islands, the British had a vested interest as well.

No airfields were close enough to the Marshall Islands to provide a base for regular surveillance of these mandated islands. Wake Island was a seaplane base. Both Kingsford-Smith and Ulm, veterans of World War I, were British patriots, i.e., "God, King, and Country." That the United States and Australia were joined in an intelligence exchange in 1937 as per the article in *Smith's Weekly* (next page) is evident. Sufficient evidence to classify Ulm's flight as pseudo-military is lacking. At Oakland, his overnight use of the United States Navy hangar, with a naval guard, prior to his 6 December 1934 departure, seems suspicious as does the request of the Australian government that the United States send a search ship to Johnston Island, 650 miles from Oahu, to look for Ulm and his crew. These facts are not conclusive. More likely, in 1934, Ulm, in his zeal to promote his land-based trans-Pacific air line, might have approached both the British and the United States military authorities with the potential for using the route for overflights of the mandated islands. Also, Earhart, having met Charles Ulm, must have given some early thought in late 1934 to the potential of flying the Pacific in a twin-engine airplane because later she planned a route somewhat similar to Ulm's course southwest to Australia, but used Howland instead of Fanning Island.

THE BRITISH TRANS-PACIFIC CONNECTION

To thoroughly appreciate the position of the British, or United Kingdom, in the Central and Southwest Pacific relative to the rivalry between that nation and the United States in establishing a national versus a privately-owned airway across the Southwest Pacific from North America to Australia must be reviewed. Great Britain made no secret of the fact that she had designs for a worldwide "All-Red" air line similar to previous ship lines both naval and merchant; cable; wireless communication; world-girdling enterprises; and the ultimate air transport.

With the commercialized Vickers Vimy bomber which was flown across the Atlantic nonstop in 1919 and the flight of another Vimy departing London in 1920 and flying across four continents, Europe, Africa, Asia, and Australia, to Sydney, Great Britain was years ahead of competitors. These early empire-girdling flights pointed

the way to rapid transport of priority mail, premium cargo and super-class passengers to the far reaches of the British empire in days instead of weeks. Unfortunately, progress on those worthwhile goals was slow, even with government backing of one chosen air carrier, a heavy subsidy for its routes, and procurement of specialized civil aircraft.

The "All-Red" round-the-world air route had low priority, trailing far behind routes to Europe; London to Capetown, South Africa; London to India; and the trans-Atlantic one. With the shift in 1935-36 from civil to military aircraft production, due to the threat of the Axis dictators, the trans-Pacific route was not developed until after World War II. Unfortunately, with full knowledge that they could not themselves complete the Pacific air routes expeditiously, they selfishly chose to block United States acquisition of terminal rights in the South Pacific until reciprocal landing privileges were granted in Hawaii and on the West Coast. Personnel in the U.S. State Department knew that granting Hawaiian landing rights to the British could lead to requests from other countries such as Japan, and was militarily unfavorable.

Although Australians were amiable to the stalling, New Zealanders decided they could benefit from an additional trading partner and possible military ally. Correctly interpreting Britain's promises of protection in the event of a Pacific war as an idle proposition, two successive governments, conservative in 1935 and labor in 1936, granted Pan American Airways landing privileges at Auckland. New Zealanders did not regret this momentous pre-World War II decision. The United States, not Great Britain, provided protection for their home islands and mandates and stopped the southern advance of the Japanese Navy toward Australia and New Zealand. After World War II, the British and United Kingdom Pacific Islands, recaptured at great cost in American lives and ships, were returned to their pre-war owners.

Kingsford-Smith opened up the airway from the West Coast of North America to Brisbane, Australia, with refueling stops at Hawaii and the Fiji Islands. This 7,000-mile flight in 1928 over the world's largest ocean in a secondhand Fokker tri-motor was one of the most daring flights of Aviation's Golden Age. Australian-born, he measured the odds and, with a courageous crew and an aircraft with an airspeed of 100 miles per hour, tackled the relatively uncharted course. His landfalls were thousands of miles apart, navigational aids were practically nonexistent and airfields were improvised. Weather conditions en route were practically unknown and unreported. There was no cabin heat, no warm meals and no smoking in the aircraft. In the jet age, a Boeing 747SP can cover that distance routinely in 14 hours, and a San Francisco, Honolulu, Suva, and Sydney flight is considered a "milk run" on several scheduled airlines. Kingsford-Smith's role has not been forgotten as attested to by naming the Kingsford-Smith International Airport at Sydney, Australia, in his honor.

Kingsford-Smith and Charles Ulm, his former copilot in 1928, made another major advance in promoting the southwest-northeast trans-Pacific airway in late 1934. Following their successful 1928 trans-Pacific flight, Kingsford-Smith and Ulm established an airline called AMA in southern Australia. This commercial venture failed due to the loss of a British-built Fokker aircraft and the worldwide depression of the 1930s. In that decade no Australian national airline existed

PRICE 4d

Smith's Weekly

GERMANY'S LOST COLONIES AND MUSSOLINI'S VISIT TO HITLER. SEE PAGE 7.

FOUNDED BY JOYNTON SMITH — The Public Guardian

Vol. XIX, No. 33 (Copyright) 1 ** Saturday, October 16, 1937.

Registered at the General Post Office, Sydney, for transmission by post as a newspaper.

U.S.A. *does* AUSTRALIA *a Secret Ser...*

AMELIA EARHART SEARCH MADE THE OPPORTUNITY

Plane Observers Over Japanese Pacific Bases

TIP WAS GIVEN OUR DEFENCE DEPT.

FIRST IMPRESSIONS

'RIME Minister's' baby-bonus song : "Just before the battle, mother, I was thinking most of you."

APSANIAS.

APPAYER claims that 50 per cent. of Australia's politicians are useless. He's about half right.

UILDING costs have risen fifteen per cent. More than ever now, man will be able to build his beloved a dear little home.

APAN indulges in plane murder.

R LYONS celebrated his birthday in September. But he'd like many appy returns in October.

OME of these politicians are already suffering from "I" strain.

TATED that Germany will protest against a British M.P. who described Hitler and Mussolini as gangsters. A protest may also be expected from Chicago.
— S. P.

RS. DON BRADMAN was fined for fast driving. Bowlers would like similar powers to deal with Don's fast swing.

(MORE ON PAGE 7)

WHEN W. M. Hughes, at the Peace Conference, insisted that Japan have no island mandates in the Pacific below the Equator, he was long-sighted.

But even with what Japan has, her strategists have not been idle. Australian defence authorities know all about this now. U.S.A. observers seized the opportunity offered by the search for Amelia Earhart. They swept wide enough to make a scrutiny of Japanese naval activities in islands in the groups under control of Nippon.

UNTIL now the real story has been withheld of the desperate international intrigue, bracketing Australia, that went with the search for ill-fated Amelia Earhart, when that intrepid aviatrix crashed into the Pacific somewhere near the Phoenix Islands.

IT is a story of military tactics that went hand in hand with that search—hand in hand with the terrific expense of £500,000 spent on American naval planes.

American planes did more than just search for Amelia Earhart. They cut a wide swathe over the Pacific and circled near the Caroline and the Marshall Islands.

Here Australia comes into the picture. The grim threat of war appears a little closer when it is realised that the groups of islands, and another (Yap), controlled by Japan, lie right at Australia's northern door.

Under cover of the search for the missing aviatrix, America's naval aircraft were anxious to glimpse two of the islands, believed by military experts to have been fortified by the Japanese. The Australian Government now knows more about that search than has been disclosed publicly.

No one is permitted to land on the Japanese controlled islands. Missionaries who previously conducted religious propaganda among natives there have been forbidden to return.

The islands are held by mandate given to Japan when that country was a member of the League of Nations. Now she is no longer a member — but she holds the islands in an iron grip. The position of the islands and their possible fortification in the Pacific were matters of grave concern to America, and to Australia.

With an examination of the accompanying map it can be seen that this group of islands dominates the Pacific—close to Honolulu, close to the Philippines, and equally close to New Guinea and Queensland.

When Japan struck so suddenly at China, and its war machine blackened Shanghai, the doctrine of naked force was revealed. The "it can't happen nowadays" theory was bayonetted out of existence.

Australia's interest lies in the fact that quietly and with the usual lack of publicity Japan has been working to get closer to the Commonwealth, equipping Japanese bases admirably suited for an expedition into the Pacific.

While this does not allege that Japan is feverishly waiting to strike into the Pacific, military circles are perturbed by the knowledge that fortified islands have been so effectively prepared nearby.

The knowledge does not add to a feeling of security, when armies march into foreign countries practically without warning these times, and start to "mop up."

As a matter of military precaution plans are always drawn up awaiting a "mythical" invader. In Australia the experts are not the only ones who know of the country's weakness in case of attack. Most people know it as well as Japan's experts would also know it. It is of the store of military knowledge that every country keeps handy.

Japan's mandate over the Caroline and the Marshall Islands, plus the taking over (peacefully) of YAP, are matters probably forgotten in the general rush of events. Military men became aware of the fact with the seeping through of news that there is a prohibition on visitors.

This is grim news to the war department. It means that there are military occupation, fortification, bases, and war material. Prying eyes are not permitted to see in cases like these.

So when Amelia Earhart went down and her faint distress signals located her plane around the Phoenix Islands, the search for her gave the pretext that was needed. Sentiment comes second to secret service.

U.S.A. naval planes swept over the waters around Phoenix Islands and then took a wide turn and went farther on. They circled on, covering the areas in which the Caroline and Marshall Islands are to be found.

Naval flying men are admirable observers. It is their profession.

America poured out money on this search. Allowing for the human interest, the search was so costly that only those on the inside even guessed at the purpose of the expenditure of 2,500,000 dollars—in our currency, £500,000!

It was the opportunity not to be missed, a real excuse to fly over Japan's islands-by-mandate, to observe what the waters contained. To-day the Australian Government has been apprised of some of the knowledge gleaned. With the world situation as it is, and with Australia's neglect of defence over the years, the knowledge came as a godsend—paid for by the U.S.A.

YAP ISLAND is close to the Equator. If a line were drawn from Japan to the Caroline Islands, and then continued to the Equator, it would strike YAP. The latter is outside NEW GUINEA—and not so far, after that, from QUEENSLAND.

The MARSHALL ISLANDS are between the CAROLINES and HONOLULU, hence America's interest. From the Carolines to New Guinea is little farther than from Tokio to Shanghai. The map tells the story—and it is a chapter which brings Japan to Australia's back door.

Feverish interest in the Earhart search acted, with shrewd newspaper reports, as a blanket over this astounding aspect of the U.S.A. flights. The facts are known in the proper quarters, which are admittedly perturbed over the Japanese situation in the Pacific.

Even if Japan had no ambitions in the Pacific, other than safeguarding her lines of communications, the proximity of fortified islands would be disturbing enough.

Military men declare that Japanese naval men in charge; that they are excellent sampans for scouting and raiding thinly settled places and that Japanese navigators know the Queensland coast in every detail.

Theoretically an attack by sampans would permit of these vessels loading light tanks and supplies for putting ashore without difficulty. Some of the sampans draw only 2ft of water, making approach to land an easy matter for the landing of tanks and light supplies.

An Australian who was formerly a high official in the Commonwealth diplomatic services tells "Smith's Weekly":—

(CONTINUED ON PAGE 2)

Grim News For War Department

OUR PACIFIC NEIGHBORS—Or should it be Our Neighbors in the Pacific?

[Map labels: SHIKOKU, KYUSHU, JAPAN, TAIWAN, PHILIPPINES, YAP, MARIANNE ISLANDS, MARSHALL ISLANDS., CAROLINE ISLANDS, MANDATE TO JAPAN, TROPIC OF CANCER, PACIFIC OCEAN, EQUATOR, MANDATE TO GT. BRITAIN, NAURU IS, MANDATE TO AUSTRALIA, DUTCH EAST INDIES, NEW GUINEA, CORAL SEA]

Although both the U.S. and Australian governments denied spying activities, this Australian gazette type tabloid "let cat out of bag" in the Oct. 16, 1937 edition.

(Via Elgen Long)

Between 10 and 12 independent businessmen, operating on scant budgets, competed for sustaining government airmail contracts. After AMA failed in the early 1930s, Kingsford-Smith and Ulm parted company, but retained the tantalizing concept of the trans-Pacific link in the British "All-Red" airway around the world.

Charles T. P. Ulm with crew members Littlejon and Skilling at Oakland, California, before takeoff for fatal flight toward Hawaii.
Photo credit - Smithsonian Institution's National Air & Space Museum Negative #87-2477 (from Queensland Newspaper)

Captain Charles T.P. Ulm flew across the Pacific with Sir Charles Kingsford-Smith in 1928. After seven years of pioneering air routes in the South Seas, Ulm lost his life in December 1934 pioneering a trans-Pacific air route.
Photo credit - Smithsonian Institution's National Air & Space Museum Negative #87-2478 (from Queensland Newspaper)

Taylor, the copilot/navigator, plotted an alternate course to Fanning Island where arrangements had been made to smooth the tidal flats on the lagoon side of the southern rim of the island and provision aviation fuel. After calculating course and remaining fuel, Kingsford-Smith decided to continue to Honolulu and landed at Wheeler field with only a small margin of fuel. A crack in the main fuselage fuel tank was rewelded before the flight continued to Oakland.

Altair Speedster--The Altair was a sport-model design that enabled Lockheed to meet requirements of private fliers and commercial airline operators. Carrying two or three persons, it was equipped with a hand cranked retractable landing gear. In 1934, Sir Charles Kingsford-Smith and his copilot, P.G. Taylor, flew their *Lady Southern Cross* from Brisbane, Australia, to Oakland, California, covering the 7,356 miles in less than 55 hours' flying time. The Altair's trans-Pacific flight was made at cruising speeds of 200 m.p.h.
Altair Speedster - 1931
Wing Span - 42' 9"   Length - 27' 1"   Height - 9' 3"
Photo credit - Lockheed - California Company

By 1934, both Kingsford-Smith and Ulm were in positions to further this cherished dream by demonstration flights. Kingsford-Smith decided to fly his Lockheed Altair, which was procured for him by solicitation in Australia, to compete in the 1934 England to Melbourne, Australia race. Unfortunately, a series of accidents forced him to abandon plans to fly in the heralded MacDonald race, so he elected to cross the Pacific Ocean, departing from Brisbane and going via Suva, Fanning Island (if necessary), Honolulu, and on to Oakland, California. Sir Charles Taylor was selected as his copilot/navigator and the Pacific crossing was successfully completed in November. Two incidents marred an otherwise uneventful flight. A tailspin, caused by accidentally cracking the landing flaps at a high rate of speed, caused their aircraft to fall some 6,000 feet before the cause of the spin was discovered and corrected.

Sir Charles Kingsford-Smith flew from Brisbane, Australia, to Oakland, California, in a single-engine Wasp-powered Lockheed Altair in November 1934. Sir Gordon Taylor was "Smithy's" copilot/navigator/radio operator. Not many persons would consider flying 7,000 miles over the Pacific Ocean in a single-engine landplane.

Photo credit - Lockheed - California Company

Meanwhile, Charles Ulm had been trying to promote expansion routes for Australian air lines on the Asian mainland. Unsuccessful at this, he journeyed to England to promote United Kingdom aviation at London, the financial fountainhead of the Empire. He was successful in obtaining backing for a trans-Atlantic crossing from England to the United States. His luck ran out, however, as the airplane was severely damaged on a tidal flat chosen for takeoff when a high tide swamped it during the night.

Ulm's final venture was assured by his finding sponsorship for a trans-Pacific flight from Vancouver, British Columbia, to Australia. Obviously, the correlation between the final link in the "All-Red" cable made in 1902 and the "All-Red" airline had caught the fancy of supportive investors to augment his own capital. Money and determination alone, however, do not guarantee success. In a few short weeks, Ulm acquired a relatively inexpensive twin-engine wooden Airspeed Envoy with Lynx engines, equipped it with fuselage tanks to give it a range of more than 2,500 miles, and assembled a crew of two. The airplane was shipped by steamer to Montreal, Canada, assembled, and flown by Ulm and his copilot/navigator to Burbank and Oakland, California.

Australian aviator Charles T.P. Ulm's Airspeed Envoy *Stella Australus* at Oakland, California, prior to ill-fated flight over Pacific Ocean toward Oahu, Hawaii, in early December 1934. Although Ulm reached the vicinity of Oahu, he ran out of gasoline and ditched in the ocean without sighting the Hawaiian Islands.

Photo credit - Museum of Flight, Seattle, Washington

Ulm's Airspeed Envoy which he hoped to fly from Oakland to Sydney, Australia, in late 1934. Route was to Oahu, then a tidal flat airstrip on British Fanning Island. Next stop was Suva in the Fiji Islands and from there to Auckland, New Zealand. The final leg was across the Tasman Sea to Sydney, Australia.
Photo credit - Museum of Flight, Seattle, Washington

There he was joined by an Australian who was hired as a navigator for the 7,000-mile flight. Many potentially weak elements existed in this endeavor. The aircraft, though thoroughly conventional in design, was relatively new and unproven as was the Airspeed Company. The primary consideration seems to have been the relatively low cost, 4,000 pounds, due no doubt to the wooden construction. The three-member crew had neither flown together nor had they flown the aircraft over water. The brief flight from Montreal to Oakland was unsatisfactory as a trial for the proposed flight to Australia. Fuel consumption, mixture economizing, oil provisions, and fuel crossfeed were all virtually untried and unknown.

Charles Ulm eventually arrived at Oakland, where takeoff with a full load of 600 gallons of fuel almost ended disastrously. Finally, with no arrangements for radio range assistance at San Francisco, a fateful mistake, he took off. Searchers believed the aircraft passed through the Hawaiian chain, but crew members drowned before they could be rescued. A rubber life raft could well have saved their lives. Unfortunately, Ulm did not help the cause of a trans-Pacific route to Australia using land planes, but dealt it a blow which, along with Earhart's equally rash venture, held it back for many years. Any comparison between Ulm and Kingsford-Smith reveals that Ulm was not a giant of a man. He left too much to chance and didn't plan the flight for contingencies and provide for emergencies. The clincher was his statement to the press at Oakland prior to his departure. When asked, "Why don't you carry a rubber raft?" He replied, "Don't worry, I won't even get my feet wet."

The British Airspeed Envoy was introduced in 1934 as a small transport aircraft of wooden construction. It was sold worldwide in the 1930s and became the military Airspeed Oxford during World War II.
Photo credit - Smithsonian Institution's National Air & Space Museum Negative #87-2480 (from advertisement in Flight Magazine, May 6, 1937)

Aerial overhead view of Airspeed Envoy in flight. Envoy was same size as Lockheed Electra, but much lighter because of wooden construction.
Photo credit - Smithsonian Institution's
National Air & Space Museum Negative #87-2482

THE ROLE OF THE BRITISH FREIGHTER
M. V. *MOORBY*

Well-known is the fact that the M. V. *Moorby*, a British freighter, participated in the Earhart search almost from the time the first notification to mariners was sent. The only other commercial ship in the Central Pacific equatorial area at that time was the S. S. *Golden Bear*, of United States registry and en route from Tarawa (British Gilbert Islands) to Hawaii. The radio operators aboard that vessel acknowledged the distress call, but the ship did not become a search participant because of a serious lack of fuel. Most researchers have assumed that the *Moorby*'s strategic location just east of the Japanese Marshall Islands was just a fortuitous event and that she was engaged in her normal commercial duties. In June 1937 the ship was en route from Vancouver, British Columbia, to Australia via Tarawa and Fiji. Several facts are worth noting relative to the strategic position of the *Moorby* east of the Marshall Islands on 2 July 1937 and approximately 400 miles north of Howland Island on 4 July 1937. The *Moorby* was the only commercial vessel used during the official period of the search. Almost immediately, *Moorby* personnel agreed to participate in the search although it was unusual for a tramp steamer to be engaged in such activity. Although only one radio operator was aboard, he continued to monitor the aviation

frequencies and heard the well-known "dash" messages. For a merchantman to listen to anything but maritime frequencies was unusual. *Moorby* personnel responded quickly to the request of the United States Coast Guard to converge on the point 281 miles north of Howland on 4 July 1937. Finding nothing, the captain requested and received permission to resume normal pursuits.

The *Moorby*, along with the British warships H.M.S. *Achilles* and H.M.S. *Wellington*, was the third British ship to be strategically located during the Earhart mission. Like so many other aspects of the Earhart episode previously investigated, the *Moorby* role deserves further study. A check of the "Port News" column of the *Vancouver Sun* in June 1937 indicates that the *Moorby* arrived at Vancouver at 1900 9 June and departed 13 June at 2200. At its customary speed of 10 knots, it should have been in the harbor at Tarawa before the end of June. Instead it was east of the Marshall Islands.

In view of the activity of the *Moorby* in the Central Pacific, an examination of her itinerary appears justified. She was owned by the Ropner Shipping Company, Ltd. On 1 May 1937 she arrived at Norfolk, Virginia, with a load of manganese ore from the Ivory Coast. Norfolk, of course, is the headquarters of the United States Atlantic Fleet and manganese ore is used in armor plate. *Moorby* sailed "in ballast" (holds empty) and transited the Panama Canal on 16 May. There were several stops en route to Vancouver. On 27 May in the afternoon she dropped anchor just inside the breakwater at San Pedro, California, and departed at midnight the same day. During the 1920s and 1930s, San Pedro, California, was the home port of the United States Navy Pacific (Battle) Fleet. Leaving San Pedro on 27 May she should have arrived at Vancouver, some 1,200 miles away, by the end of May. Instead the arrival date was 9 June. As no commercial seaport had logged her in for this nine-day period, the conclusion was that after Norfolk and San Pedro, another United States Navy facility claimed her. Only two of these were en route: Mare Island at Vallejo, California, and Bremerton, Washington.

The transit times between ports are also an important indicator of merchant ship activity. As *Moorby* was designed for a constant speed of 10 knots, she could cover 240 nautical miles per day, except in heavy weather. On the trip south from Norfolk to the Panama Canal, *Moorby* covered the 1,822 nautical miles at her design speed. On the trip north from Panama to San Pedro, however, the speed was increased to 10.5 knots, for her 11-hour stopover at San Pedro.

These deviations from the normal operating pattern of a ship are significant to the actual role of the *Moorby* in the Earhart mission. Now apparent is that the mid-1937 cruise of that ship was anything but routine for a tramp freighter. Thus, it was necessary to determine her activity based on her known itinerary and contemporary events in the areas in which she was operating.

After leaving her home port of Cardiff, the *Moorby* was loaded with a cargo of coal which she transported to the Ivory Coast, an African colony. Taking on a load of manganese ore, she crossed the Atlantic Ocean to Norfolk, the cargo becoming part of a stockpile of strategic metals being purchased by the United States government and stored by the United States Navy. Norfolk port records show that the *Moorby* never returned to Norfolk until after World War II, so this delivery was a chartered operation, not routine. When the *Moorby* left Norfolk on 7 May 1937, the local shipping column showed her destination as the "high seas," a common dodge used almost exclusively for warships, in peacetime, when the destination must remain secret. Shown by available evidence is that the *Moorby* was under charter for the United States Navy and carrying out some type of covert mission. At Panama, she passed through with empty holds, but this did not preclude assorted deck cargo. This explains why her destination was withheld at Norfolk. Too many persons there knew what her deck cargo was. If the destination had been given as the Pacific Ocean, questions might be asked later.

The reason for the increase over design speed from Panama to San Pedro, and seldom would a freighter captain do this, was to arrive on time for her 11-hour stop at San Pedro, where she would off-load her deck cargo to a harbor lighter, or barge, for subsequent reloading elsewhere within the harbor. In summary, the *Moorby* had a date to meet another ship which was on a schedule. This meant a passenger liner, because in peacetime freighters and warships normally don't hold to tight schedules. The following day, the Matson Steamship Company cruise ship *Lurline* sailed for Honolulu on a five-day run. By this time employees on this ship were used to loading aircraft on the aft tennis deck, having been involved with Earhart flights across the eastern Pacific and the return of her damaged Electra to the West Coast. The difference here was that the airplane was from a British freighter and the airplane was undoubtedly British, too.

The nine-day delay between the San Pedro and Vancouver stops had to be at a naval facility because she didn't enter any commercial harbor on the West Coast. Mare Island Naval Shipyard in upper San Francisco Bay was the logical naval facility to accommodate the *Moorby*. Because of her subsequent station east of the Japanese Marshall Islands on 2 July 1937, it becomes apparent that the *Moorby* was being fitted with the same kind of radio homing, communication, and navigation equipment which had been installed on a United States submarine used for picket duty in the Southern Marshalls for the Earhart flight.

After that nine-day delay at Mare Island, the *Moorby* resumed her cruise to Vancouver. Upon arrival there, her shipping agent called for a two-day loading schedule. Even the Vancouver longshoremen, working nights and over the weekend, couldn't work a miracle. Thus, four days later the ship left port for a great circle cruise to Tarawa, Fiji, and Australia. By 1 July she was in position off Wotje Atoll in the Eastern Marshalls. In 1937 Wotje Island was the radio listening post and radio direction finding station for Japanese Naval Intelligence and a forward staging area for the Imperial Japanese Navy (IJN). Therefore, it was a prime target for aerial reconnaissance.

HIGHLIGHTS OF THE BRITISH CONNECTION

The following factors are considered relevant in establishing British participation in a concurrent operation which included an overflight by Earhart of the southern Marshall Island of Jaluit and an overflight by a British reconnaissance airplane of the eastern Marshall Island of Wotje.

1.   Joint United States and British cooperation existed in the Eritrea overflight to satisfy British strategic reconnaissance requirements.

2.   Considerable evidence exists relative to the capture of female and male Caucasian fliers before World War II in the Marshall Islands. They may have been taken to Saipan. An aggregate of at least 50 man-years of research and investigation in this direction was made by Fred Goerner and many others.

3.   Later covered up by the United States Navy was the radio message intercepted by the *Achilles* regarding the two stations including KHAQQ, received from the Phoenix Island area.

4.   The British (New Zealand) Navy participated in the 8 June 1937 Solar Eclipse expedition on Canton Island and later in the Earhart search.

5.   A major Japanese move in the Orient was imminent concerning the United States/United Kingdom/China sphere of influence.

6.   There was precedence for British flights in the Pacific as demonstrated by Kingsford-Smith and Ulm, in the 1920s and 1930s.

7.   Four men from the *Achilles* went ashore at Canton Island on 8 August 1937 and established a radio station which was maintained for several years.

8.   The switch of Earhart's landing place from Canton Island to Hull Island. A landing party from the *Swan* went ashore on Canton on 10 July 1937 to remove personnel and equipment and supplies left behind by the *Avocet* on 10 June.

9.   Politically involved were members of the United States "War Cabinet," Roosevelt, Morgenthau, Leahy, and members from the United Kingdom "War Party," Churchill, Eden, and Cooper. Significant cooperation among United States, British, and New Zealand navies occurred after Japan's departure from the 1936 Naval Conference in London.

10.   Considered important military reconnaissance targets in 1937 were Jaluit, Wotje, and Eniwetok in the Marshall Islands.

11.   The active cooperation of the New Zealand Navy in the "Earhart Search" is suggestive of Commonwealth involvement and interest.

12.   For aerial spying, the British had a predilection for using the Lockheed 10 as evidenced by cameras in the one used by Prime Minister Chamberlain during flights to Germany.

13.   In the article in *Smith's Weekly* was evidence of mutual United States/United Kingdom activities.

14.   The British flight used Fanning Island for departure and Canton Island as a destination for security reasons.

THE BRITISH OVERFLIGHT

It is now possible to define the "North of the Equator" mission involving an airplane which overflew the Japanese Marshall Islands prior to World War II. The key factors are the location and interview of a reliable, educated on-site witness and by identifying the true role of the British freighter M. V. *Moorby* during the covert operation. As the airplane was known to have sheared off one wing on impact landing in the ocean off Mili Atoll, it most certainly was of wooden construction. A British twin engine airplane of this type was previously used (in 1934) for long-range over water flying in the Pacific, which established a precedent for the later flight. As the British were recognized as being quite conservative in the 1930s, and under the limited time constraints known to be available, it appears evident that following established

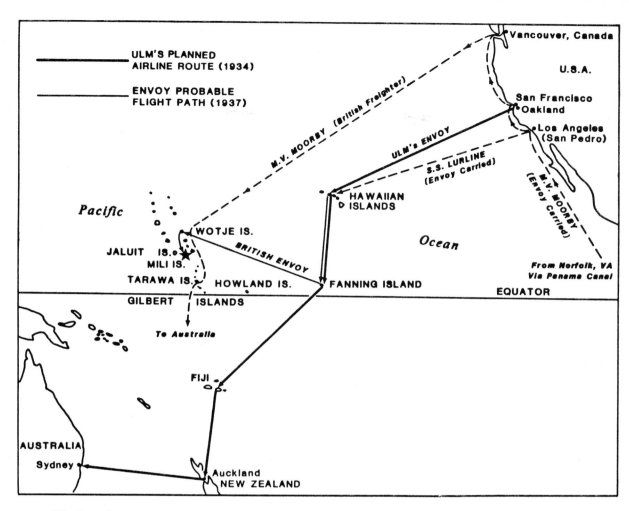

Ulm's planned airline route (1934) and British Envoy flight path (1937)

precedent would command major consideration by mission planners.

It has been publicly known since the 1944 invasion of the Japanese Marshall Islands by United States military forces that an airplane flown by a white Caucasian couple (man and woman) overflew the islands prior to World War II and they were forced to ditch their airplane in the ocean adjacent to Mili Atoll. After five decades of continuing research by individuals over most of the globe, legitimate, educated witnesses have been located and interviewed by South African author Oliver Knaggs (and several others) to add more important facts to help solve this part of the Earhart disappearance mystery. Knaggs interviewed two Marshallese residents present in the Marshall Islands in 1937. One was named Bilimin. His testimony was confirmed by another eye witness named Tomaki. They were both at Jaluit Atoll which was the principal island of the Marshall Islands in pre-war years. They had both been involved in the Japanese search for Earhart by the Imperial Japanese Navy (IJN) survey ship *Kamoi*. Their testimony clearly establishes the following: the woman aviator with blond hair below the ears was not Earhart, the male companion with blue eyes was not Noonan (who had steel gray eyes), and the airplane which sheared off a wing was not the metal-built Electra which never lost a wing in its entire service life covering more than 50 years. Despite the

repeated efforts to tie Earhart, Noonan, and an Electra to this episode, very clearly these researchers are trying to "put the glass slipper on the ugly stepsister."

A modest amount of research on British airplanes available in 1937 and precedent in recent British (and Commonwealth) Pacific Ocean crossing efforts, identifies the Airspeed Envoy as a wooden-structured twin-engine cabin aircraft of the same size as the Lockheed Electra, although much lighter and selling for about half the price of the all-metal Electra. Further, Charles T.P. Ulm had previously (in 1934) modified an Airspeed Envoy for long-range Pacific Ocean flying by installing fuselage fuel tanks to give it a range of more than 2,500 miles. Additionally, because the wooden-structured airplane was designed for worldwide use, it was equipped with detachable outer wing panels so that it could be carried aboard freighters or passenger liners as deck cargo. This airplane was in serial production at Portsmouth, England, which was the principal home port of the Royal Navy and adjacent to Southampton, which was the main shipping port for passenger and merchant ships leaving southern England. In a few weeks, an Airspeed Envoy could be taken off the assembly line and the long-range tanks installed as had been previously done in Ulm's ocean-hopping Envoy. After completion and local factory acceptance testing, the Envoy would be shipped across the Atlantic Ocean by liner, freighter, or fast naval auxiliary

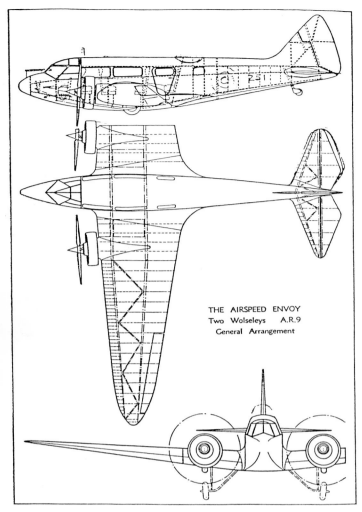

THE AIRSPEED ENVOY
Two Wolseleys A.R.9
General Arrangement

"ENVOY" 5,300 lbs.

DIMENSIONS:

	British:	Metric:
Total Span	52′ 4″	15.95 m.
Span without Extension Planes ...	15′ 6″	4.72 m.
Span, Tail Plane and Elevators ...	14′ 6″	4.42 m.
Overall Length	34′ 6″	10.5 m.
Overall Height of Aircraft ...	9′ 6″	2.9 m.
Overall Height of Aircraft (Prop. Vertical)	9′ 6″	2.9 m.
Wheel Track	12′ 5″	3.78 m.
Engine Centres at Prop.	12′ 7.4″	3.85 m.
Total Area Main Planes with Ailerons	339 sq. ft.	31.5 sq. m.
Total Area Ailerons (2)	26.2 sq. ft.	2.42 sq. m.
Total Area Fin	7.45 sq. ft.	0.693 sq. m.
Total Area Tail Plane ...	23 sq. ft.	2.14 sq. m.
Total Area Rudder ...	15.8 sq. ft.	1.47 sq. m.
Total Area Elevators (2) ...	26 sq. ft.	2.42 sq. m.
Wing Chord at Fuselage ...	9′ 3″	2.82 m.
Mean Chord	6′ 9″	2.06 m.

Mean Dihedral 5°

Incidence ··· 2° at root section with 2° washout along
extension plane

5300 lbs.	Wing Loading ...	15.6 lbs. per sq. ft.	76.1 kg./sq. m.
	Power Loading ...	13.1 lbs./h.p.	5.875 kg./ps.

Twin-engine Airspeed Envoy had wooden propellers in most civilian versions. Later Mark numbers had full chord N.A.C.A. engine cowling as in this Mark III version of 1936.
Photo credit - Alexander Turnbull Library, Wellington, New Zealand

Airspeed Envoy, Mark III Convertible, civil transport; military light bomber/trainer. Thousands were built under Commonwealth training program of World War II as Airspeed Oxfords and flown worldwide.
Photo credit - Davis Collection, Alexander Turnbull Library, Wellington, New Zealand

Typical cockpit layout of military version of Airspeed Envoy/Oxford series
Photo credit - Alexander Turnbull Library, Wellington, New Zealand

to Norfolk, Virginia. There it would tie in with the M. V. *Moorby* itinerary for transport to the Pacific Ocean via the Panama Canal to San Pedro, California, there to be trans-shipped via the S. S. *Lurline* to Oahu, Hawaiian Islands, for Central Pacific use. After reassembly at Wheeler Field and local test flights, the Airspeed Envoy could be flown 1,000 miles south and landed on the semi-secret tidal flat airstrip on the lagoon side of the south rim of British Fanning Island. From Fanning Island, a synchronized takeoff westward for a thousand miles and guidance inward by picket ship M.V. *Moorby* would place the Envoy over Wotje Island, which was a prime military base for the IJN.

The identity of the British female pilot is unknown at this time, but the prime suspect is Beryl Markham. She fits the description of the woman seen at Jaluit whom the Japanese had picked up at Mili Atoll far better than Earhart. The very secretive nature of Beryl Markham's activities after her 1937 trans-Atlantic flight is well known. Whether she was expatriated by the Japanese after capture, or a surrogate established for her alleged sojourn in southern California, for 20 odd years, is unknown. Some day soon some Markham biographer who picks up her life where the *West With the Night* autobiography ends (1936) may clear up her activities. Needless to say, her male companion could have been any one of a thousand military aviators who was slight in build and long in flying experience.

An appraisal of available evidence indicates an "overlay" mission. The use of diversionary tactics is used during major missions to confuse persons in the target area and divert attention in several directions. The United States was not the only country with a vested interest in the Japanese Mandated Islands, but U.S. concern was almost entirely strategic. Britain had strategic as well as commercial interests, the latter notably in the Gilbert and Ellice Colonies and Nauru Island. Those possessions were a few hundred miles from the Japanese Mandated Islands and were, in fact, captured within a matter of months after the opening of hostilities in the Pacific in December 1941.

The detour of the Earhart flight over Eritrea was undoubtedly to acquire aerial intelligence for Britain, because the United States had little military or political interest there. Relative to the covert cooperation between the United States and the United Kingdom, a brief review is necessary. First, at the London Naval Conference in 1935, Japanese delegates refused to renew prior commitments and left. This action made war in the Pacific not a matter of if, but when. The invasion of Eritrea by Italian troops in 1935-36 brought the Royal Navy to almost total mobilization in the Mediterranean and adjacent areas. Only Neville Chamberlain's appeasement policies averted a shooting war. Many persons, both inside and outside British government circles saw Italy, Germany, and Japan for the threats they were. Churchill had strong allies within the Chamberlain government, namely Anthony Eden, the Foreign Secretary, and Duff Cooper, First Lord of the Admiralty (see Cooper, Duff, *The Second World War*, First Phase). They became the nucleus of a war party opposed to Chamberlain's appeasement policies. Both Eden and Cooper resigned after the Munich "agreement" of "Peace in Our Time." The United States counterpart was Roosevelt's War Cabinet with early members being the President, Henry Morgenthau, Jr., Secretary of the Treasury from 1934 to 1945, Secretary of the Navy Swanson, and Admiral William Leahy, Chief of Naval Operations from 1937 to 1939. The go-between was Bernard Baruch who, periodically, crossed the Atlantic during the 1930s to coordinate policies of Roosevelt and Churchill (see Baruch, B., *The Public Years*). Available evidence indicates that Churchill's War Party bypassed His Majesty's Government and the Prime Minister and worked through the military forces. Since the buildup of the Royal Air Force had started in 1935, and a top level military decision had been made to forego a large "continental army," the development of a strategic bomber force was underway. As the success of strategic bombing depended upon selection of targets and assessment of target damage, both of which are augmented by aerial photography, one of the areas under development was mounting high resolution aerial cameras in bombers. One of the airplanes with demonstrated capabilities included the Lockheed 10. The Lockheed Electra Model 10A, purchased by British Airways, which was used to transport Chamberlain to Munich, had aerial cameras beneath the floorboards. Thus, photos of the Siegfried Line and other German military targets were taken. Also, a British civilian, Sydney Cotton, performed pre-World War II aerial reconnaissance using cameras mounted in an Electra, one of three purchased by the RAF.

The far-reaching network of the British Admiralty, Foreign Office, and Colonial Office has been identified in the Western Pacific, and precedent for strategic military aerial photographic capability noted.

Most likely, the Royal Navy developed the operational plan and partially funded the mission which was based on the Kingsford-Smith trans-Pacific crossings of the mid-1930s and the attempted crossing by Charles Ulm. The airplane was an Airspeed Envoy built and modified at Portsmouth, England, test flown, and crated. It went by water to Honolulu and was then flown to Fanning Island.

BRITISH PARTICIPATION IN THE FLIGHT AND SEARCH

A logical definition for the British Connection is beginning with the better known aspects of British participation in the Earhart flight and subsequent search. These are well known over the past decades and have undergone considerable clarification during that lengthy period. Perhaps the only significant change in recent years is the Nauru Island landfall, which although present from the start, was not recognized as significant until the last 15 years. The British Connection is similar in many respects to the collective United States government agencies, the personnel of which in the early 1960s asserted that "no information whatsoever on the Amelia Earhart episodes, classified or otherwise" was held. In 1967, after the enactment of the Freedom of Information Act (FOIA), this was proven to be a monumental lie. Likewise, the United States Navy claim of only giving limited assistance to the operation in the form of two picket ships for weather reporting and radio support during the flight was patently false.

The extent of British participation is generally restricted in most accounts to airfield support in the Sudan, India, Burma, Singapore, and the Commonwealth of Australia and its New Guinea (Lae) mandate. The British and Commonwealth communication network was used to forward radio messages and weather information to Lae via Naval radio Tutuila at American Samoa.

Standard Airspeed Envoy had single vertical tail, but a variant was built with twin rudders. In this configuration, with internal fuel tanks in the cabin as in Ulm's Envoy, it was an Electra surrogate.
Photo credit - Smithsonian Institution's National Air & Space Museum Negative #87-2481

British (Commonwealth) participation in the search is usually believed to have been restricted to two ships, H.M.S. *Achilles* and M.V. *Moorby*, which just "happened" to be in the general vicinity of the search area. Belated support was also afforded at the Tarawa and Ocean Islands in the Gilbert Group by the regional administrator.

In concert with involved United States government agencies (FDR administration), the United States Navy, and the United States Coast Guard (under the Treasury Department), nautical activities regarding the United Kingdom and the Commonwealth countries of Australia and New Zealand have never been acknowledged as to overt and/or covert participation. Why had persons in the above countries been reluctant to admit anything about the Earhart flight and her disappearance? This is the question which needs to be answered in the "British Connection." The following key points are worth examining.

1. Pre-flight participation consisted of use of the communications network via Suva, Fiji Islands. Weather reporting was included in the British service. No participation was evidenced relative to the Gilbert and Ellice Colony. Of the utmost importance and worth noting is that Ocean Island was immediately available for reprovisioning the *Ontario*. Thus, the claim of that ship being unavailable for the search is false.

2. British activities relative to the flight segment included the *Wellington* taking on fuel from the *Achilles* in the harbor at Pago Pago on 26 June 1937 and a radio watch undertaken on aviation frequencies.

3. British participation during the search included duties for personnel aboard the *Achilles* and *Wellington*.

4. At Putnam's request the sand spit east of the Gilberts was searched by the British.

5. During and after World War II, the searches continued in the Pacific Islands for some trace of the missing fliers.

Why did an overreaction occur in high places in this country regarding Earhart's actions during the overflight of the Marshall Islands? Weren't the fliers who apparently ditched near Mili Atoll reported to have been a "white Caucasian-appearing couple?" During World War II, American military men weren't looking for Earhart and Noonan. They were looking for the British fliers! Churchill depended on Roosevelt to initiate a search for that couple because at that time predominantly United States forces invaded the Japanese mandates of the Caroline, Marshall, and Mariana Groups.

A BRIEF REVIEW OF THE BRITISH CONNECTION INCLUDES:

1. Overflight of Italian East Africa.
2. Intelligence exchange with Australians vis-a-vis Japan (pre-World War II).
3. The British High Commission for the Western Pacific Islands at Suva, Fiji Islands. Information on communications, weather, and naval operations. Commonwealth activity in the Gilbert and Ellice Colonies, the Phoenix Islands, and the Line Islands.
4. The Nauru Island Connection. Proof that Earhart altered her route.
5. The United States/New Zealand Solar Eclipse Expedition in June 1937 to Canton Island. U.S.S. *Avocet* and H.M.S. *Wellington*.
6. The British (New Zealand) warships H.M.S. *Achilles* and H.M.S. *Wellington*.
7. The British agent on Hull Island, Captain John W. Jones.
8. The Odyssey. Captain Jones' boat. Hull to Sydney Island.
9. The Fanning Island Connection. North-of-the-equator flight.
10. The London Connection. Churchill. Eden. Cooper. The Trans-Pacific Air Line Connection.

OVERFLIGHT OF ITALIAN EAST AFRICA (ERITREA)

One of the more perplexing questions regarding Earhart's first flight attempt was whether she was doing reconnaissance, aerial or otherwise, for the United States government, or agencies thereof, or other interested parties. This question has been debated since Earhart was reported "missing." Those persons involved with the flight and those in governmental circles who know what happened have remained silent. Many have died. Some individuals claim to have heard radio messages from Earhart while she was overflying some of the Japanese Mandated Islands. Radio amateurs said they heard radio traffic, overflight messages which were subsequently classified, and sent from the *Itasca* to Coast Guard headquarters in San Francisco.

For five decades the "official" viewpoint has remained that she was lost, ran out of gas and ditched in the vicinity of Howland Island. A small group of researchers still endorse this belief. A number of researchers base their conclusions in large part on a book draft by Captain Laurance Safford, USN, titled "Amelia Earhart's Last Flight: A Tragedy of Errors." In this unfinished manuscript, Safford, who knew very little about aircraft, based his beliefs on a false premise. Apparently Earhart never received a weather message from Ocean Island. This message was that at 12,000 feet the winds were from the east at 30 knots. Therefore, he assumed that she was bucking 30-knot head winds throughout the second half of the flight. He concluded that she went down, out of gas, just east of the Gilbert Islands and west of the International Date Line, far short of her destination. His assumption was that she carried no fuel reserve and that flying against the unexpectedly severe head wind depleted the fuel supply. This assessment is not too surprising from a ship's officer of a one-dimensional service. Trips are from A to B at 15 knots and whatever weather occurs en route is accepted. Surprisingly, a number of other persons believed this illogical premise.

Most of the debate surrounding the aerial reconnaissance has been centered on the Japanese Class C mandate of Micronesia composed of the Caroline Islands, the Marshall Islands, and the Mariana Islands with the exception of Guam, which was United States territory. In *Amelia Earhart, The Myth and the Reality*, Dick Strippel hypothesized that with Guam 100 miles to the south of Saipan and the Marshall Islands within easy flying distance from Wake Island, any meaningful military aerial reconnaissance which necessitated periodic coverage for comparative analysis, could have been launched from these islands. The Marshall Islands were closest to the United States territory of Hawaii and the initial "target" in the U.S. Orange War Plan. Since the Marshalls are relatively close to Howland Island, they would have been the logical goal if Earhart's mission had been photo reconnaissance.

Another potential target on Earhart's world flight warrants close scrutiny as a positive target for aerial reconnaissance. Additionally, the myth that Earhart, allegedly being a "pacifist," would not indulge in aerial spying is also exposed as nonsense. The country involved is Italian Eritrea on the Red Sea. A careful look at her route chart, the fuel allocation chart, and the text in *Last Flight* is revealing.

Mussolini, the Italian dictator, used Eritrea as the northern springboard for the invasion of Ethiopia (October 1935 to May 1936). The first airport in Eritrea that Earhart visited was at Massawa, the closest port city to Italy. A majority of the troops and supplies for the invasion had passed through that port and airfield. Fuel location charts, dated 1 February 1937 by George Palmer Putnam had identified three airports in Eritrea: Massawa without a fuel cache, Assab with a fuel cache, and Asmara with a line drawn through the name. Earhart landed at Massawa, remained overnight and then flew on to Assab to refuel. Taking off for Assab she overflew the RAF base at Aden 175 miles away where there was another large fuel cache for a lengthy nonstop flight to the British base at Karachi, India.

Approval from Italian authorities for landing in Eritrea was late in arriving. The airfields at Massawa and Assab were approved in time for the second flight. A landing at Asmara, reported to have the largest airfield in Africa, was not allowed. Asmara, located 40 miles inland from the Red Sea and 7,000 feet above sea level on the Hamasien Plateau, was the principal bombing base used by the Italians against Addis Ababa in Ethiopia, and was a prime target for British aerial reconnaissance. Accomplishing this had been a goal of the British since 1935 because all three of these bases in Eritrea were on the British "Life Line of the Empire" through the Red Sea from Port Said to Aden. Additionally, Earhart had a personal interest in the possible reconquest of Eritrea because of her friendship with the "Flying Mollisons," Jim and Amy, who, in turn, were closely associated with Emperor Haile Selassie who was deposed during the Ethiopian War of 1935-36.

The flight over Eritrea was a detour from the normal global flight path. Initially, she planned to fly between the three RAF bases at Khartoum, Aden, and Karachi and fuel was provided at each one. When Italian authorities, including Air Marshall Italo Balboa, approved landings at Assab and Massawa, plans for a detour were made. Why?

Since 1935, the RAF had been making reconnaissance flights eight miles offshore over the Red Sea past Assab and Massawa, but they had been unable to penetrate the 40 miles into the interior to photograph the airfield at Asmara, the Eritrean capital.

If the "cover story" in *Last Flight* is carefully noted, Earhart wrote, "We flew not far from Asmara, 7,000 feet high, Eritrea's capital." Then, "Later I learned that on this Hamasien plateau is being constructed a large new airport . . ." and "as visibility was good . . ." What she did not write is that the airfield had already been through a major war and was reported to be the largest one in Africa. Further, the airfield was only five miles south-southwest from Asmara. With good visibility and the Electra flying "not far from Asmara" they most certainly could have seen both Asmara and the nearby airfield. Noonan, by pre-arrangement with the RAF airfield personnel at Khartoum, Anglo Egyptian Sudan, would have acquired an aerial camera for oblique shots from the RAF and secured it beneath the floorboards until reaching Karachi, India, where it was returned to the British RAF personnel. Interestingly, British Imperial Airways used flying boats for north/south traffic through Khartoum and those were landed on the Nile River. Flying boats were used on almost the entire route from London to Capetown in the 1930s because of the many rivers and lakes south of Cairo. The route became oceanic along the eastern coast of Africa on the Indian Ocean and turned inland further south.

Where is the documentary proof? Where are the signed confessions? Where are the photographs? International spying, by nature, is highly secretive and always has been. In the Powers U-2 incident and the KAL 007 incident, claims were made that navigational instruments malfunctioned. In the records of British espionage, a clearly-established RAF interest in Eritrea dated back to 1935. By 1939 Cotton was flying over the interior of this country in his long-range Lockheed 12 which had been purchased for him by the RAF and modified for photo reconnaissance. Earhart was interested in the defeat of the Italians there because of the Mollisons. If the RAF wasn't involved in Earhart's obvious detour to fly near the Asmara airfield for reconnaissance purposes, a good opportunity would have been missed. British objectives were to maintain the life line of the Empire, reconquer Ethiopia, and drive the Italians out of East Africa, all of which was accomplished in 1942.

BRITISH PARTICIPATION ACTIVITIES

The activities of the *Achilles* and the *Wellington* from 25 June to 9 July 1937 are worth noting, both individually and together. Apparently, both were involved in aeronautical matters during this period and beyond. Their arrival at Pago Pago on 25 June was timely and coincidental with Earhart's planned arrival in the islands north of Samoa. The significant fuel transfer from the *Achilles* to the *Wellington* (220 tons) in view of the stringent fuel economy measures being enforced, almost certainly meant a gift of oil to the New Zealand Navy. The five-day standby at Apia, Western Samoa, from 26-30 June 1937 indicated a wait for some anticipated event. The scheduling precludes this being the skipper's unplanned illness at Canton Island and hurried departure on 8 January 1937. A brief visit to the Tokelaus, which was followed by five days at Apia harbor, is indicative of some highly important anticipated event that overshadowed a routine visit by the acting commissioner of Western Samoa to the Tokelaus.

British light cruiser H.M.S. *Achilles* was en route from American Samoa to Honolulu when its radio operators picked up Earhart's radio messages from the Phoenix Islands. These signals were also picked up by radio station on Nauru Island.

Photo credit - Alexander Turnbull Library, Wellington, New Zealand

It should be apparent that the British High Commissioner did not commit half of his navy in support of Earhart's "civilian" stunt flight. The positioning of a light cruiser and modern escort vessel of the British Navy within close steaming distance of the Phoenix Group meant some covert activity was anticipated. Usually, radio operators on foreign naval vessels don't monitor aviation frequencies of 3105 and 6210 kc. The *Wellington*, rather than the *Achilles*, was to be the on-site ship. If the British aircraft didn't reach Canton Island or the Electra didn't quite make Hull Island, the *Wellington* crew could make a timely search for either. As it happened, the *Wellington* wasn't needed. Earhart made it to Hull Island and the British airplane went down north of the equator in the Japanese Marshall Islands. Quite possibly a radio operator in the Gilberts received a message from the pilot of the British aircraft giving the approximate location before the ditching.

The *Achilles* proceeded toward Honolulu after leaving supplies for the shipwrecked "sailors" and moving Burns-Philp store goods from Hull Island to Nassau Island, which is northeast of American Samoa.

U.S.S. *SWAN* LANDING PARTY ON CANTON ISLAND

Why did a landing party from the U.S.S *Swan* go ashore on Canton Island on 10 July 1937? Neither the ship's log nor United States Navy track charts show a landing party going ashore there. In the Honolulu, London, and Auckland newspapers, however, were articles which included information about this landing. *Swan* was an airplane tender and, like her sistership *Avocet*, was attached to PatWing2 at Pearl Harbor. When the *Avocet* left Canton Island on 10 June 1937 after the solar eclipse party departed, several things remained: two naval ratings, the radio installation erected on the island, and an aviation fuel cache of 1,000 gallons. The assignment of *Swan* personnel on 10 July 1937 was to recover personnel, equipment, and the fuel cache left a month previously by the U.S.S. *Avocet*, to ascertain if any fuel had been used, and note any airplane tire tracks on the island. The entire fuel cache was retrieved, and no evidence of tire tracks was seen.

When the *Achilles* stopped by Canton on 2 August 1937 on the return trip from Honolulu to Auckland, four naval ratings and radio equipment were taken ashore. Both countries had reneged on their diplomatic agreement to maintain the status quo of the island until ownership was resolved between the United States and Britain. After radio approval was received from the High Commission Office at Suva, a four-man occupation force was landed from *Achilles* on 2 August 1937 to establish possession of the island by occupancy.

THE BRITISH WEATHER REPORTING NETWORK

A baffling aspect of the Lae, New Guinea, to Howland Island leg of Earhart's flight was the weather network. While the weather was known for hundreds of miles at each end of the flight path, for the crucial center portion neither Nauru nor Ocean Island weather reports were officially solicited or received. These locations were only a few degrees off Earhart's flight path and turbulent weather was often encountered there. Generally from Lae to Ocean Island the winds were westerly and from there to Howland were easterly. Where these opposing winds came together, unstable and variable weather often occurred. Oddly, the reports from Fanning and Christmas

Islands, a thousand miles away, were part of the Earhart weather network. While the critical and mid-course weather at Ocean was not supplied to Earhart, the Fanning weather, of little consequence, was provided. The weather from Fanning, however, could have been useful on Earhart's later scheduled flight from Howland to Honolulu. In the *Itasca* radio log was a query to San Francisco Coast Guard Headquarters, "What has happened to our Fanning Island weather forecasts?" Actually, Pan American Airways (PAA) had established the weather station on Fanning in early 1937 to support the first Honolulu-to-Auckland flight via Kingman Reef and American Samoa in March of that year. A suitable radio station was established to transmit the weather to Honolulu. Though Fanning Island was a "cable" station, several members of that crew were trained to make weather observations and transmit forecasts by radio. The facility only operated when needed to support PAA flights and not on a regular basis. A total of three belated weather forecasts were received from Fanning Island, and they were relayed by the cable station supply ship, the S. S. *Dickenson*, some 200 miles north of Fanning. One might suspect that the radio messages from Fanning were not weather related at all, but encoded notification to mission personnel that the Fanning Island "bird" was ready to fly.

One can't help but compare this bungled weather and communications arrangement when the available and vitally needed facilities were ignored and weather a thousand miles east of Howland was included in the net. On the PAA flight from Honolulu to New Zealand in March 1937, a compact Adcock high-frequency D\F range finder had been mounted on the PAA support ship *Northwind* at Kingman Reef. It brought in the PAA clipper ship to a 500-yard long sand spit in mid-ocean, but that was civilian efficiency. The *Itasca* D\F was worthless on Earhart's flight. Small wonder that the government effort has been called a "tragedy of errors."

THE AUSTRALIA AND NEW GUINEA CONNECTION

Originally planned by Commander Clarence W. Williams, USNR (Retired), Earhart's final route around the world had had many changes. How much of this was covertly motivated and how much was genuine indecision is uncertain. It is difficult to see how an alleged course across the North Pacific with aerial refueling over Midway Island, as noted in naval correspondence, with a Tokyo, Japan, landfall, conforms to an "equatorial" route. Among other routes discussed were those through Brisbane, Australia, and Port Moresby, New Guinea. Rabaul, New Britain, which had the best airfield in the New Guinea area, wasn't even considered. Initially, in March 1937, her route westward was across the Middle East and the northern part of Africa. This was north of Arabia and followed the British, French, and Dutch air routes. It continued to Cairo, Egypt, and thence along the northern continental shore of Africa, and then south along the Atlantic shore to Dakar. By 1 February 1937, all of these diversions, real or covertly inspired, had been cancelled and the "real" route decided. Fuel and oil were provisioned along the route by the oil interests.

Two principal developments made the equatorial route possible. The first was the switching of a Department of the Interior project from Jarvis Island, where it belonged, to Howland Island to accommodate Earhart. The second was the benevolence of the British

Royal Air Force during the planning of the March 1937 flight. The British set up a southern route between the RAF base at Karachi and Aden which would bypass Arabia. The course line went from the RAF base at Aden to the RAF base at Khartoum, Anglo Egyptian Sudan.

The Eritrean "detour" came after Earhart, taking advantage of her friendship with Italian Air Force Marshal Balbo, received permission to land there. The flight between Khartoum and Karachi would have broken new ground regarding air routes, as the legs from Lae to Howland to Honolulu would have. These were never completed and were the only "new" mileage on Earhart's alleged world airway she was pioneering on her world flight. During World War II, after the reconquest of Italian East Africa, the routes between Khartoum, Aden, and Karachi became important for military air transport, with many B-25s flown through Persia to Russia. Following the war, the same routes were opened to commercial carriers. Thus the 1,920-mile segment of her flight did pioneer a future useful air route. To keep up pretexts, Earhart used the fuel cache at Assab to avoid a direct flight to the RAF base at Aden. How ridiculous and so obvious was the duplicate fuel and oil cache 175 miles away. The cover story of the possibility of "contrary winds" at Aden might fool the uninitiated, but the RAF used the base extensively, regardless of hypothetical or real hindrances from meteorological phenomena.

From Karachi in West India, Earhart followed the established Imperial Airways route through Calcutta, Rangoon, and Singapore to Port Darwin, Australia. One minor deviation was a landing at a Dutch East Indies military and commercial base at Bandoeng. The subsequent route from Port Darwin to Lae, New Guinea, a former German colony mandated to Australia after World War I, followed a route used by New Guinea airlines.

Most of the flight from Oakland eastward to Lae had been over established air routes, had used reasonably good airports, and used 87- and 100-octane fuel from the United States prepositioned along the route. She had done predominantly daytime flying with prearranged or volunteered mechanical assistance. Under these conditions, radio contact was unnecessary and navigation was mainly by dead reckoning and pilotage. The South Atlantic crossing had required celestial navigation and involved only flying at night. At Lae, with 22,000 miles behind her, the remaining 7,000 miles were the real challenge. Denied her was efficient assistance which might have been offered by governmental agencies. The difference between the efficient civilian PAA trans-Pacific flights in March-April 1937, which were highly successful, and dismal July support of Earhart's ocean flight is appalling. The Australians at Darwin and Lae provided support as had been done at other Commonwealth stops.

THE BRITISH HIGH COMMISSIONER
FOR THE WESTERN PACIFIC ISLANDS

In the 1930s, when the sun never set on the British Empire, the British High Commissioner for the Western Pacific Islands was looking out for British interests half a world away from England. His headquarters were at Suva, Fiji Islands, the "crossroads of the Southwest Pacific." Using the "All-Red" cable network which circled the globe, London was only a few minutes away. The British trans-Pacific cable went from Vancouver, British Columbia, passed through Suva

where a relay station and terminal were located, and continued to Sydney, Australia. By the 1930s, a wireless communication network connected the British Empire. Regarding communications, Suva was favorably situated with radio/cable United Kingdom outlets and commercial and naval ships from Australia and New Zealand, Honolulu, and the United States Navy stopping at the harbor. In addition, the High Commissioner had de facto control over the itinerary of four of His Majesty's warships on loan to the Royal New Zealand Navy. In the late 1930s, these were: *Achilles*, *Leander*, *Wellington*, and *Leith*.

The area of the High Commissioner's jurisdiction covered the western Pacific islands and a significant part of the central Pacific islands. His territory included Australia and New Zealand and the sphere of naval interests extended north above the Hawaiian Islands. A number of islands within those boundaries, however, were owned or claimed by other powers. The northern boundary extended along the equator to the Japanese-mandated Caroline and Marshall Islands. The British-ruled territory extended north of the equator in two places, the Gilbert Islands and the northern islands of Fanning and Washington.

Although vast oceanic distances were involved, the land area was relatively small. Travel in the 1930s was primarily by ship, and generally slow and irregular. Airline development was begun with both east-west and southwest routes across the Pacific. Australian air pioneers were attempting to reduce the typical three-week transit time by steamer to five or six days by air with overnight stops at connecting islands.

Politically, in the early days of the territory, during the late 19th century, the High Commissioner, usually a lord, was located in Suva and had jurisdiction over all British Islands. Later, in the 20th century, until the seat of government was moved to the Solomon Islands, the High Commissioner was also the governor of the Fiji Islands. This brief overview of British interests in the western and central Pacific is essential to a full understanding of their involvement in the critical last stages of Earhart's flight which flew through the British-controlled islands.

Names such as Khartoum, Karachi, Singapore, Port Darwin, Lae, Suva, Fanning Island and the Phoenix Islands kept appearing with reference to the flight and the subsequent search. Additionally, Captain John Jones, who met Lt. Lambrecht on the lagoon at Hull during the search of the Phoenix Islands, and the KHAQQ radio intercept by a radio operator aboard the *Achilles* on 2 July 1937 are all British-connected facts of Earhart's last flight.

Few, if any, of these factors have been examined in depth and most have been dismissed as inconsequential. A thorough investigation, however, has proved them to be highly relevant. The leg east from Khartoum is revealing. The Port Darwin stop is significant. The flight past Nauru Island is of interest. The meeting with Jones on the lagoon at Hull was the crux of the USN search and its true significance was denied to the public because the information had been withheld from the Imperial Japanese Navy. The Fanning Island airfield opens a new dimension and an explanation and rationale for the "above the equator" activity on 2 July 1937 relative to the British overlay flight.

THE NAURU ISLAND CONNECTION

Neither Nauru Island nor Ocean Island was included in the weather network for Earhart's flight. The

British escort ship H.M.S. *Wellington* spent May and June 1937 in vicinity of Canton Island, first with New Zealand Solar Eclipse party. After refueling from the H.M.S. *Achilles* in Pago Pago harbor, she stood by for duty in Phoenix Group.

Photo credit - National Archives Negative #80-G-410142

Ontario, on station south of Nauru as a mobile checkpoint, was so close to the above two islands that the difference in miles on a long flight would have been almost negligible. As to the "ship in sight ahead" being the *Myrtlebank*, one might assume that this was a coded message for seeing the lights of the phosphate mines on Nauru and an overt message to convince the IJN that she was on course with the *Ontario* in sight.

THE BRITISH PHOENIX CONNECTION

The British Phoenix Island Group consisted of eight islands below the equator. In the early part of the 20th century, both Howland and Baker Islands were sometimes considered a northward extension of the Phoenix Group. Prior to 1935, their connection was purely academic because, following the depletion of the high grade of guano in the 19th century by the United States and British commercial interests, the islands were forgotten. In 1935, events changed the lethargy of the Central Pacific. The Imperial Japanese Navy became more aggressive. Military rivalry became ongoing between the United States and Britain in 1935 and subsequent years over ownership of strategic central Pacific islands useful as landing places for both land and seaplanes. Howland, Baker, and Jarvis were occupied by the United States in 1935.

THE BRITISH WARSHIPS
H.M.S. *ACHILLES* AND H.M.S. *WELLINGTON*

The comprehensive accounts of the search for Earhart contain references to the *Achilles*. Few have read anything about the *Wellington* in connection with activities in the Central Pacific or the Earhart mission. In spite of the fact that the communications department on the *Achilles* made the only positive radio intercept from the Earhart airplane on 2 July 1937 hours after it had terminated its flight from Lae, this important fact has been ignored. The reasons are similar to those associated with Jones at Hull Island. He was British and, therefore, would be hard to trace. These suppositions are both untrue. Secondly, their impact was not inconsequential. These activities were to divert attention from the prime area and parties most involved. The *Wellington* had been at Canton Island with the New Zealand Solar Eclipse Party of 8 June 1937, three weeks before Earhart was scheduled to land at Howland, some 300 miles northwest. In this area, 300 miles would be considered "nearby," "in the vicinity."

Aboard the *Wellington* and *Achilles* were naval officers and civilian specialists who were surveying islands from Midway Island, northwest of Hawaii, to Sunday Island, a day's steaming from Auckland to islands as far east as Pitcairn. The H.M.S. *Leander* was also used for this purpose from 1937 to 1941. The survey was to assess islands for landing fields and/or seaplane bases. To understand the roles of the *Achilles* and the *Wellington* in the Pacific Ocean, a brief review of the New Zealand Navy in the 1920s and 1930s is necessary. In World War I, New Zealand had no navy and might not have had one until World War II except that British Lord Jellicoe[1], the hero of Jutland, decided to retire from the admiralty and accept the post of Governor General in New Zealand. Naturally, a former Royal Navy person of his stature could not tolerate a country, no matter how small, that had no navy. Beginning in 1920, a succession of H.M.S. vessels were loaned to New Zealand and local recruits were gradually trained as crews. A few selected officers were also commissioned after being trained in Australia or British naval schools. Some of the early cruisers loaned to New Zealand were intercepted on the way to the breakers yard. By the mid-1930s, two light cruisers of recent vintage, the *Achilles* and a sister ship, the H.M.S. *Leander*, were stationed in New Zealand. Two other ships there were the H.M.S. *Wellington* and the H.M.S. *Leith*, escort ships 250 feet long having small caliber cannons. All had predominantly British crews. The principal port of the New Zealand Navy was at Auckland, while naval headquarters was at Wellington, the capital.

The command structure of this four-ship navy was unusual. Although the Senior Naval Officer at Wellington was in tactical command of the ships, the British High

---

1 Agar, Augustus (Captain, Royal Navy). *Showing the Flag*. London: Evans Bros., Ltd., 1962.

Commissioner actually had the final approval of overall deployment of all H.M.S. ships in the Western Pacific. In the 1937 era, almost all cruises began or terminated at Suva, Fiji Islands. Exceptions were joint tactical operations to the west with the Australian Navy or the annual cruise to the islands of French Polynesia far to the east and scattered British islands. Another pertinent factor was the huge area of responsibility of the New Zealand Navy.

Since 1920, a close rapport had existed between the New Zealand Navy and the Unites States Navy in American Samoa. British, or Western, Samoa was a New Zealand Class C mandate. Administering a colony of its size and population was a challenge to a small country such as New Zealand, the officials of which had no previous experience in overseas administration except for the military occupation of the German colony of Western Samoa during World War I. Apia had been a significant port since the middle of the 19th century but was bypassed by the major British and American ocean liners after 1920. The British sea route to Australia went through Suva. The American routes were from Pago Pago to Suva to Australia and from Auckland to Pago Pago on the return trip north.

The New Zealand Chief Administrative Officer of Western Samoa was the counterpart of the Naval Governor of American Samoa. The respective philosophy of governing the two "colonies" was completely different. Western Samoa was profit-oriented while American Samoa was a native-oriented protectorate. In the 1920s and 1930s, respective administrators made annual, or occasionally more frequent, visits to the territory in their jurisdictions. Additionally, a New Zealand government steamer made monthly visits to Wellington, Auckland, Suva, and Apia. The Royal Navy vessels also made Apia a port of call on all trips north from New Zealand. Because American Samoa was administered by United States naval personnel, the New Zealand Navy, both officers and enlisted men, considered it a first-class liberty port. A stop at Apia was almost always coupled by a corresponding visit at nearby Pago Pago. Before World War II, no direct diplomatic relationship existed between Wellington, New Zealand, and Washington, D.C. Communications were accomplished via the British ambassador, the United States Navy at American Samoa, and the frequent visits by New Zealand warships. This was a "sidedoor" diplomatic channel that Roosevelt, for one, was not adverse to using.

In the years immediately prior to World War II, the New Zealand Navy consisted of four excellent ships. These two cruisers and two useful escort vessels were scheduled for lengthy summer and winter cruises over territory patrolled by the New Zealand Navy. Every year at least one visit by a warship was made to each British island possession in the High Commissioner's domain. Frequently, he went on a cruise to make personal visits as the need arose. The annual itinerary of each ship was planned in advance and was approved by him in his de facto role as Royal Naval Commander in Chief, Pacific Ocean.

Itineraries could be changed to some degree if some unexpected event occurred. Due to strict allocation of fuel, deviation from a planned itinerary had to be approved by the Senior Naval Officer, the Commander of the New Zealand Navy, the New Zealand Naval officer in Wellington, and the British High Commissioner at Suva.

When modern naval radio communication became a reality, an emergency authorization was only a few radio messages away. The May through August 1937 itineraries of the *Achilles* and *Wellington* relative to the Northern Phoenix Islands are worth examining.

The *Achilles* radio intercept from KHAQQ on 2 July 1937 is known because it was released to the press. Its interpretation is especially important because the captain emphatically denied its receipt after his ship arrived at Honolulu. Also, his Hull Island reference was deleted in further references, thus revealing its sensitive nature.

The actions of both the *Achilles* and *Wellington* are important from 25 June 1937 until their returns to port in August. On 25 June, they were both in Pago Pago harbor, American Samoa. On this date, according to a previously-arranged schedule, Earhart was to depart from Lae, New Guinea. The Commander of the New Zealand station was aboard the *Achilles*, so exactly one-half of the combat force of the New Zealand Navy, including its flagship and only flag officer, was in an American port on this particular date. The *Wellington* was refueled from the *Achilles*, taking aboard 220 tons of fuel oil. This, for a ship with a total capacity of 250 tons of fuel oil, indicated that the *Wellington* had been low indeed on oil. Those 220 tons of oil were not needed for her to complete her cruise and return to Auckland. She was being readied for some hard steaming and departed Pago Pago after dark to make the short trip to Apia, Western Samoa. As a local pilot was required to enter Apia harbor, she did so the following morning. With full tanks and in radio contact with the High Command at Suva and the Commodore commanding the New Zealand Navy, in nearby Pago Pago, she stood by for five days until departing Apia on 30 June 1937. That day Earhart arrived at Lae. Instead of the ship following her schedule of going east, she went north to a position just south of the Phoenix Islands. After it became known that Earhart had safely landed at Hull Island, and the British airplane was down in the Marshalls, the *Wellington* was directed to resume her normal cruise.

According to the *Achilles* log, she also departed Pago Pago on 30 June 1937, but this is in conflict with the captain's comments when arriving at Honolulu a fortnight later and at Auckland a month later. At those times, he said that the *Achilles* had stopped to leave supplies at Hull Island to succor some shipwrecked sailors. *Achilles* log entries are not supportive of this statement.

Achilles left the U.S. naval station at American Samoa and headed northward toward Honolulu for a "good will" visit. On 2 July 1937, she was southeast of the Phoenix Islands and made the KHAQQ radio intercept which the Commander released by radio to the press.

A number of questionable factors are obvious regarding the *Achilles* and her activities: (1) the fuel transfer; (2) the five-day layover; (3) the monitoring of aircraft frequencies; (4) the release of the Earhart message to the press; (5) the release of Hull Island information to the press; (6) the refueling at Honolulu with comparatively expensive United States fuel oil; (7) the retraction of the KHAQQ transmission; (8) the taking of civilians off Hull Island; (9) the taking of a British radio operator to Christmas Island; (10) the stops at Fanning Island, Canton Island, and Hull Island; (11) identifying Captain John Jones as a British official; (12) the repeat of the "shipwrecked sailors" story regarding Hull Island; (13)

British-owned Fanning Island, 1,000 miles south of Hawaii, had tidal flat airstrip which was prepared in 1934 for the trans-Pacific flight attempts by Kingsford-Smith and Charles Ulm.
Photo credit - National Archives Negative #111-SC-11888

the conflicting dates between the log and what actually occurred; (14) the mention of the wrong island (Nassau) in the *Achilles* report concerning the shipwrecked sailors when it was Hull Island.

One can only conclude that the involvement of the New Zealand Navy in the Earhart search was substantial, and that there must have been British interests at stake as well. The planned arrival of the British overflight airplane at Canton Island could have been the real reason.

THE BRITISH AGENT AT HULL ISLAND

The search for Amelia Earhart and Fred Noonan officially extended from 2 July to 18 July 1937. As described elsewhere, it was conducted by one United States Coast Guard cutter, several United States naval ships, and many aircraft. During this period millions of square miles were searched and only two white men contacted: the resident manager at Hull Island on 9 July and the deputy resident manager at Beru Island in the Gilberts on 14 July. The Hull Island contact was made by naval personnel Cadet Wilson and Lt. Lambrecht when the latter landed an O3U-3 floatplane on the lagoon. The resident manager at Beru, Gilbert Islands, was contacted by a landing party from the Coast Guard cutter *Itasca* while those islands were being searched. From a diplomatic standpoint, approval for these searches was never requested from the appropriate British sources by the U.S. State Department. British sovereignty over the Gilbert and Ellice Colony was recognized by the United States. The May 1937 annexation of the Phoenix Group as an extension of this colony, however, was not recognized by the State Department, that is, the Roosevelt Administration in July 1937. After the search of the Gilbert Group and the Phoenix Group had essentially been completed, permission was requested of the resident administrator at Ocean Island for the previously conducted search.

A brief report of the encounter between Lambrecht and Jones was released to the newspapers. Not given in this were Jones' name, his employer, his tenure on the island, his nationality, or the nationality of

the natives. All that was reported was that some 40 natives were in residence on the island being directed by an unidentified white manager, who said he had not seen or heard an airplane, and had not heard of Earhart's flight from listening on his radio receiver. Also, he had exhibited great surprise when told that the floatplane had not come from Honolulu, but had been launched from a nearby warship. According to the newspaper account, the men parted company and Lambrecht flew back to the *Colorado*. Apparently nothing of significance was officially attached to this encounter. The intent of the newspaper release was to acknowledge that it had occurred, negate its importance, and divert further attention from that episode.

Lambrecht wrote an eight-page report on the aerial search from the battleship *Colorado*, but this did not become available for more than 30 years, when the FOIA came into effect. The actual events during this encounter on the lagoon at Hull Island and what was reported to the public were diametrically opposed. The overseer told Lambrecht that his name was Captain John W. Jones, that he was from Apia, Western Samoa, that he worked for Burns-Philp South Seas Company, and that the natives were from the Tokelau Islands, just south of the Phoenix Group. He further stated that he had a high-powered radio transmitter which he used to keep in touch with the outside world. The story given to the press was a cover-up. The *Colorado* fliers had found a high-powered transmitter which undoubtedly was the source of the radio emissions from the Phoenix Group. Yet, no further investigation was made, and the existence of the radio was kept secret by naval orders.

Both documentary and first-person evidence are existent for the preceding statements. When one of the four *Colorado* fliers, Capt. William Sullivan, USN (Ret.), was interviewed, he recalled that it was well known aboard the *Colorado* after the Hull Island flight that the white resident manager had a "high-powered radio transmitter on the island."

When the USCG cutter *Taney* stopped at Hull Island four months later, Jones went aboard and reported the same story. This evidence was included in the cruise report of the *Taney* for October 1937, a document which was classified for more than 30 years. Not classified was Jones' presence on Hull Island. The late Edwin H. Bryan, Jr., of the Bishop Museum in Honolulu identified Jones in a 1942 book *American Polynesia and the Hawaiian Chain.*

Captain John Jones' beautiful daughters, Jane and Heather, born, respectively on Hull Island in 1937 and 1938. Daughters said that their father was working as an agent for both British and United States naval intelligence while on Hull Island from 1937 to 1940.

Photo credit - Via Heather Jones

THE CAPTAIN JONES-UNITED STATES NAVY (TUTUILA) CONNECTION

When interviewed, Jones' two blood daughters, Heather and Jane (married names withheld by agreement) stated that their father was an active agent for both British and United States naval intelligence while at Hull Island from 1937 to 1940. The truth of this is easily established from records in the New Zealand National Archives with reference to British authorities in the Western Pacific area. Documents which can be cited include:

    1. H.M.S. *Achilles* cruise report, May through August 1937.

    2. Request for "legal" radio for Hull Island, PIM reference.

    3. Royal Navy reference to Jones as "Phoenix Island" resident manager.

    4. Jones' report to the High Commissioner on use of Hull Island as a landing field (New Zealand State Archives).

    5. Further activities:

        a. Union Jack in evidence October 1937 (USCG *Taney* cruise report).

        b. Jones rehired by British authorities in 1938.

        c. Radio communications with Canton Island and Ocean Island.

        d. Integration of Gilbert natives and retirement of Tokelau natives.

In available records, little documentary evidence exits that Jones was actively employed as an intelligence agent by the United States Navy through the naval station at Pago Pago. Such documents, if available, were still classified as of 1987. Sufficient actions of the United States Navy and United States Coast Guard prove that Jones was indeed an intelligence agent for the United States Navy. One action was the *Colorado's* trip from Honolulu on 4 July 1937 and another the floatplane landing on the Hull lagoon on 9 July. One definite topic of conversation on board was, "Where did the spurious radio signals received on the aircraft frequencies come from?" When Lambrecht returned to the ship after talking to Jones at Hull, he knew their source was Jones' high-powered radio. This and other facts learned from Jones, including his name, were not released to the public. Prior to 1987, one of the four surviving aviators from the *Colorado* revealed that it was well known aboard the ship (after the lagoon landing) that Jones had a high-powered transmitter on Hull. He had to be the source of the signals.

This cover-up, directed from Washington D.C., is proof that Jones was, in fact, working for the United States Navy. The same information was recorded in the *Taney* log. The *Taney* cruise reports of 1937 and 1938, during which stops at Hull Island were logged, were classified "confidential" for 30 years, thus protecting this sensitive information.

In addition to these obvious USN and USCG cover-ups which prove collusion between Roosevelt, Morgenthau, and a foreign national (British citizen), other indications exist that Jones was in radio contact with Naval Radio Tutuila in June and July 1937. Information regarding the safe landing site on the lagoon at Hull, and moving Earhart and Noonan to Sydney Island before the arrival of the floatplane from the *Colorado*, indicate prior knowledge only obtainable by U.S. naval radio contact from Tutuila, American Samoa.

While the British intelligence case can be proved with documentation, the U.S. Navy case is more illusive. During interviews, it has been established Jones' daughters were of that opinion. Jones' visits to ports such as Suva, Fiji, Pago Pago, and his earlier trips aboard a New Zealand inter-island ship as a maritime officer, acquainted him with many South Seas ports. After 1933 and the repeal of Prohibition in the United States and its possessions, beer and liquor were not only legal but inexpensive, especially at the U.S. naval station at Pago Pago. The nearest foreign port of call was Apia in American Samoa, a mere 65 miles away. As radio operator at the Western Upolu plantation, where he worked, his Morse Code "fist" was well known to radio operators at the U.S. Naval Station.

Backup transportation by coastal motor vessel from Savaii Island across to Upolu Island and along the northern coast to Apia and from there to Pago Pago was often used to make connections with the Matson liners S. S. *Monterey* and S. S. *Mariposa* on their runs between Honolulu and Australia/New Zealand.

Jones was a veteran of World War I due to his service in the British merchant marine. Because the "red" ensign in wartime became part of the Royal Navy "white" ensign, he was entitled to wear his Maritime Captain's uniform with World War I campaign ribbons. In full dress uniform, he would have been a welcome guest at the USN Officers' Club at Goat Island in Pago Pago Harbor.

Lagoon at Fanning Island harbored secret tidal flat airstrip of 6,000 feet. This was available from 1934, when prepared for Kingsford-Smith and Ulm, and used infrequently until 1970.
Photo credit - National Archives Negative #80-G-11886

In 1936 Jones attracted considerable attention in the Samoas by sitting on a maritime court of inquiry on the loss of the motor vessel which steamed between Apia and Pago Pago. Because this vessel had been a major link between the two harbors and took passengers for the American liners, the naval governor of American Samoa was concerned with the outcome of that proceeding.

Thus, the white communities of both Samoas shared much common ground and a maritime officer at one port would most certainly be most welcome at the other. Periodic visits of the naval station ships at Upolu (Apia) and New Zealand (British) warships at Pago Pago on their annual summer and winter cruises were common occurrences. Actually, Jones was initially employed at Hull Island by Burns-Philp (South Seas) Co., Ltd., with headquarters at Suva, Fiji Islands. The company was a subsidiary of Burns-Philp (Sydney, Australia), and had retail stores at both Apia and Pago Pago in the 1930s.

Within this framework, Jones was certainly known to the naval officers at Pago Pago. Just why Burns-Philp decided to send him to Hull Island and Sydney Island as plantation manager in May 1937 with Tokelau natives and knowing that the British had annexed the islands to the Gilbert and Ellice colonies and were going to colonize the productive ones with excess Gilbertese natives, is not clear. The company must have known that its investment would soon have to be sacrificed to the "crown." They couldn't recoup their start-up costs before the British took over and the price paid for "improvements" would be minimal.

One can only surmise that a covert deal between the British and Burns-Philp was arranged so that the Crown could establish a presence on the islands to preclude colonization by the United States. Shown in

New Zealand archival records is that the British regarded Hull Island, not Canton Island, as a superior land/sea base for aircraft in 1936-37.

If Jones' blood daughters are correct, he was also acting as an agent for the United States naval authorities at Pago Pago while at Hull Island. He had a good plantation management background and was a radio operator strategically located 600 miles north of that naval station. Initially, as a civilian and free agent, he could have agreed to keep in radio contact with United States naval authorities. Just as Jones disliked and distrusted German nationals because of his World War I experiences, he liked and trusted persons from the United States, according to Heather, his elder daughter. No documentary proof can be offered that Jones was in radio contact with the United States Navy, but the following evidence can be given:

1. Earhart knew where to land on Hull Island.
2. She also knew how to positively identify it from the large copra shed with the conspicuous red roof on the west point of the island.
3. Lambrecht knew he could land safely in the lagoon.
4. A cover-up of the encounter on the lagoon occurred both before and after World War II.
5. Jones experienced a rapid (four month) promotion from a civilian to Deputy High Commissioner of the British Western Pacific Islands.
6. After his return to Upolu Island, Western Samoa, he was rehired by New Zealand Crown Estates (Western Samoa).

THE BRITISH-FANNING ISLAND CONNECTION
Fanning Island was well known in the early part of this century for two reasons. First it was a key link on the

Entrance to English harbor in lagoon at Fanning Island. British cable relay station at Fanning Island linked Vancouver, British Columbia, with Suva, Fiji Islands in world-girdling "All-Red" cable network.
Photo credit - National Archives Negative #80-G-409700

Pacific Ocean "All Red" cable system which circled the globe. Second, the cable station had been attacked, the cable cut, and the facilities damaged soon after the beginning of World War I. Not much was heard from Fanning thereafter until World War II began. Then, according to the British War Plan, New Zealand provided a small defensive force to protect the cable station from a repeat performance as had occurred during World War I.

Not until 1932 was the potential of Fanning Island as an airport first visualized. The first person to designate Fanning as a potential refueling point between Hawaii and the Fiji Islands was the noted Australian navigator Harold Gatty. Fellow countrymen Kingsford-Smith and Ulm had "made arrangements" to use Fanning as a possible refueling stop on their respective trans-Pacific flights in late 1934. The 6,000 foot runway on the tidal flats on the lagoon side of the southern rim of the atoll was prepared

for both men and aviation fuel stocked there. Not used by the fliers in 1934, the site remained as an emergency airfield until the mid-1960s when the lessees of the former cable company facilities built a strip for light aircraft on the northwest rim of the island.

Kingsford-Smith's flights across the Pacific from east to west in 1928 in a tri-motored Fokker named the *Southern Cross* and the November 1934 west-to-east crossing from Brisbane to Suva to Hawaii to Oakland in the *Lady Southern Cross* have been summarized previously in this book. Ulm's unsuccessful attempt to make an east-to-west trans-Pacific crossing in December 1934 is much more germane. Since the early 1920s, both he and Kingsford-Smith had been trying to close this final 7,500-mile "Pacific Gap" on the "All-Red" airline. Trans-Canada Airlines ended at Vancouver and Australian Airlines extended to Auckland, New Zealand. Neither Kingsford-

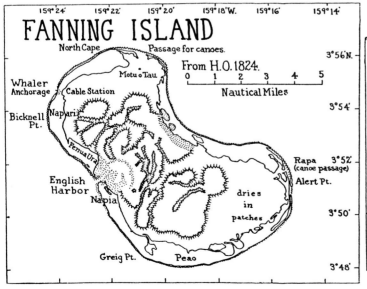

Overt (Commercial) map of British Fanning Island

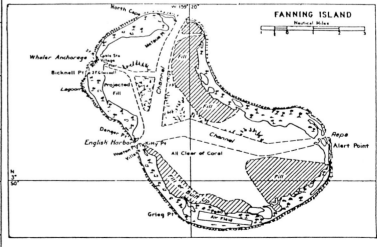

Covert (Military) map of British Fanning Island showing hidden 6,000 foot airstrip, 1934
(U.S. Office of Naval Intelligence Report)

Smith nor Ulm were wealthy, and the $500,000 needed for equipment to start such a service was far beyond their grasp. All they could hope to do was demonstrate the feasibility of making the crossing on donations and their own capital resources.

Ulm became interested in an Envoy built by the newly-established Airspeed Company of Portsmouth, England. This was a twin-engine cabin-type transport with fuselage tanks for extended-range operation. Most important, it was constructed of wood, and a cable inquiry brought the astounding news that the factory price was only £4,000 ($20,000) or about half of any similar aircraft which could be used for his trans-Pacific flight. Ulm's bank loans were guaranteed by the Australian government to purchase the aircraft, equip it with overwater navigational instruments, install fuselage tanks holding 600 gallons of gasoline, and pay en route and flight expenses. He had located an affordable airplane, knew that the tidal airstrip on Fanning would be available, and that summer weather prevailed below the equator. Unfortunately, in his hurried preparation, he cut too many corners. Most importantly, his disdain for carrying a rubber raft was both his and his crew's undoing.

Beyond Ulm's reckless behavior for attempting a flight without thorough preparation was the fact that just as he was trying to promote a landplane route southwest across the Pacific, he, paradoxically, caused the exact opposite to occur. PAA flying boats took over across-the-Pacific routes. Earhart's two failures to make Howland Island in March and July 1937 and the onset of World War II delayed commercial landplane crossing service for the Pacific Ocean for essentially a decade.

THE LONDON CONNECTION

To present a detailed analysis of the interrelation between His Majesty's Government (HMG) in London and the Western Pacific Islands half a world away is beyond the scope of this book. Prioritywise, the Western Pacific was far down on the British list in 1937. Of interest here is the connection between these remote outposts of Empire and London. Also included is a brief outline of the potential for further investigation by interested parties.

From 1935 on, a steady deterioration of national relationships in Europe continued until total war broke out in September 1939. In 1935-36 Mussolini, Italy's fascist dictator, invaded Ethiopia, and in May 1936, that territory was united as Italian Northeast Africa. During the Italian invasion, the Mediterranean Fleet of the Royal Navy went on full war mobilization and was reinforced by units from around the world. At home, the German arms buildup under Hitler, particularly the air arm, finally had loosened enough money from the British government to start the "home chain" RAF Stations and begin to procure RAF Fighter Command aircraft. Later in 1936, Civil War broke out in Spain between Loyalist forces supported by communist Russia and fascist forces supported by Hitler and Mussolini.

With Europe occupying center stage, news of the Western Pacific was relegated to the back pages of London newspapers. In 1935, the RAF obtained a realistic portion of defense funds, the Royal Navy received the largest portion, and the British Army became the doormat of the services. Aerial reconnaissance was not forgotten by the RAF after World War I, and steps were initiated in 1935 to continue this lost art. Italian Eritrea was a paramount target of RAF interest in the years just prior to World War II and by 1939 the need for specially-equipped aircraft for the long-range photographic missions was recognized and funded. Because a few bombs, delivered by German Zeppelins, had fallen on England in World War I, the English feared massive air raids. Their strategic planning called for maintaining the balance of power on the mainland and bombing the European dictators into submission in the event of open war. The tremendous cost in lives and materials which had occurred in the static trench warfare of World War I was to be avoided at all costs.

The use of Australian civilian Sydney Cotton and the purchase of proven United States aircraft for aerial espionage may come as a surprise to some Britons. In 1939 three Lockheed 12s were procured by the RAF for this operation, passing two on to French Air Force Intelligence for the same purpose. The RAF high-level decision to "buy American" to procure suitable aircraft was a departure from standard practice. The importance of foreign aerial reconnaissance was recognized and considerable funds were spent on covert aerial reconnaissance of potentially strategic targets in the years prior to World War II.

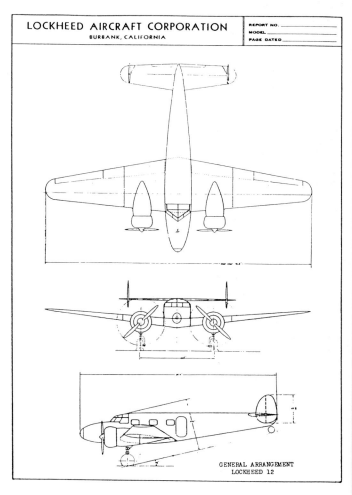

3-View Drawing of Lockheed 12

In the Pacific, the Commonwealth countries of Australia and New Zealand were working in cooperation with the United States Navy. In early 1937, information on the planning of Earhart's mission had most certainly reached the Royal Navy, the Royal Air Force, and joint military intelligence planners in London. With aerial spying on potential opponents' territory in Europe and Africa acknowledged and the United States/Australia/New Zealand connection known, there were reciprocal espionage activities in the Pacific, as well.

Lockheed Electra Model 12 was used by British Air Intelligence expert Sydney Cotton. Three airplanes of this type were purchased by the Royal Air Force in the late 1930s.
Photo credit - Lockheed - California Company

An interesting pattern can be seen developing. In 1937, Anthony Eden was Foreign Secretary and Alfred Duff Cooper was First Lord of the Admiralty. Both were senior proteges of Winston S. Churchill. These three men were key members of the so-called "British War Party." This "shadow government" could have been more involved in covert foreign affairs in 1937 than the British government itself. Eden and Cooper were ideally situated to implement Churchill's directed foreign policy against the dictators.[2, 3, 4]

The intent here is to present a brief background of pre-World War II covert foreign activities conducted from London. Some have been acknowledged, but others may still be under security restrictions. The full extent of Churchill's behind-the-scenes control of British affairs, including his years-long relationship with Roosevelt (prior to World War II) has barely been documented.

As previously discussed, persuasive evidence from 1944 onward suggests that a Caucasian woman and man overflew the Marshall Islands in 1937. This couple was not Earhart and Noonan, and their airplane was not an Electra. The British have commercial interests in the Pacific many times greater than the United States. Considering prior involvement in the Eritrea overflight in Northeast Africa, an extension of aerial espionage to the Pacific appears logical. This period involved an exchange

---

[2] Eden, Anthony, *The Eden Memoirs—Facing the Dictators*. London: Cassel & Company, Ltd., 1962.

[3] Cooper, Alfred Duff. *Old Men Forget*. London: Rupert Hart-Davis, 1953.

[4] Churchill, Winston S. *The Second World War—The Gathering Storm*. Boston: Houghton Mifflin Co. 1948.

of technical information among the Royal Navy, the Royal Air Force, and the U.S. Navy. Although the RAF had been experimenting with photoflash bombs since World War I, they lacked General George Goddard's synchronization equipment to make nighttime aerial photography practical.

SUMMARY OF THE BRITISH CONNECTION
1. Goerner, Gervais, Devine, Davidson and others have written books promulgating the north-of-the-equator theory.
2. Of importance is the KHAQQ intercept made by the radio department aboard the *Achilles* on 2 July 1937 and its repudiation by request of the United States Navy.
3. The *Achilles* and *Wellington* stood by in early July in their own self interests and not entirely those of the United States.
4. Canton Island was the alternate for Earhart, but it was subsequently withdrawn and Hull Island substituted.
5. Putnam was misled by Roosevelt in this regard and Earhart was betrayed by her husband in agreeing to a government request of conducting the Marshall Island overflight.
6. By 1935, the necessity had risen for restoration of RAF espionage flights over foreign countries.
7. Cooperation with RAF in one theater (Africa) ties in with cooperation in another (Pacific).
8. In 1944, interest in Earhart's fate was revived. During the invasion of the Marshalls, United States military men were instructed to look for evidence of a Caucasian couple having been there prior to World War II.
9. Military targets in the Marshalls and Carolines were of interest. Civilians employed by Roosevelt as intelligence agents included Willard Price in 1935 (Truk), Amelia Earhart in 1937 (Jaluit), Dr. Archbold (Truk) in 1938, and Vincent Astor (Marshalls) in 1938.
10. Planning two takeoff points in an overlay mission required dual approaches and dual departures. The Fanning Island airstrip was of paramount importance.
11. Available to the British was Fanning Island with its airfield, fuel cache, radio for communications and weather reporting.
12. Amelia Earhart's target, Jaluit, was paramilitary. Early sectors of Japanese air routes in the Pacific Island mandates were operative and the status of the eastern terminal at Jaluit was important.
13. Overlay operation with dual penetration would give double exposure to photoflash bomb use.
14. The evaluation of suitable aircraft by the British centered on the availability and use of an Airspeed Envoy and its prior conversion for long-range operation.
15. Realistic training for the flight was impossible because of time limitations.
16. British military support of the Commonwealth countries of Australia and New Zealand was expected in the event of a Pacific war.
17. In 1937, PAA personnel operated radio and weather stations on Fanning. This would have been useful in supporting a flight from the tidal flat airstrip.
18. The members of the eclipse expedition who had been left on Canton Island by the *Avocet* were picked up in July 1937 by the *Swan*.

Island of Wotje in Eastern Marshalls was Japanese radio listening post in 1937. Wotje Island and Eniwetok Island were military points of interest in 1937. World War II military buildup on Wotje Island used every square foot of space to maximum advantage. Wotje was frequently bombed, but never invaded by United States Forces in World War II.

Photo credit - National Archives Negative #111-SC 206927

19.   There was an overflight of Wotje from the *Lexington* to "recover" the lost British aerial photos (*Smith's Weekly* evidence).

20.   The *Achilles* was diverted to Canton (and Hull) in August 1937 on its return trip from Honolulu and a four-man radio station installed on the island.

21.   During the diversion of the *Achilles* to Hull Island in June 1937, specialized PX and personal supplies from Pago Pago were delivered for the use of the "shipwrecked sailors," who were Earhart and Noonan.

22.   The U.S.S. *Swan* landed a party on Canton to retrieve the personnel, the aviation fuel cache, and equipment left by the *Avocet* in June.

23.   The Japanese reaction to the captured couple has been speculated on by several authors. The British mission could have left Fanning, overflown Wotje and a possible second target in the Marshalls, and then turned southeast toward Canton. This couple could have ditched their plane near Mili Atoll, prepared their raft to reach the nearest island, and buried their film canister there.

*   *   *

A continuing surface surveillance of the Marshalls was conducted by U.S. submarines approaching from the east in the morning sun, or by the use of periscopes while submerged. Most activity in the lagoons, however, could only be seen using aerial surveillance. Long-distance oblique photography was possible. By 1937, however, nighttime aerial photography and infra-red techniques to penetrate foliage were available. To penetrate lagoons via rubber rafts launched by a submarine would have been possible but dangerous.

Many long-time Earhart researchers, some with a quarter century of work concerning the above-the-equator Saipan theory, are reluctantly shifting to a below-the-equator rationale. Some of them insist that the Japanese were saturating the area below the equator as well as the area adjacent to the Marshall Islands. If not Japanese naval ships, then Maru freighters and sampan fishing vessels were used. The fact is that only one nondescript merchant tramp freighter of any description was seen in the 250,000 square miles covered by the United States Navy search. It was such an inconsequentially small cargo "tramp" steamer that it wasn't even identified by the *Lexington* force.

The area above the equator was well traveled compared to the corresponding area below the equator. Only a few ships which sailed adjacent to the Phoenix Island Group in 1937 were Matson Line and British passenger steamers en route to Honolulu to the Antipodes via Pago Pago or Suva. Also, H.M.S. *Leith*, H.M.S. *Wellington*, or H.M.S. *Achilles* (British warships on loan to the New Zealand Navy) were infrequently in the area. Copra-collecting schooners such as the A.S. *Makao* which struck a coral head and foundered off Hull Island on 25 May 1937, a colonial steamer used by the British Gilbert and Ellice Colony, and possibly an errant tramp steamer carrying nondescript cargo may have passed through the area. No one fished these waters commercially in 1937. This area was definitely not Japanese-frequented in 1937. United States naval ships known to be in these waters during June and July 1937 were the U.S.S. *Avocet*, the U.S.S. *Colorado*, the U.S.S. *Swan* and the USCG cutter *Itasca* (in equatorial waters) and the USCG cutter *Taney*. Additionally, the U.S.S. *Preston* and U.S.S. *Smith* (new *Mahan* class destroyers) passed by the Phoenix Group on a shake-down cruise to New Zealand and Australia in February and March 1937.

What hasn't been considered by many researchers is that above-the-equator activities and below-the-equator operations are entirely different entities and not interrelated. Once this fundamental idea is recognized, the solution to the Earhart disappearance becomes possible.

Roosevelt conducted his covert operations verbally and few records remain. Therefore, documentary proof has been lacking and details concealed from United States citizens and the world at large for 50 years. Positive reference to documents most relevant to the Roosevelt administration has been identified, but these secret documents cited haven't been released, even under the FOIA, or their existence acknowledged. The cover-up continues to this day.

To accomplish her goals, Earhart had to trust some influential persons, including President and Mrs. Roosevelt, her husband, George P. Putnam, Paul Mantz, Eugene Vidal, naval officers (Admirals Murfin and Leahy, and the governor of American Samoa, M. Milne).

To a greater or lesser extent, all of these persons of influence betrayed her by using her talents for their own purposes. Noonan, who shared her fate, did not deserve to be a victim of this international intrigue.

Adequate documentary evidence exists to tie in the British Commonwealth nations of Australia and New Zealand from 1937 onward with justified concern regarding the Japanese Mandated Islands. This is not surprising when a map of the area shows the northernmost Gilbert Islands about 200 miles from the southernmost Marshall Islands. The distance from Jaluit, the Japanese capital of the Marshall Islands in 1937, to British Butatari (Makin Island) is only 200 miles. The capital of the British Gilbert and Ellice Colony in 1937 was Ocean Island, which along with Nauru, was rich in phosphate deposits and was a prize indeed.

Intelligence gathering in the Marshall Islands became difficult after 1936. The London Missionary Society, commercial merchants, and trading schooners with British merchant skippers were good sources of information. The Japanese, however, declared certain islands which previously had been unrestricted, off limits to commercial vessels. Wotje and Eniwetok in the Marshall Islands were thus designated in 1935. Vincent Astor tied his yacht alongside Kings' Wharf in Suva Harbor in May 1938. He reported to the British High Commissioner as Roosevelt's emissary. He learned that two prior British requests for entry into the Marshalls had been rejected by the Japanese. Astor's request was also rejected. He was advised to return to Honolulu by way of the Gilberts, Tarawa, the capital, and Ellice Island, and to talk to the inter-island traders who had been going into the Marshalls. The captains of these ships, who had been sailing these waters for years, knew which islands were off limits. From natives who traveled between the islands, they received much useful information. In mid-1938 Vincent Astor was able to piece together an overview of the Japanese preparations on Jaluit, Eniwetok, and Wotje Islands.

Although there were no airstrips in the Gilberts, Walrus amphibian aircraft with folding wings could be transported by cargo ship to the Gilberts and make short flights into the Marshall Islands. The *quid pro quo* of the *Smith's Weekly* reported exchange of information is not known relative to Australia, but the Walrus was originally developed there for the Australian Navy and they took delivery of the first 30 aircraft.

The four New Zealand warships were under the British High Commissioner's direction and were sent throughout the Central Pacific. As *de facto* commander of these British units of the Royal Navy, their activity was in the Crown's interests. It appears illogical that they would have been employed to support Earhart if there wasn't concurrent British covert participation in the Central Pacific.

Part Five

Summary and Conclusions

Trans-Pacific airlines were covert factors in Earhart flight. Pan American Airways clippers with 150-knot speeds eclipsed the steamers with speed of 15 knots. Japan's merchant fleet of ocean liners and marus were losing Pacific Ocean passage supremacy in middle 1930s.

Photo credit - Pan American Airways

SUMMARY AND CONCLUSIONS

SUMMARY

This summary encompasses the world flight attempts in March and May-July 1937, the searches, the aftermath (called the Odyssey), and the British Connection concurrent (Royal Air Force) overflight of the Marshall Islands. Previously, considerable material regarding the world flights and searches has been published in newspapers around the world and by several authors, but in inadequate detail and scope. New material is covered in the sections called "The Odyssey" and "The British Connection." In addition to the above major topics, a large number of relevant subtopics have been included. Although important, prior researchers have largely ignored them.

These subtopics include governmental jurisdictions of major significance encountered during the world flight, including the British High Commissioner of the Western Pacific Islands and the Commonwealth governments of Australia and New Zealand in the Southwest Pacific. Also covered are British (or Western) Samoa, Governor M. Milne of American Samoa, His Majesty's Government in England, and the Winston S. Churchill "shadow" government. Included is the overflight of Italian Northeast Africa (Eritrea). Finally, the roles of Franklin D. Roosevelt, as Commander in Chief of the United States Armed Services, and Secretary of the Treasury H. Morgenthau, Jr., as head of the United States Coast Guard in 1937 are discussed.

Also, domestic and foreign governmental influences, technical details of the Lockheed, its equipment, and the flight parameters are examined in depth. The foregoing are discussed relative to involvement with Pan American Airways, the United States overseas airline in the 1930s; Lockheed, the aircraft manufacturer; Paul Mantz, the technical advisor and instructor pilot; the mission equipment and installers; and flight coordinators.

The configuration details are followed by the maritime and military service involvement of the United States Coast Guard, United States Navy, United States Air Corps, and the United States Naval Reserve components which "ghosted" the flight from start to finish. Technical personnel and airport representatives and their roles (and recollections) are given. The British resident agent at Hull Island and his participation in post flight activities are discussed in considerable detail.

Movie stunt flier Paul Mantz and Amelia Earhart were staunch friends and he was her mentor on the West Coast from 1935-1937. His reported salary as technical advisor was $100 a day.
Photo credit - Paul Mantz Collection

Concurrent activities north of the equator which represent a significant part of the "British Connection" are defined. The overlay mission is explained with the support of more than 50 man years of Japanese Mandates overflight research by contemporary authors of books and articles about Amelia Earhart.

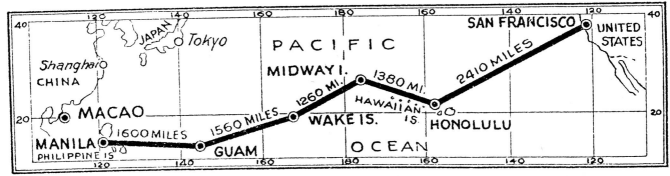

**Pan American Airways Central Pacific Ocean (East/West Route).
U.S. military used these commercially built facilities.**

SOURCES OF INFORMATION

Data associated with historical research are at three levels:

1. Contemporary documentation published at the time of occurrence or shortly thereafter.

2. Archival records from five continents.

3. First party interrogation of persons associated with the flight, search, and aftermath who could be expected to have some special insight or interpretation as to what actually transpired.

Finally, there are "leaks" where individuals, through human error, released covert information. Also, subordinates of insiders not cleared may inadvertently expose information never intended for the public domain. All of the above sources have contributed to the Earhart/Noonan disappearance and are presented in this volume.

Throughout the text, pertinent documental records are cited as well as official archival records. Listed in the bibliography are contemporary publications believed to be the most relevant.

The material presented in Part One offers a very brief review of the Mandates problem in the Pacific in the decades prior to World War II. The wild claims of fortification of the Japanese Mandates in the 1920s and 1930s were part of a war hysteria fostered by certain groups whose aim was to misrepresent the actual events. As Captain Zacharias, USN, was to say in 1945, "Their apparent secrecy was to keep us from finding out how little they (the Japanese) had done not how much they had done."

A brief review of the development of Pacific Ocean airways is presented to illustrate the damage Earhart and Ulm had done to plans to develop a landplane route to New Zealand via Jarvis and American Samoa. Both Roosevelt (through the United States Navy) and P.A.A. did everything they could to block a landplane route because their efficiency was bound to make their favored flying boats obsolete.

WORLD FLIGHT ATTEMPTS

The world flight descriptions are based on Amelia Earhart's book *Last Flight* and contemporary local accounts from newspapers in Los Angeles (Burbank), Oakland, Honolulu, Miami and elsewhere in which reporters covered Earhart when she was in their area. During the past 50 years, most surviving direct participants in the Earhart

Newspaper cluster of photographs depicting the world flight attempt. Shown are the Electra, Amelia Earhart, the *Itasca*, Howland Island, and Fred Noonan. Cluster of photographs taken from New Zealand Herald, July 5, 1937.
Photo credit - New Zealand Archives

145

episode have been interviewed and their "on the record" comments documented. In particular, these are the six-day Java layover (Francis O. Furman), Darwin overnight stop, (Moye Stevens, Sgt. Rose), the Lae, New Guinea, activities (Collopy, Balfour), the very vital Nauru Island flyby, and other local activities which Earhart scarcely mentioned, such as the Eritrea (northeast Africa) overflight. These are all covered in detail in this book.

To carry the flight to its termination after Nauru, a detailed assessment of the known (1937) targets in the Marshall Islands in H. O. 184, *Naval Air Pilot—Pacific Islands*, 1936, the bypassing of Howland and Baker Islands with the radio message charade, the flyby of Gardner Island, and the final approach to Hull Island are all a matter of documented records from the United States and foreign government national archives.

H. O. No. 184

NAVAL AIR PILOT

PACIFIC ISLANDS

PREPARED BY THE HYDROGRAPHIC OFFICE UNDER THE AUTHORITY OF THE SECRETARY OF THE NAVY

JANUARY 1936

UNITED STATES
GOVERNMENT PRINTING OFFICE
WASHINGTON: 1935

Naval Air Pilot - Pacific Islands, 1936
Hydrographic Office (USN) report shows defensive features of strategic Pacific Islands

THE SEARCHES

The United States Navy search is well documented to give the government viewpoint. Although the search, activated by Roosevelt and the United States Navy, was proclaimed adequate by the government, Putnam continued on his own by requesting that the British and Japanese governments search the Gilberts and Marshalls long after the official July 18th termination of United States government efforts.

The apparent hostile relationship between Great Britain and the United States relative to British commercial and U.S. strategic interests in the Pacific in the later 1930s now appears to be foolhardy and self defeating. Japan was not a paper tiger, but a threat to all Occidental nations and interests in the Oriental sphere. Admiral Yarnell, USN, once stated the true situation in the Pacific during his tour as head of the United States Asia Station based at Subic Bay in the Philippines, when he said it all depends upon how distant one was from the Far East. Those at the Asia Station knew the Imperial Japanese Navy was a serious threat, one the United States was ill-equipped to counter. At Honolulu (14th Naval District) the feeling was that the Japanese would stay in their "own waters"—that is, west of the International Date Line and north of the equator. How false an assumption this was relative to the Japanese strategic and economic penetration of the Western Pacific all the way to Australia, throughout the Philippines and Dutch East Indies, and other relevant areas is now evident. The Imperial Japanese Navy used the prerogative of having naval personnel on board any Japanese ship in their merchant marine. On the West Coast, Admiral William Halsey and others resented the oil and scrap iron going to Japan right under the guns of the Pacific Fleet, but few of them felt the United States fleet was inferior to the IJN in any respect. In Washington, D.C., a month before the Pearl Harbor attack, Secretary of the Navy Knox said, "If Japan dared to attack us, we would lick them in thirty days."

The 1930s feud between Pan American Airway's Juan Trippe and Great Britain was another factor in the unsettled North Atlantic route fiasco. The truth was that the British didn't have the aviation equipment to compete in both the Atlantic and Pacific. With their long routes from London to South Africa, Australia, and the European centers of population, they lacked adequate aircraft for the projected Atlantic route and Pacific route in the late 1930s. Building adequate civil aircraft was well beyond their means, particularly with the buildup of the RAF starting in 1935. Not only was a large fighter force under construction for home defense, but a long-range strategic bomber force was planned for use in lieu of an Army Expeditionary Force (AEF) on the continent. With no means of competing with Trippe, the ploy was to delay, obstruct, misrepresent, propose untenable reciprocal agreements, have studies conducted by multi-governmental committees, and use all the tools of imperial bureaucracy to impede progress. Very little is said about conflicts of interests in British politics, but the majority of the ruling class are wealthy persons who have their family money invested in a number of large companies. It would be difficult to envision a Prime Minister bankrupting a company in which his family had had a vested interest for a century or two and which was a cornerstone of that family's wealth.

After the United States Navy search ended, follow on operations were initiated by Putnam in the Gilbert (British) and the Marshall (Japanese) Islands. There were a number of reports of civilian yachts being employed in 1938 and 1939 for searches of islands in the South Central Pacific, but no concrete evidence was found. (Putnam, Dimity etc. cited.)

Amelia Earhart and manager/husband George Palmer Putnam. She was second of four wives before his death in 1950.
Photo credit - Smithsonian Institution's National Air and Space Museum Negative #82-8669

In 1940, the schooner *Yankee*, with Captain Irving and Electra Johnson in command, was used to check the Gilbert and Ellice Islands, but that is all. During U.S. Navy Service in World War II, Johnson also kept his eyes and ears open, but to no avail. From 1944 on, stories were circulated, many, no doubt, inspired by the parody motion picture *Flight for Freedom*. Some still persist. The subsequent desecration of graveyards on Saipan by Goerner and others and the Marshall Islands searches by Oliver Knaggs and Vincent Loomis are well-known, but nothing connecting Earhart with these islands was positively established. The search continues. The airplane did go down in 1937 and someday all or part of it may be found.

THE ODYSSEY

Secondary classified (confidential) documents from military sources supplemented by complimentary documentation make it appear certain that Earhart and Noonan landed on Hull Island at the termination of her flight on 2 July 1937. Interviews with four of the six naval aviators who flew off the *Colorado* provide conclusive evidence of a significant suppression of the truth which constitutes a deliberate cover up. Three of them wrote accounts. In the *Honolulu Star Bulletin* was a detailed article about the *Colorado* search featuring the fliers' participation.

A real breakthrough was identifying the British resident manager at Hull Island and the subsequent unraveling of his activities. This was accomplished through a number of sources:

1. Edwin H. Bryan, Jr., (Bishop Museum, Honolulu) Records of the Islands of American Polynesia.
2. Various *Pacific Island Monthly* (PIM) issues from the 1930s.
3. Consular Agent McKenzy at Apia, Western Samoa.
4. Vital records from Apia, Western Samoa.
5. Captain John W. Jones' blood daughters.
6. "Jonsey's" business associates in Apia and Suva, Fiji Islands.
7. National Archives records at Suva (Fiji Islands) with information on the M.V. *Makoa* and Captain Jones.
8. New Zealand (Navy/Air Department records) National Archives at Wellington.
9. Cruise reports from United States Coast Guard vessels.
10. Burns-Philp (South Seas) Ltd. Archives at Sydney, Australia.
11. Reports by the British High Commissioner of the Western Pacific Islands.
12. Apia newspapers on Captain John W. Jones' activities from 1936 to 1965.

John W. Jones' daughters, Heather and Jane, stated that he was working for both British Intelligence and United States Naval Intelligence prior to World War II (1937-1940). This is established by documents in the British case.

1. Cruise report of the H.M.S. *Achilles*.
2. Activity report of the *Achilles*.
3. Log of the *Achilles*.
4. Letters by and to the High Commissioner at Suva, Fiji Islands.
5. Union Jack seen flying on Hull Island in October 1937 (by *Taney*) after Jones was appointed British manager of Phoenix Island Group.

In the latter United States case, Jones was recruited by the Navy to act as an agent at Hull Island. Evidence exists that M. Milne, the Governor of Samoa, was working with the Office of Naval Intelligence regarding the Japanese Mandated Islands and recruiting of maritime seamen (ship's captains) as favored targets and Jones was one person well qualified.

Somebody from the U.S. Naval Station at Tutuila contacted Jones in 1937 after learning of his assignment on Hull Island after the British takeover in the Phoenix Islands. Rogues of the type represented by Franklin Roosevelt are difficult to trap by documentary evidence. Who can fire the Commander in Chief when he hides behind a well-planned veil of secrecy to cover up his misdeeds?

"By their fruits you shall know them." This is the only way international conspirators can be identified. Both the United States Navy on 9 July 1937 and the United States Coast Guard on 10 October 1937 had Jones' admission that he had a high-powered transmitter ashore. He wasn't afraid to acknowledge this to United States naval aviators or to the Coast Guard, a United States international law enforcement agency, when he knew, as a maritime officer, that transmitting fraudulent distress signals was a violation of international law with severe penalties.

Conversely, when faced with this evidence as reported by Lt. Lambrecht to Captain Friedell, nothing whatsoever was done. The fact that Friedell was under direct orders coming from Naval Radio Arlington (Washington, D.C.) had a lot to do with his decision. Four months later, a United States international law enforcement agency had Jones in a compromised position, but he was given a few cold beers and sent on his way. Of course, Secretary of the Treasury Morgenthau had made the long trip from Washington to Honolulu in July 1937 to tell Coast Guard personnel how to respond in such a situation.

A master mariner, Jones knew the penalty for transmitting bogus distress signals. He was neither seeking international notoriety nor could he have expected the British government to protect him with diplomatic immunity in early July 1937 when he was a civilian working for Burns-Philp on Hull Island. Obviously, he knew he had nothing to fear from United States naval authorities because he was working for them as an intelligence agent according to his daughters.

The first leg of the Odyssey was shown in Lambrecht's report and the cruise report of the *Taney* which stopped at Hull Island on 11 September 1937. In contemporary reports the number of natives on both Hull Island (40) and Sydney Island (17 adult males) is recorded.

The second leg of the Odyssey was from Sydney Island to American Samoa. The answers to the questions of which vessel was used to transport Earhart and Noonan and on which island they were placed have been kept secret. Despite the conspiracy to conceal the major prewar acts of the Roosevelt administration, sufficient revelations have emerged. Many of Roosevelt's acts began as legitimately classified operations to keep the enemy from learning the truth. At the end of World War II, however, American citizens became the "enemies" from whom the truth must be kept. These secrets included the responsibility for the Pearl Harbor attack and extended back to 2 July 1937, or, perhaps, even earlier and to several dates between.

Learning which vessel was used to transport the fliers to American Samoa was somewhat simplified by those actually available. Although technically feasible, Jones' boat and the M.V. *Tutuila*, based at Pago Pago, were ruled too small to safely cover the 600 miles to Samoa, especially if heavy weather was encountered en route. That left the U.S.S. *Ontario*, based at Pago Pago, the USCG cutter *Taney* from Honolulu, one of the search mission destroyers (*Lamson*, *Cushing*, or *Drayton*), or a destroyer from San Diego.

The logs of all these ships were examined and senior officers on board interviewed. Eventually, by the process of elimination, only one ship was left. One destroyer, the U.S.S. *Preston* (DD-379) in San Diego fit mission requirements. Three key personnel who had been aboard in 1937 were interviewed and its record studied from commissioning until the start of naval action in World War II. The *Preston* was the ship most likely to have accomplished the designated task.

The means were available to transport Earhart and Noonan from Sydney Island to the nearest United States Territory of American Samoa. This possession consists of seven separate islands, the largest being Tutuila (where a United States naval station was located until 1951) and the smallest being Rose Island, 150 miles east of Tutuila. In descending size are Tau, Losega, Swains, and Aunu'u.

Before one of these islands was selected, details needed to be known about all of them. Then, the decisions were made as to what accommodations were necessary and on which island could they be best

provided were made. Putting on Governor Milne's gold-braided cap in 1937, and looking from a nautical viewpoint, an isolated island near the naval station was chosen. In addition to the logical process of elimination, viewing the islands and talking to the persons living on them today, was accomplished. The above process yielded the answer. This investigation, in which different known criteria were applied, meant that all except Aunu'u Island could be eliminated. The medical isolation infirmary established on the south shore of Aunu'u Island was almost ideal for the purpose of sequestering the fliers.

THE BRITISH CONNECTION

This material reverses the trend of the past 50 years which has diverted attention from the pre-World War II south-of-the-equator quest to the "northern sector" with the Imperial Japanese Navy as the villain. One would think after all these years of fruitless endeavor, that a re-evaluation of the last flight, its objectives, its suppression, and the effectiveness of the search made by the United States Navy and Coast Guard would be conducted. As noted previously in this book, the *Colorado* crew actually had the solution to the Earhart disappearance, but on instructions from Washington officials, placed tight security on their findings. So far as Earhart and Noonan are concerned, events north of the equator from 2 July †937 onward are of little consequence to their fate. This does not mean that these events can be ignored, but that Earhart and Noonan were not involved in them. The United States government, some of its agencies, the Japanese government, the Imperial Japanese Navy, and foreign governments have been known participants since 1937. Many authors have tried to fit the glass slipper on the ugly stepsister and have disregarded the basic fact that many white races were living in the Pacific Ocean area in the years prior to World War II, particularly the British who were in the Gilbert Islands only 200 miles from the southern Marshall Islands. Not only did England have a strategic military interest in the Japanese Mandates but a keen commercial interest as well. During the opening stages of the Japanese Pacific offensive, the Gilbert Island group was one of the first British territories captured.

Certainly the British had airplanes which could make overflights of the Marshalls, hundreds of RAF pilots who could fly an airplane, and slender female aviators who could crop their hair, wear a leather jacket, and fly an airplane. Not only are the British the prime suspect, but they already had been involved in the Earhart Asmara Airfield overflight in Italian Eritrea.

With the conquest of the Abyssinia in 1935-36, the start of the Spanish Civil War in 1936, and the Japanese invasion of China in 1937, the totalitarian states were waging war on three continents on which Britain had vested interests. Belatedly, H.M.G. began to buildup the RAF and RN. Strategic aerial reconnaissance, dormant for 15 years, was reactivated in 1935, and overseas photo missions against strategic targets initiated. The RAF may not have been 100 percent sold on a Marshall Island mission in 1937. They needed both the experience and updated technology. By participating in the Marshall overflight mission they would receive the technology of practical nighttime aerial photography which took the USAC more than a decade, 1926-1937, to perfect to the tactical stage. The elaborate photocell triggering device and the photoflash bombs themselves were operative. The RAF most certainly would have been interested in this technology and equipment in 1937.

From available evidence, the conclusion is reached that the RAF put an airplane over Wotje Atoll in the Marshalls on a photo mission. They made preparations in three months following Earhart's rescheduled flight by; the use of technology from Ulm's trans-Pacific flight in December 1934, a modified Airspeed Envoy, and the secret Fanning Island airstrip, with a planned landing on Canton, and, after refueling, on to Suva and Australia.

Three months were required to take a production line airplane, modify and equip it, ship it via the Panama Canal to the West Coast and from there to Hawaii and on to Fanning Island. After assembly and testing, it was ready for a flight synchronized with Earhart's arrival over the Marshall Islands. References include archival material and the precedent of the Ulm and Kingsford-Smith/Taylor trans-Pacific flights in 1934 which made the British effort possible.

The author has been interested in the Earhart disappearance since 2 July 1937, spent a lifetime in the aerospace industry, and would like to see Earhart's Lockheed recovered and restored for exhibition at the National Air and Space Museum. A diving team for photographic confirmation, salvage survey, and possible retrieval of removable exterior and interior parts would be relatively inexpensive. Salvage of the airplane with air evacuation is dependent upon preliminary search results. The author has examined archival records from Australia to England, talked to almost every known surviving participant in the flight, search, and subsequent activities, including many parties unidentified or ignored by others. Also acquired were most relevant documented records from four governments: United States, Great Britain, New Zealand, and Australia. A determination of the state of aeronautics in 1937 was made and the true political situation in the Central and South-Central Pacific in 1937 ascertained. The geography of all the Central Pacific Islands was studied and conversations with experts on these islands recorded. The author has visited many of the islands. After studying all of the above findings and separating fact from nonsense, in official records and personal accounts, the author has reduced the search area from several million square miles of ocean to an area 100 yards by 400 yards and 220 feet deep.

During the years 1982 to 1987, the author studied USN historical records for operations during the pre-World War II years and interviewed naval personnel from three-star rank to apprentice seamen and visited with the civilian head of the USN historical operational archives, USMC historians, and USCG historians. Interviewed was a USN photographer who served with PatWing2 on Ford Island in 1937. This naval technician removed an aerial camera from Earhart's Electra on 20 March 1937, on the evening of the crackup. The author interviewed two three-star admirals and several destroyer captains from DesRon2, who, in 1937, both overtly and covertly, participated in the flight and postflight phases. The author has talked to many others who have stated there is no mystery at all. They, however, have been restrained in one way or another from revealing what actually happened.

A few months after Earhart's disappearance, a story was circulated which received wide attention. She had been on an intelligence mission for this country in the course of which she had been forced down in the Marshall Islands, then under Japanese rule. The story continued that the woman flier had been captured and executed by the Japanese. The belief that Earhart met her fate in Japanese hands lingers to this day. According to rumors printed in this country during the past 50 years, she was supposed to have been forced down near a Japanese-controlled island and imprisoned. After this, she was presumed either to have died or been executed.

Japanese records on espionage matters have been studied. If Earhart had been captured, the fact would most likely have been in their files. Japanese officers, even in remote areas, did not take action in such matters without informing headquarters. If she did fall into Japanese hands and was disposed of by local military authority, it would have been a precedent-shattering incident.

If a white woman aviator had been on an intelligence mission, she may have been captured and imprisoned by the Japanese. If so, it is one of the best kept secrets in the Pacific. The following quote was found in "First Lady of the Air" by Francis and Katherine Drake, in *Reader's Digest* (May 1951): "Judging by the radio signals, the lost plane was not 100 miles from Howland. Somewhere near journey's end the needle of the gas gauge sank against the stop. In the uncaring desolation of the deep, Amelia's luck ran out." An article titled "Radio Slip-Up Seen Costly to Earhart" by C. B. Allen, *New York Herald-Tribune* Aviation Editor, appeared in that newspaper on 8 July 1937. He said:

"Out of a welter of conflicting opinions by radio experts concerning the authenticity of distress calls and "carrier wave" signals supposedly received from the Earhart-Noonan plane since it was forced down in the Pacific last Friday, and from a study of the messages exchanged by the Coast Guard cutter *Itasca* with the ship while it was still in the air, there emerged yesterday a tragic picture of technical slipups that are believed to have brought the fliers to grief at a time when the last of their fuel supply was being consumed and they were striving desperately to locate their tiny, mid-ocean objective of Howland Island.

"Her reason for dispensing with a transmitting wave length universally used by ships at sea which might have easily spelt the difference between success and failure, if not between life and death, on her long flight across the Pacific, was explained by Miss Earhart before her take-off from Miami as being due to the fact that neither she nor Capt. Fred Noonan, her navigator, were competent to send and receive messages in radio code. This is used exclusively in the 500 kilocycle band. Miss Earhart decided to depend entirely on her two radio-telephone frequencies—6210 kilocycles for day transmission and 3105 at night.

"'Our radio is equipped to transmit either voice or code,' she said, 'but if we wanted to use the 500-kilocycle channel, it meant that we would have to take along a 250-foot trailing wire antenna which would have to be reeled out after every take-off and reeled in before each landing. If either Fred or I could use the key, it would be different, but, since we can't, the antenna would be just one thing more to worry about and we've got plenty of things now to keep us busy, what with watching fuel-consumption gauges, winding up the wheels and letting them down again for a landing and the hundred and one other things a pilot has to remember during landings and take-offs.'"

That the *Itasca's* commander was ignorant of this fateful decision is readily apparent both from the text of his official report to Washington and from the note of irritation that its tersely factual style does not wholly disguise.

The tragedy of all this was that the *Itasca* was wholly powerless to tune the standard marine wave-length direction finder to either of Earhart's high frequencies which she "insisted" on using for the desperately sufficient reason that they were all she had.

NOONAN AND EARHART DECLARATIONS OF DEATH

California court records show that Mrs. Mary Bea Noonan and her husband-to-be, Harry B. Ireland, petitioned the Alameda County Superior Court on Monday, 20 June 1938, to declare Fred Noonan legally dead. This hearing was in the Alameda County Courthouse at Oakland, California, before Superior Court Judge Allen. The petition was based upon a "seven-page photostatic copy of the Coast Guard communications with Amelia Earhart and radiograms subsequently sent during the search for her plane." This evidence was considered sufficient to declare Frederick J. Noonan officially dead. On Friday 24 June 1938, Mrs. Mary Bea Noonan and Mr. Harry B. Ireland were married in Carson City, Nevada. They resided in Santa Barbara, California, for the rest of their lives.

Despite the fact that notice of Noonan's "death" appeared between 24 and 26 June 1938 in Los Angeles, San Francisco, New York City, and Oakland newspapers, it was relegated to the back pages and attracted little attention. In peacetime the U.S. Coast Guard was part of the Treasury Department. Mrs. Noonan had obtained the Coast Guard records from the San Francisco District Office.

In January 1939, in a Los Angeles Superior Court, Earhart was also declared legally dead. Putnam, however, obtained U.S. Navy records from Washington, D.C. Apparently, he was unaware, due to different "sources" of records, that Mary Bea Noonan had preceded him in gaining freedom to remarry.

This indicates how Mrs. Noonan was able to remarry six years earlier than the normal seven-year wait required. Photostatic records from the San Francisco Coast Guard District would not have been released to a civilian without approval from Washington. Secretary of the Treasury Henry Morgenthau would have released them with Roosevelt's approval. Putnam received USN records six months later. Although F.D.R. apparently did not intercede overtly or covertly in the court's action, some command may have come from the attorney general's office. Logically, this could indicate that F.D.R. and a few other administration officials knew that Noonan was dead prior to one year after the last flight and that Earhart died after July 1937. Neither the alleged "vicinity of Howland Island" or "while a captive of the Japanese" would have been acknowledged in open court by Washington officials.

THE DEMISE OF AMELIA EARHART

The actual demise of Amelia Earhart is a story over and above her last flight. In available records is the evidence that she survived the wheels-up landing on the sand covered platform reef at Hull Island and that her voice was heard on radio in the early morning on 3 July 1937. Thus, between that date and 5 January 1939, when she was declared legally dead in California, she passed away. Since she had expired prior to the court hearing, archival records state that this occurred sometime during the spring of 1938.

A number of clues relative to the cause of her demise are supplied in large part by her own statements as well as observations by her close associates. Clues are also found in documentary evidence, with interpretation, and present a logical and plausible explanation of those final months. The following material is directed to those with open minds who are willing to look at the record and form an unbiased opinion based upon something other than preconceived notions. Enough is known about Noonan's background, personal situation, character weaknesses, and his alcoholism to predict the cause of his death. The problems which led to his death were basically physical, although his frustration at being incarcerated lowered his inhibitions so that when alcohol became available, he relapsed into an alcoholic state which led to his demise. In 1937 and 1938, medical knowledge and psychological attention, even if the authorities had been sensitive to the captives' personal needs, would have prevented the almost inevitable result. Government authorities, however, could be accused, if subject to public scrutiny, of neglect. How Noonan would respond to a "protective custody" situation was predictable. Had the human factor and his access to intoxicating beverages in sufficient quantity to be injurious to his well being been considered, corrective action might have been taken. The human factor is seldom considered in bureaucratic judgments and decisions. Communication between Pago Pago, American Samoa, and the secret cabal in Washington, D.C., was deliberately diluted through so many intermediaries that the actual originating source was concealed.

Earhart's death is more complex and, very likely, a mixture of mental and physical ailments complimenting each other, which led to a gradual deterioration. A general background of her "mentality" has been documented and while far from adequate presents a case to build on.

1. Could not stand confinement even in a gilded cage.
2. Provider for family members.
3. One person's "paradise" is another one's prison.
4. Mixer and shaker—personal view of herself.
5. Devoted "middle age" to molding public opinion to her viewpoint.
6. Particularly susceptible were young women who opted for her different and innovative lifestyle options.

While this brief psychological profile is far from adequate to predict exactly how Earhart might react to protective custody, it is possible to consider the other side of the coin, "her custodians."

In this case, the custodians were the socialistic bureaucrats of 1937 Washington, D.C. The Earhart incident was their creation, and it was unsuccessful because of governmental mismanagement. In the 50 years of liberalism, 1937-1987, those who don't wear the rose-colored glasses and deliberately misrepresent the facts, realize that once a bureaucrat bungles, the only recourse is to bungle his way out.

Reaction in Washington to Noonan's death was predictable. His drinking problem had been overlooked, and when he was "left alone," he reverted to his old habits. Once this error was known, the second realization was, "We could be held responsible for negligence in not providing adequate medical care to the detainees and it must never be known that we were the guilty parties. Keep it quiet, classify it, destroy records, and pledge everyone to lifetime secrecy."

Predictable overreaction occurred. We can't let this happen to Earhart. She has important connections in the

United States and embarrassing questions could be asked. We must provide her with more adequate medical attention forthwith. On the U.S. mainland, a state of virtual 24-hour house arrest would have to be imposed because she might escape or contact someone outside the plot, plus perhaps bringing even more custodians into the conspiracy of secrecy. A geographical compromise was found in a small sparsely-populated island, 18 miles away from the naval station and one mile from the larger island. Unfortunately, in many Big-Brother solutions to a complex problem, human factors receive scant consideration. The move to Aunu'u Island might have been the ideal solution from their point of view, but it was fatal for her. Her problems were both physical and mental. Perhaps a naval doctor could have helped her physically, but only a skilled psychologist could have adequately diagnosed her problem. Thus, even bringing her to Aunu'u Island, did not mean that adequate medical care was available.

The conditions on Aunu'u Island were:

1. Prevalence of primitive surroundings.

2. A state of house arrest was maintained using native Fita Fita guards.

3. Earhart had lost her gentle Tokelau companion, who had been with her since protective custody began at Sydney Island, and received an autocratic type of jailor at Aunu'u Island.

4. Her hidden psychological problems remained undiagnosed.

5. The loss of Fred Noonan and, to a lesser extent, her native companion, were major tragedies.

Earhart had no real attachment for Noonan, but he represented the only link with her past life. That loss would have been a shattering blow. The substitution of a Samoan female jailor instead of her former gentle, compassionate companion would also have a negative effect. The cooks on Aunu'u, trained in the Samoan manner, made lots of meat dishes with half-cooked pork, a common staple. In Amelia's incapacitated state, after months of detainment, the switch to a significantly different diet was catastrophic. Always a picky eater, her only recourse was to eat very little or not at all. Severe depression, the food, insufficient medications of the right kind and too many of the wrong kind, were tantamount to a regressive downward spiral. Under these circumstances, a person's will to live becomes a paramount factor. Faced with an existence of seemingly endless confinement and detached from all that was important to her, she was undoubtedly destitute.

Her fate had been sealed by fiat. Mental health techniques known in the 1980s and drugs which combat depression were generally unknown in 1937. Exactly which combination of factors resulted in her demise is unknown. She most likely died on Aunu'u Island in the spring of 1938 and was interred there in an unmarked or coded marked grave until several years after the war.

CONCLUSIONS

Historically the background for the Earhart world flights centers around the southwest trans-Pacific airline route from the West Coast to Honolulu and on to Australia. A route across these 7,000 miles of ocean was initially pioneered by Sir Charles Kingsford-Smith and Charles T. P. Ulm in 1928. During the 1932-1935 period three well known Pacific Ocean pioneers worked diligently to make the southwest crossings a commercial reality. These were aerial navigator Harold Gatty (Tasmian by birth), Charles

T. P. Ulm (Australian) and Eugene Vidal who was then the U.S. Air Commerce Secretary. The personal papers of these three airline pioneers have been studied and are quite revealing. Harold Gatty's personal papers are in the Library of Congress and the Fiji Central Archives at Suva. Charles Ulm's personal papers are located at the Mitchell Library at Sydney, Australia, while Eugene Vidal's papers are divided between the U.S. National Archives (Air Commerce Secretary) and University of Wyoming, Laramie (private papers).

Pioneer Pacific Ocean flier Charles T. P. Ulm (center) and crew members, George M. Littlejohn (right) and John Skilling (left) planned trans-Pacific Ocean crossing from the West Coast of America to Australia to establish a commercial airline across 7,000 miles of ocean in 1934.

Briefly, Harold Gatty started working on the trans-Pacific route planning in 1932. In 1934 a private airline called South Seas Company was formed with Donald Douglas, the airplane builder, and eventually TWA participated as well. The main interest was a flying boat route from the West Coast to China and a land plane route from Honolulu to Australia. Gatty's work, which was conducted in Washington, D.C., soon became known to the State Department, the U.S. Navy and later in the year to the President, Franklin D. Roosevelt. Archival records show that Secretary of the Navy Swanson, Admiral William D. Leahy, Chief of Naval Operations, and Boggs of the Department of State seized upon this civilian effort as a means of circumventing the Washington Naval Treaty of 1922, which prohibited construction of bases in the Western Pacific. The ploy was to have civilians build the bases with covert government assistance. The initial plan (mid 1934) was for the construction of a joint US/Australian route from Hawaii to American Samoa (U.S.) and to link up with a southern (Australian) route from Australia to Suva in the Fiji Islands. Jarvis was to be used as an airfield between Oahu and American Samoa. Initially, the lengthy 2,400 mile leg from Hawaii to the West Coast would depend upon commercial steamer to make the five-day voyage until suitable commercial aircraft became available.

The Australian government was approached in the

summer of 1934 urging their participation in the scheme. Charles T. P. Ulm was the most experienced airline executive so he was given the job of establishing the Australian route. The Douglas DC-2 airliner was the designated airplane for the inter-island land plane route. It has been determined from an examination of Charles Ulm's personal papers that because he had no collateral of the usual type it was necessary for the Australian government to guarantee the payment of the loans necessary to establish the airline and to finance a demonstration flight on the selected route. Australian Prime Minister Lyons was the official who authorized the loan guarantee for Ulm's bank loans. Ulm's plan was to fly an airplane over the selected route to demonstrate to the public that the airline was feasible. As the Douglas DC-2 was not immediately available from the British Airspeed Company (which had the English rights to manufacture the airplane), Airspeed suggested using a modified long range version of their twin engine Envoy passenger airplane then going into production. With his government guaranteed bank loans, Ulm was able to purchase the airplane and hire a crew to accompany him over the selected Pacific route. Ulm's personal papers also establish that he was the one who selected the intermediary landing strip on a lagoon tidal flat on the south rim of British Fanning Island some 1,000 miles south of Hawaii. Working with Fanning Island cable station personnel (who were mainly Australian), Ulm was able to pick a suitable site (6,000 feet long), have the surface smoothed out and provide a cache of aviation gasoline for the projected flight.

Typical Airspeed Envoy in foreign service as transport.
Photo credit - Smithsonian Institution's National Air & Space Museum Negative #87-2479

This temporary tidal flat airstrip was to be used intermittently up until 1970 when a small private airstrip was constructed adjacent to the cable station grounds on the island's northwest corner. Ulm's demonstration flight in December 1934 ended tragically when the Airspeed Envoy airplane, on the 2,400 miles from Oakland to the Hawaiian Islands, failed to make a landfall due to faulty navigation. Earhart became acquainted with Charles Ulm and his airplane for extended range flight in December 1934 when they were both preparing their respective airplanes for the Oakland-to-Hawaii ocean crossing. It is therefore no surprise that Earhart's Pacific Ocean crossing airplane for her world flight attempts was similar in many respects to Ulm's range augmented specially equipped Airspeed Envoy of December 1934. Following Ulm's flight preparation stay at Burbank, he flew up to Oakland for the trans-Pacific crossing. Earhart flew north by commercial airliner to see Ulm's departure and wish him well on his flight to Australia. It was known at Union Air Terminal where Pacific Airmotive was preparing Ulm's Envoy that he was

receiving advanced state-of-the-art equipment from the East Coast from parties unknown but suspected. The Australian government wasn't the only one interested in the flight. Ulm's effort to reach Australia with the covert assistance of two governments was undoubtedly the event which triggered Earhart's planning for her eventual world flight effort.

The third party was Air Commerce Secretary Eugene Vidal. In 1935, using a government budget set up to promote the advancement of commercial airplanes and equipment, Vidal set out to prove the practicality of using land airplanes over large stretches of ocean as an alternate to the inefficient flying boat.

Using the original Douglas DC-1 leased from TWA, Vidal equipped the Douglas airliner with the latest in radio location, navigational equipment and started flying progressively longer over water distances out of the Oakland airport. Just as the program was certain to achieve success, funds for its support were vetoed and the program was terminated. As Congress had appropriated the money for the program in the first place, it was apparent that it was the executive branch of the government that killed the program.

Amelia Earhart with U.S. Air Commerce Secretary Eugene Vidal and Paul F. Collins. Earhart continued research begun by Vidal in overwater flying and radio compass equipment when Vidal's overwater tests using Douglas DC-1 were terminated by Washington in 1935.
Photo credit - National Archives

By the end of 1935, both Ulm's and Vidal's efforts to establish land plane routes over the Pacific had failed. It is apparent that the flying boat advocates had prevailed. Although Vidal's effort was killed by administrative edict, Vidal opened up a new avenue of attack. He knew it was the U.S. Air Corps who were the most interested in establishing air force capability over water. Earhart and

Putnam learned of the angle from Vidal, who was a close personal friend and prospective business associate. He advised Earhart that the U.S. Air Corps might be willing to sponsor a test airplane to verify radio direction finders over long ranges. The end result was Earhart's Lockheed Electra, a so-called "flying laboratory." Proof of this is established by the fact that during the month of October 1936 after the Bendix air race, the Earhart Electra spent a month at Wright Field, Ohio, testing an advanced Bendix Automatic Radio Compass and marker beacon radio navigational aide for the Air Corps. This clearly supports the contention that the U.S. Air Corps was the actual sponsor of the Earhart airplane and the agency most likely to profit from her confirming the efficiency of the land plane for over-water flying. It appears certain that not only did the Air Corps underwrite a substantial part of the original capital cost for the airplane but also most of the $25,000 refitting cost after the Luke Field wipeout on the first world flight attempt.

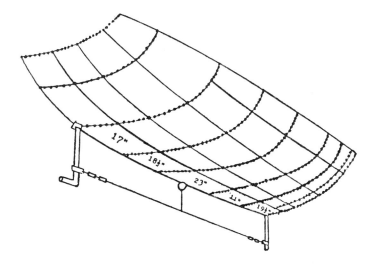

The Electra's Secret Marker Beacon Antenna
Graphic credit - Paul Rafford, Jr.

Not only did these three prior efforts contribute to the Earhart world flight endeavor, but they also set the precedent for the British overflight of the Marshall Islands in 1937. Ulm's range augmented Airspeed Envoy, the availability of the Fanning Island 4,000-foot tidal flat airstrip, radio homing, direction finding and other mission-oriented equipment such as aerial nighttime photoflash technology played a major factor in the overflight.

WORLD FLIGHT ATTEMPTS

Sufficient evidence has appeared in the past half century to substantiate the contention that both world flight attempts were aimed at overflying the Japanese Mandated Pacific Islands. The Earhart civilian espionage mission was not conducted in isolated context. Continuing penetration of this restricted area was carried out by Americans Williard Price in late 1935 and Dr. Richard Archbold in 1938 in a civilian version of the Consolidated PBY and Roosevelt's millionaire associate Vincent Astor in his steam powered yacht S.S. *Normahal,* also in 1938. Both Earhart's and Dr. Archbold's airplanes used the existent high technology equipment of that period and the newly perfected nighttime photoflash technology

developed by the U.S. Air Corps and the best radio communication and radio navigation aids available. The nighttime overflight limitation in peace time required suitable weather to disguise the "thunderclap" and brilliant flash of light caused by the photoflash bomb. Scattered tropical squalls or thunderstorms were ideal for this purpose although the target area had to be sufficiently clear to enable aerial photography. The needed weather requirements were not uncommon in the tropics; however, the local weather over the designated target was conditional upon its suitability to perform the desired aerial reconnaissance.

It is now known that the weather was unsatisfactory in March 1937 and the overflight cancelled. This is borne out by the switch from a later afternoon takeoff from Hawaii which would have enabled the overflight. A dawn takeoff would have precluded a detour over the Marshalls and arrival near Howland during daylight hours. On 2 July 1937 there was a wide weather front passing through the Marshalls so a nighttime detour from the announced great circle flight path to overfly the Southern Marshalls was accomplished.

Strategic target islands in the Marshalls in 1937 are well known from a large number of overt and covert sources. The U.S. government targets of interest were Eniwetok, which was an Imperial Japanese Navy submarine base opposite Wake Island and Wotje Island which was a I.J.N. forward staging area and radio intercept and D\F station. Jaluit Island as the administrative center was a pseudo-military target.

The assignment of Marshall Island targets would include U.S. Navy PBY Patrol aircraft over Eniwetok Atoll from nearby Wake Island, the Earhart Electra long range airplane over Jaluit Island approaching from the southwest, and a British civilian aircraft from the east overflying Wotje Island. The capability of the U.S. Navy PBY (and Dr. Richard Archbold's civilian PBY) and the fuel tank augmented extended range Model 10E Electra and British Airspeed Envoy were satisfactory for the overflight missions. The demonstrated high technology of these aircraft was complimented by using the latest in aerial reconnaissance equipment: military aerial cameras and the U.S. Air Corps photoflash bombs and electronic synchronizing apparatus to enable nighttime aerial picture taking. State-of-the-art radio direction finding and communication made the overflight possible.

Archbold's civilian PBY (GUBA II) in New Guinea, 1938.
Photo credit - San Diego Aerospace Museum

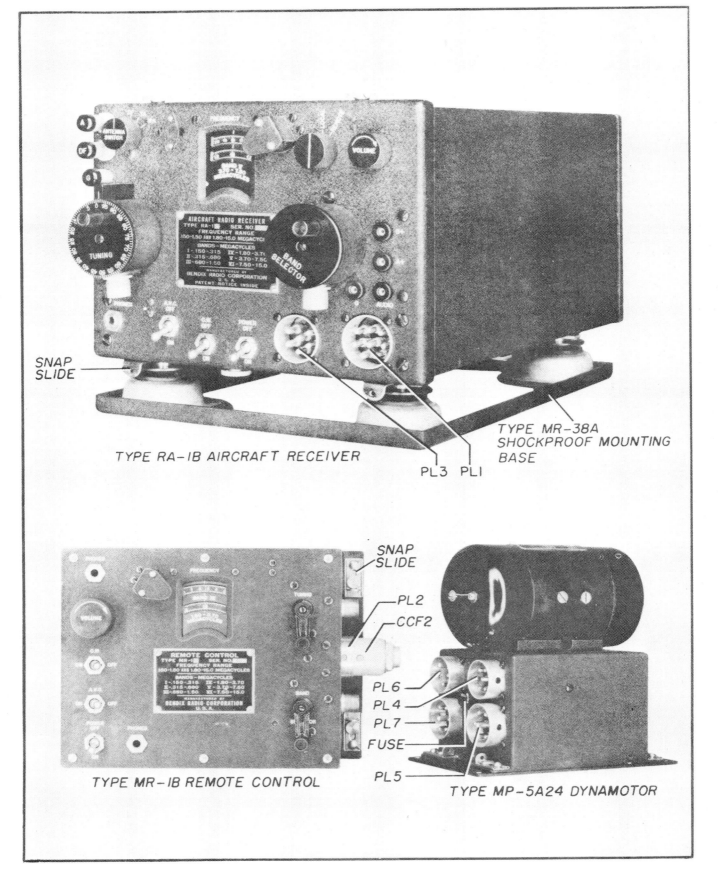

SNAP
SLIDE

TYPE RA-1B AIRCRAFT RECEIVER

TYPE MR-38A
SHOCKPROOF MOUNTING
BASE

PL3 PLI

SNAP
SLIDE

PL2

CCF2

PL6
PL4
PL7
FUSE
PL5

TYPE MR-1B REMOTE CONTROL

TYPE MP-5A24 DYNAMOTOR

Production version of Bendix RA-1 all-wave receiver supplied by U.S. government to the Earhart and Dr. Richard Archbold expeditions, both of which overflew Japanese Mandated Islands in 1937 and 1938.
Via Vernon Moore, Bendix Project Engineer

UNITED STATES PATENT OFFICE

1,936,595

AUTOMATIC PHOTOGRAPHIC APPARATUS

George W. Goddard, Rantoul, Ill.

Application July 15, 1929. Serial No. 378,361

7 Claims. (Cl. 67—29)

(Granted under the act of March 3, 1883, as
amended April 30, 1928; 370 O. G. 757)

The invention described herein may be manufactured and used by or for the Government for governmental purposes, without the payment to me of any royalty thereon.

The invention relates to photography and in particular to apparatus for taking flashlight pictures at night.

It has been the practice heretofore in flashlight photography to set the camera shutter in open position as for a time exposure. Then the flashlight is set off to illuminate the subject and the camera shutter is subsequently closed. In the use of this method in aerial photography, the resultant pictures are streaked due to automobile headlights, electric signs, and other sources of ground illumination. Similarly, in ground photography, any sources of light other than the flashlight, or reflecting surfaces, will cause streaks in pictures taken by the old method. When the subject to be photographed is a group of persons, for instance, any movement on the part of one of the persons will produce a blur in the picture. With the proposed new method, the picture is a snapshot and therefore the speed of the shutter prevents this blurring.

In the application of this invention to aerial photography, the flashlight must necessarily be produced by the explosion of an aerial bomb released from the aircraft over the terrain to be photographed at suitable altitude. In experimentation wherein personnel on board the aircraft attempted to impart snapshot operation to the camera shutter manually, after the bomb had been released and exploded, it was found that the shutter was operated too late, due to the comparatively slow reaction time of the operator in response to the visual stimulus produced by the flashlight. It is therefore an object of the invention to utilize light-sensitive mechanism capable of operating the shutter automatically upon explosion of the flashlight bomb at a speed unattainable by human agency.

A further object is to provide time-controlled mechanism for exploding the flashlight bomb in aerial photography after it has been released from the aircraft and has reached the most desirable position with respect to both the terrain to be illuminated and the aircraft-carried camera.

A still further object is to provide means for use in aerial photography to prevent premature operation of the camera shutter due to sources of light other than the flashlight bomb.

It is also an object to provide a flashlight bomb which will be reliable and efficient in operation. Other objects will appear as the following description is read in connection with the accompanying drawings in which:

Fig. 1 is a perspective view of a studio camera with the improved flashlight apparatus arranged for use in connection therewith:

Fig. 2 is a fragmentary sectional view of the airplane in which the apparatus is mounted, showing the details of construction of the light-sensitive camera operating mechanism;

Fig. 3 is a fragmentary sectional view of the flashlight bomb, showing the time-controlled mechanism for exploding the light producing charge.

Fig. 4 is a cross-sectional view of one of the powder trains which extend into the flashlight powder charge of the bomb;

Fig. 5 is a diagrammatic view of the flashlight apparatus mounted in an airplane, three successive stages of the use of the apparatus being shown; and

Figure 6 is a diagrammatic view of the electric circuits of the camera operating apparatus.

The invention will first be described in its application to ground photography due to the fact that this form of the apparatus is less complex than that used in aerial photography and is thus best suited for description in the introductory explanation of the invention.

Referring to Fig. 1 of the drawings, the numeral 6 designates a camera of the kind ordinarily used in taking flashlight pictures in any location where the ordinary light is insufficient for instantaneous exposure. The camera has a shutter 7 controlling the admission of light to the plates or other sensitized material.

The numeral 8 designates a flashlight holder which may be of any type suitable for use in connection with the camera just described. This holder should be capable of being fired manually at will and should be positioned relative to the camera so as not to be included in the field of view of the camera but in a position where maximum illumination of the subject to be photographed may be accomplished.

In order to cause instantaneous operation of the camera shutter at the time of the production of photographic light by the flashlight holder, a photo-electric cell 9 is mounted in such a position relative to the holder that light rays from the flashlight will enter the cell. This cell may be mounted on the camera as shown, or may have any other desired support. It is not intended to be limited to any particular type of cell, it being necessary simply that some cell be utilized which will be sufficiently fast in its response to light

Nov. 28, 1933. G. W. GODDARD 1,936,595

AUTOMATIC PHOTOGRAPHIC APPARATUS

Filed July 15, 1929 3 Sheets-Sheet 2

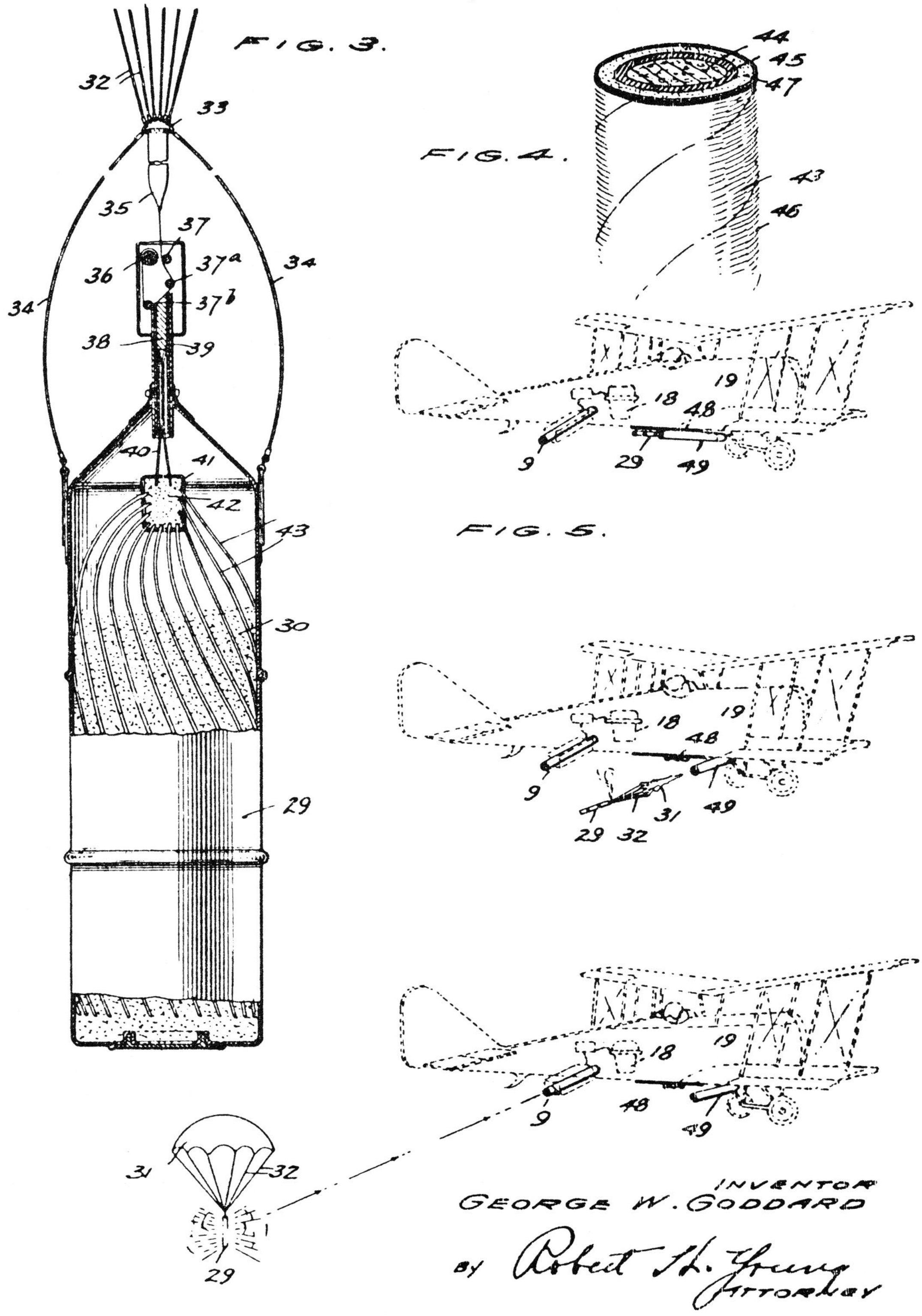

FIG. 3.
FIG. 4.
FIG. 5.
INVENTOR
GEORGE W. GODDARD
BY Robert H. Young
ATTORNEY

General George Goddard, U.S. Air Corps, Patent Illustration of Photoflash Bomb and Electronic Control Equipment (1926-1929)

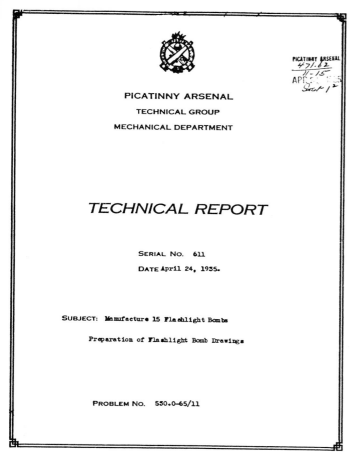

PICATINNY ARSENAL
TECHNICAL GROUP
MECHANICAL DEPARTMENT

TECHNICAL REPORT

SERIAL NO. 611
DATE April 24, 1935.

SUBJECT: Manufacture 15 Flashlight Bombs

Preparation of Flashlight Bomb Drawings

PROBLEM NO. 550.0-65/11

**Reduction of front cover of
PHOTOFLASH BOMB REPORT, 1935
U.S. Army Ordnance Picatinny Arsenal (Dover,
New Jersey) manufactured high technology
photoflash bombs for nighttime aerial
photography from 1935 onward.**

Other possible targets were Jaluit Island which was the eastern terminus of the long anticipated Japanese Mandates airline promised since 1934. Of course, the strategic targets in Italian Eritrea were the east-west railroad, fortifications and the large military airfield in the suburbs of Asmara, the capital city. Additionally, the two Red Sea Italian airfields were of strategic interest to the British because they were situated right on the so-called "lifeline of the empire" route of seaborne commerce and passenger transport.

THE SEARCHES

The government search for Earhart and Noonan was conducted by the U.S. Coast Guard (then under the Treasury Department) and the U.S. Navy from 2 July - 18 July 1937. It cost (reportedly) $100,000 for fuel and a total of 4,000,000 depression dollars when all costs were included. The search covered over 250,000 square miles of Central Pacific Ocean both below and above the equator. The primary ships involved were:

Lexington (CV-2) - $44 million aircraft carrier
Colorado (BB-45) - $33 million battleship
Swan (AVP-7) - Aircraft tender
Ontario (AT-13) - American Samoa Station Ship
Itasca - C.G. Cutter based on West Coast

The search covered the Phoenix Island Group, the British Gilbert Islands west of Howland and the International Date Line plus going 400 miles above the equator. The search was declared unsuccessful. Only one small freighter was seen in an area the size of the state of Texas.

Other nations also participated in the search, including the Japanese Imperial Navy ship Koshu, a 3,000 ton survey ship that searched the southern Marshalls. The New Zealand Navy ships Wellington and Achilles and the British freighter M.V. Moorby also participated in the search.

The search was initiated by the USCG cutter Itasca and within a few hours the U.S. Navy, on orders from Roosevelt and Admiral Murfin, was authorized "to use all available naval facilities." The Colorado was dispatched from Honolulu and the Lexington (with a three destroyer escort) was sent from the West Coast. Three Colorado float planes and 62 scout/bombers from the Lexington participated. A PBY patrol craft was sent from Pearl Harbor but was forced to turn back. The U.S.S. Swan joined the search, but the U.S.S. Ontario, which had been on station near Ocean Island during Earhart's overflight returned to its station at American Samoa. A government HYPO distress call was sent out. Two ships responded, S.S. Golden Bear (which could not participate) and British freighter M.V. Moorby, which was just to the east of the Marshall Islands. Control of the search shifted to the USN on 6 July 1937.

The above summary gives the overt facts of the military search. Subsequently the U.S. government asserted that an adequate search had been accomplished and that no trace of the fliers, their airplane or life raft was found. The official verdict was that the fliers became lost, failed to find Howland Island and ditched in the ocean approximately 100 miles northwest of Howland Island. This government edict has not changed over the past half century. In making this declaration, the nation's foremost woman aviator's piloting was blamed for the loss of the airplane after the ditching and for the inept radio communication. All radio intercepts by the Pan American Airways' D\F stations, a British warship and British freighter, commercial radio stations, competent radio engineers/amateur radio operators were declared invalid to support the government edict.

COVERT ACTIVITY

The evidence which has surfaced during the past five decades shows that most of the government's claims were false. The real intent of the search was to convince the Japanese government and the Imperial Japanese Navy that the overflight of the Marshall Islands was a failure resulting in the fliers being lost at sea. Actually the government knew where the Earhart airplane was throughout the flight from takeoff to landing. Radio messages for the Earhart airplane were heard throughout the flight on a hourly basis. In short, Earhart was never lost but flying a preprogrammed course with variable options as to the mission and designated alternate landing sites; Baker, Canton and Hull Islands.

Far from being unsuccessful, the Colorado fliers located the high powered radio transmitter at Hull Island which was sending out the bogus distress signals on 3105 kc that were heard all over the Pacific Ocean basin. Also, the fliers notified the Colorado commanding officer that Sydney Island should be searched because of native huts evident and no natives visible. The suspicion was that the residents were hiding inside their huts. All of these

157

findings were covered up (on orders from Washington) and a completely fictional report made public that nothing whatsoever was found.

THE ODYSSEY

The key to the Earhart disappearance is connected to Hull Atoll and the British resident manager of the island's copra enterprise. Captain John William Jones, RNR, arrived at Hull on 21 May 1937 as a civilian employee of Burns-Philp (South Seas) Company, Ltd. His home base was Apia, Western Samoa, some 65 miles west of the U.S. Naval Station on Tutuila Island, American Samoa. Within two months Captain John Jones was promoted to Deputy High Commissioner of the British Western Pacific Islands with jurisdiction in the Gilbert and Ellice Island Group and British administration manager of the Phoenix Island Group.

Captain John W. Jones, R.N.R., as an officer on New Zealand interisland steamer *Maui Pomare* (circa 1932).
Photo credit - Via Heather Jones

Captain Jones remained in this capacity until 16 January 1940, when he returned to Apia, Western Samoa. Two daughters, named Heather and Jane, were born to Jones on Hull Island in 1937 and 1938. Capt. Jones died at Apia in 1965. However, his daughters have testified that he was an intelligence agent for both the British and the U.S. Navy at Tutuila during his tenure at Hull Island.

Capt. Jones was well known to the U.S. Naval authorities at American Samoa because of his Royal Navy Reserve Rank, radio communication activity from Western Samoa and frequent inter-island visits. Captain Jones set up a high powered radio station on Hull Island and maintained communication with American Samoa during his Hull Island residency. When interviewed by U.S. fliers from the *Colorado* who landed on Hull Island lagoon, Jones' radio capability became known aboard the battleship. On orders from Washington a completely fictitious report was given to the press to conceal the true island colonies a few hundred miles south of the Japanese Mandated Islands.

An evaluation of the itinerary and activity of the three British ships known to be in the equatorial region of the Central Pacific established the extent of the British involvement in the July 1937 overflights of the Marshall Islands.

British warships H.M.S. *Achilles* and *Wellington* (attached to New Zealand Navy) were both nearby the Phoenix Islands and uncharacteristically monitoring the aviation radio frequencies. The *Achilles* radio intercept from the Earhart airplane hours after the flight ended is well known. H.M.S. *Wellington* fully refueled from *Achilles* in Pago Pago harbor and was standing by just south of the Phoenix group in case assistance was needed in that area.

It was the British freighter M.V. *Moorby* which played the key role of transport for the British airplane to the West Coast for transshipment to Hawaii. After outfitting at the Mare Island shipyard and a brief stop at Vancouver, B.C., *Moorby* was standing by as a radio homing picket ship off the strategic island of Wotje in the eastern Marshalls after 1 July.

The precedents from the Capt. Charles T. P. Ulm trans-Pacific flightplan of 1934 are clearly evident. An Airspeed Envoy was modified with long range tanks, and radio navigation homing equipment and aerial cameras were installed. After assembly in Oahu, the airplane was flown 100 miles south to British Fanning Island where a 6,000 foot tidal flat airstrip had been prepared and aviation fuel stored. At the designated time the Envoy departed Fanning for the 1,200-mile trip westward to home on *Moorby* and to photograph Canton Island (Phoenix Group). The British aircraft ran into trouble and was forced to ditch in the southern Marshalls.

The identity of the British female aviator is unknown but Beryl Markham is the prime suspect. Either Markham was repatriated or a substitute established for her to cover her disappearance.

The evidence of the presence of a second airplane over the Marshalls on 2 July goes a long way toward explaining much of the conflict experienced during the past half century with the details of the Earhart disappearance. Also, the switch of alternate landing places for the Earhart airplane from Canton Island to Hull Island in the Phoenix group indicated that the British airplane got the better airfield but failed to reach it due to mechanical problems forcing them down. After the wheels up landing at Hull, the American fliers were dependent upon outside help for rescue.

Further, the involvement of a foreign government provides an explanation for the half century of security blackout and the bipartisan honoring of intergovernmental security agreements. If the Japanese had been responsible for Earhart's death it would have been role Jones had played in the last flight terminal phase and subsequent activity in transmitting bogus distress calls which were picked up all over the Pacific Basin. Four months later, in September 1937, the U.S. Coast Guard cutter *Taney* stopped by Hull Island and all of the details of Jones' activity on Hull were documented in a classified cruise report. The fact that neither officers from *Colorado* or *Taney* took any punitive action against Jones while knowing he had to be the source of the bogus "Earhart" distress signals clearly indicated the collusion between Jones and U.S. Naval authorities at American Samoa.

In recognition of Jones' daughters' testimony of his British and U.S. intelligence connections, rapid promotion from civilian to deputy British High Commissioner and obvious collusion with U.S. Naval officials regarding his true status on the island, it is obvious that some highly covert activity was taking place on Hull Island. This activity involved the landing of the Earhart Electra on the sand of the atoll's platform reef and the subsequent transport of the fliers from Hull to Sydney Islands, 60 miles to the east. After Earhart was diagnosed as having dysentery, specialists and medicine were carried aboard a destroyer from the West Coast to Sydney Island. The fliers were then taken to isolated American Samoa, the closest (and most secure) U.S. possession, and quartered at a newly constructed U.S. Naval medical infirmary on the south shore of Aunu'u Island, 18 miles from the U.S. Naval Station. Available evidence indicates that both Noonan and Earhart had died within eight months of protective custody on the island.

THE BRITISH CONNECTION

Evidence dating back to 1944-45 depicts the prewar landing of an airplane carrying a white couple (woman aviator and male companion) who ditched their aircraft in the ocean off Mili Atoll in the southeast Marshall Islands. The testimony of numerous Marshallese natives had remained essentially constant to this day. The Japanese captured the fliers and interned them in the jail on Jaluit Island. Descriptions of the fliers and their airplane clearly shows that the white woman aviator was not Earhart, the male companion was not Noonan and the airplane was not a Lockheed Electra.

With the Earhart flight termination below the equator at Hull Island, a second overflight by another airplane is indicated which ended above the equator in the pre-World War II same time frame.

What the forgoing evidence indicates is that two different airplanes conducted Marshall Island overflight missions. Further evidence suggests a simultaneous overflight from the southeast (Earhart) and from the east (a British civilian airplane). The British are the logical suspect as they had both strategic and economic interests in their revealed during the war trials after the end of WW II. If the U.S. government alone held the secret of her demise, it would have been revealed by now, probably after the enactment of the Freedom of Information Act in 1967. Only if a foreign government with its own idea of security (not in the strategic sense but in the economic sphere) would a half century of concealment make any sense.

The Earhart spy mission is an exact parallel to the U-2 affair of May 1960. Eisenhower's "Open skies" proposal was rejected and overflights of U-2 airplanes started in 1955, initially with British covert participation and subsequent cognizance of the espionage activity. The problem was of strategic importance. There was an extensive restricted area to be covered and such activities frequently entail the use of civilian cover. There was a need for the government to determine by whatever means what was happening in these restricted areas. Failure of the operation results in the civilian agent being the scapegoat with little government support.

Peacetime espionage is an endeavor in which all the major powers participate using every means available. Unfortunately, some participants, both military and civilian, become victims of the requirement to satisfy a need to know. This is the overriding factor in both the Japanese Mandated Islands in the 1930s and Central Russia in the 1950s and 1960s.

To update the Earhart/Noonan episode another generation, their disappearance could be attributed to their status as Missing In Action (M.I.A.) before United States/Japanese hostilities actually began in the Pacific in 1941.

In a sense Earhart became a victim of her own overriding ambitions. With a fatalistic attitude towards accepting the risks involved in a succession of what she called her "shining adventures," her fellow traveler, Noonan, shared her calculated risk and also paid the supreme price.

Where the analogy ends, is in the aftermath. All evidence indicates that Earhart and Noonan survived the last flight but a pretext had to be made that they were lost at sea to prevent a serious international incident. They had to drop out of sight for a indeterminate period of time until the incident blew over. Unfortunately before this period was over, both Earhart and Noonan died.

A more benevolent government could and should have found a more suitable solution to the predicament in which they found themselves. Instead the blanket of security descended to conceal their misdeeds and has remained for half a century.

To attempt to moralize the episode would be futile, indeed. All participants in covert activites have to accept the risks of being apprehended and convicted with death a likely outcome. Earhart and Noonan paid the ultimate price.

Amelia Earhart and Fred Noonan
Photo credit - Smithsonian Institution's
National Air & Space Museum Negative #71-1095

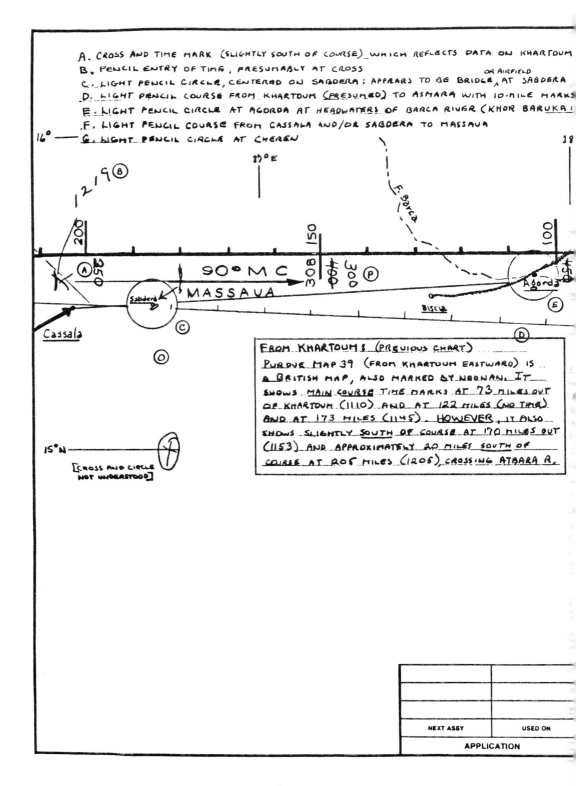

A. CROSS AND TIME MARK (SLIGHTLY SOUTH OF COURSE) WHICH REFLECTS DATA ON KHARTOUM
B. PENCIL ENTRY OF TIME, PRESUMABLY AT CROSS
C. LIGHT PENCIL CIRCLE, CENTERED ON SABDERA; APPEARS TO BE BRIDGE, AT SABDERA OR AIRFIELD
D. LIGHT PENCIL COURSE FROM KHARTOUM (PRESUMED) TO ASMARA WITH 10-MILE MARKS
E. LIGHT PENCIL CIRCLE AT AGORDA AT HEADWATERS OF BARCA RIVER (KHOR BARUKA)
F. LIGHT PENCIL COURSE FROM CASSALA AND/OR SABDERA TO MASSAUA
G. LIGHT PENCIL CIRCLE AT CHEREN

16° ────

37°E

90° M C

MASSAUA

Sabdera

Cassala

[CROSS AND CIRCLE NOT UNDERSTOOD]

15°N ────

BISCIA

Agorda

FROM KHARTOUM: (PREVIOUS CHART)
PURDUE MAP 39 (FROM KHARTOUM EASTWARD) IS
A BRITISH MAP, ALSO MARKED BY NOONAN. IT
SHOWS MAIN COURSE TIME MARKS AT 73 MILES OUT
OF KHARTOUM (1110) AND AT 122 MILES (NO TIME)
AND AT 173 MILES (1145). HOWEVER, IT ALSO
SHOWS SLIGHTLY SOUTH OF COURSE AT 170 MILES OUT
(1153) AND APPROXIMATELY 20 MILES SOUTH OF
COURSE AT 205 MILES (1205) CROSSING ATBARA R.

NEXT ASSY	USED ON	
APPLICATION		

Italian Eritrea Overflight Chart
Details on Fred Noonan's own navigational chart (at Purdue University Special Earhart Collection) clearly depict deviation from straight-line course for intelligence gathering over fortified areas, railroad and Asmara Airfield, the largest military airfield in Africa at that time.

Credit - Charles N. Hill

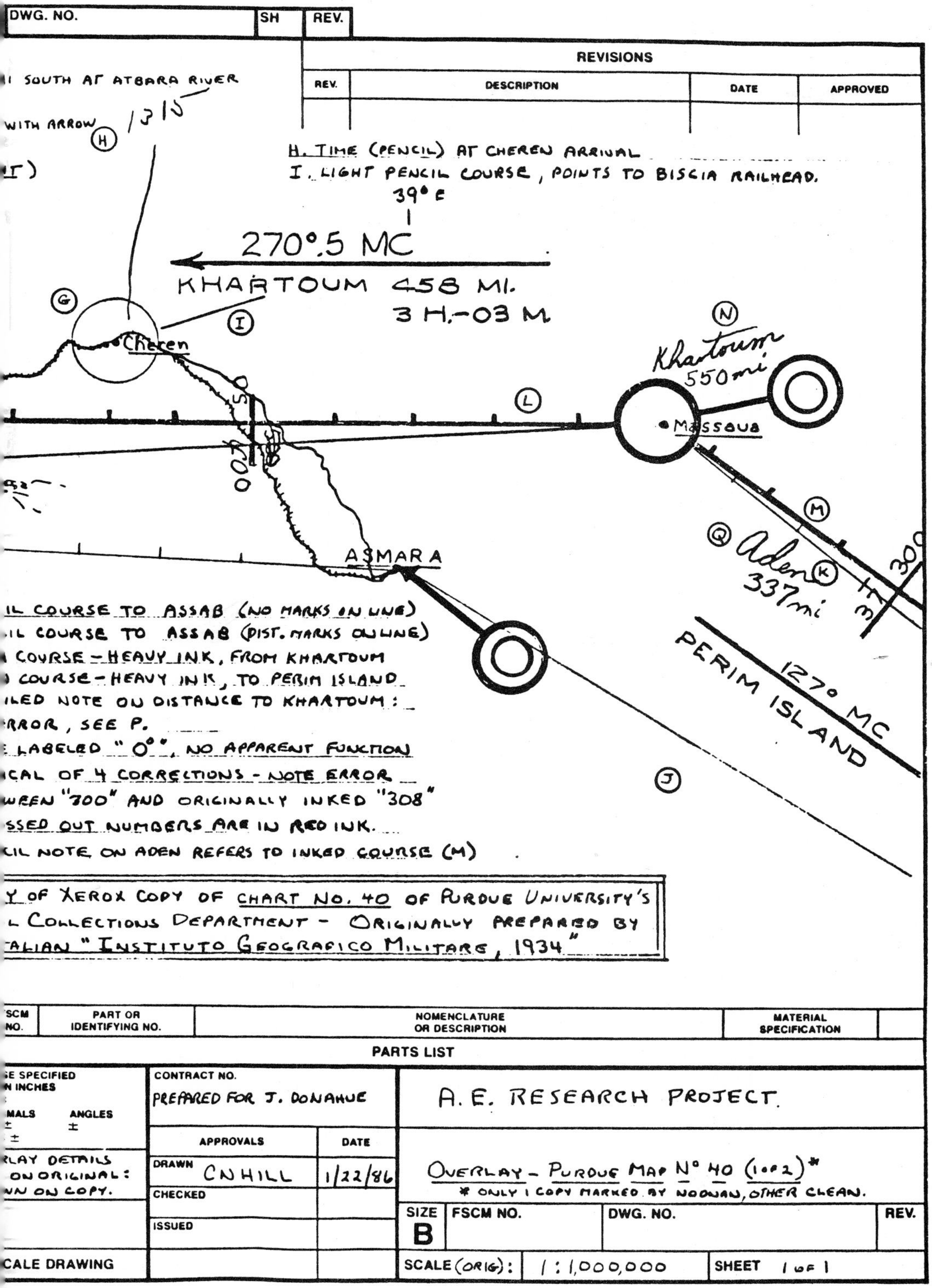

	REVISIONS		
REV.	DESCRIPTION	DATE	APPROVED

...I SOUTH AT ATBARA RIVER

...WITH ARROW (H) /3/5

...T)

H. TIME (PENCIL) AT CHEREN ARRIVAL
I. LIGHT PENCIL COURSE, POINTS TO BISCIA RAILHEAD.

39° E

270°.5 MC

KHARTOUM 458 MI.
3 H.-03 M.

(G)

(I)

• Cheren

(N)

Khartoum
550 mi

(L)

Massaua

• Massaua

Khartoum 550 mi

ASMARA

(M)

(Q) Aden
337 mi

(K)

1270 MC

PERIM ISLAND

(J)

...IL COURSE TO ASSAB (NO MARKS ON LINE)
...IL COURSE TO ASSAB (DIST. MARKS ON LINE)
...A COURSE - HEAVY INK, FROM KHARTOUM
...D COURSE - HEAVY INK, TO PERIM ISLAND.
...ILED NOTE ON DISTANCE TO KHARTOUM :
...RROR , SEE P.
...E LABELED " O° ", NO APPARENT FUNCTION
...CAL OF 4 CORRECTIONS - NOTE ERROR
...WEEN "700" AND ORIGINALLY INKED "308"
...SSED OUT NUMBERS ARE IN RED INK.
...IL NOTE ON ADEN REFERS TO INKED COURSE (M)

...Y OF XEROX COPY OF CHART NO. 40 OF PURDUE UNIVERSITY'S
...L COLLECTIONS DEPARTMENT - ORIGINALLY PREPARED BY
...ALIAN " INSTITUTO GEOGRAFICO MILITARE, 1934 "

	SCM NO.	PART OR IDENTIFYING NO.	NOMENCLATURE OR DESCRIPTION		MATERIAL SPECIFICATION	
			PARTS LIST			

...SE SPECIFIED ...N INCHES	CONTRACT NO. PREPARED FOR J. DONAHUE		A. E. RESEARCH PROJECT		
...MALS ±		APPROVALS	DATE		
...LAY DETAILS ON ORIGINAL: ...NN ON COPY.	DRAWN	CN HILL	1/22/86	OVERLAY - PURDUE MAP N° 40 (1 of 2)* * ONLY 1 COPY MARKED BY NOONAN, OTHER CLEAN.	
	CHECKED				
	ISSUED		SIZE B	FSCM NO.	DWG. NO.	REV.
...CALE DRAWING			SCALE (ORIG): 1 : 1,000,000	SHEET 1 OF 1	

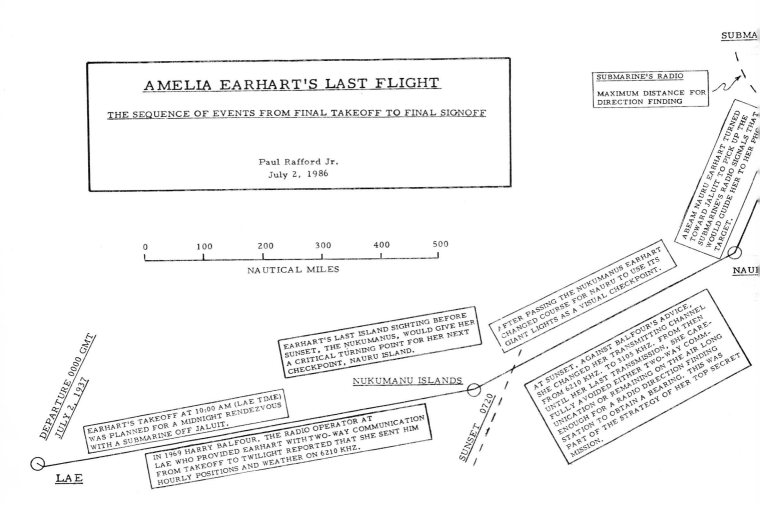

AMELIA EARHART'S LAST FLIGHT

THE SEQUENCE OF EVENTS FROM FINAL TAKEOFF TO FINAL SIGNOFF

Paul Rafford Jr.
July 2, 1986

0   100   200   300   400   500

NAUTICAL MILES

SUBMA

SUBMARINE'S RADIO

MAXIMUM DISTANCE FOR DIRECTION FINDING

ABEAM NAURU EARHART TURNED TOWARD JALUIT TO PICK UP THE SUBMARINE'S RADIO SIGNALS THAT WOULD GUIDE HER TO HER PHO TARGET.

NAUI

AFTER PASSING THE NUKUMANUS EARHART CHANGED COURSE FOR NAURU TO USE ITS GIANT LIGHTS AS A VISUAL CHECKPOINT.

EARHART'S LAST ISLAND SIGHTING BEFORE SUNSET, THE NUKUMANUS, WOULD GIVE HER A CRITICAL TURNING POINT FOR HER NEXT CHECKPOINT, NAURU ISLAND.

NUKUMANU ISLANDS

DEPARTURE 0000 GMT
JULY 2, 1937

EARHART'S TAKEOFF AT 10:00 AM (LAE TIME) WAS PLANNED FOR A MIDNIGHT RENDEZVOUS WITH A SUBMARINE OFF JALUIT.

SUNSET 0720

AT SUNSET, AGAINST BALFOUR'S ADVICE, SHE CHANGED HER TRANSMITTING CHANNEL FROM 6210 KHZ. TO 3105 KHZ. FROM THEN UNTIL HER LAST TRANSMISSION, SHE CARE-FULLY AVOIDED EITHER TWO-WAY COMM-UNICATION OR REMAINING ON THE AIR LONG ENOUGH FOR A RADIO DIRECTION FINDING STATION TO OBTAIN A BEARING. THIS WAS PART OF THE STRATEGY OF HER TOP SECRET MISSION.

IN 1969 HARRY BALFOUR, THE RADIO OPERATOR AT LAE WHO PROVIDED EARHART WITH TWO-WAY COMMUNICATION FROM TAKEOFF TO TWILIGHT REPORTED THAT SHE SENT HIM HOURLY POSITIONS AND WEATHER ON 6210 KHZ.

LAE

Lae, New Guinea, to Hull Island, Phoenix Group, Flight Chart
Credit - Paul Rafford, Jr.

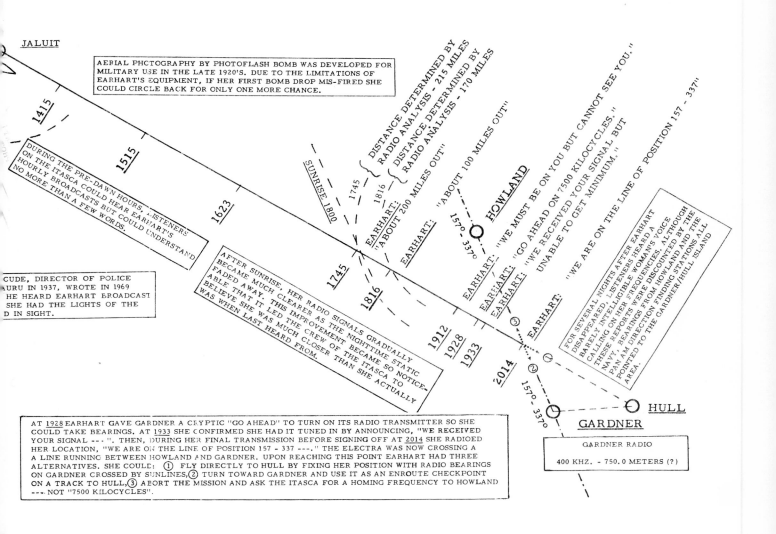

JALUIT

1415

1515

1623

DURING THE PRE-DAWN HOURS, LISTENERS ON THE ITASCA COULD HEAR EARHART'S HOURLY BROADCASTS BUT COULD UNDERSTAND NO MORE THAN A FEW WORDS.

AERIAL PHOTOGRAPHY BY PHOTOFLASH BOMB WAS DEVELOPED FOR MILITARY USE IN THE LATE 1920'S. DUE TO THE LIMITATIONS OF EARHART'S EQUIPMENT, IF HER FIRST BOMB DROP MIS-FIRED SHE COULD CIRCLE BACK FOR ONLY ONE MORE CHANCE.

DISTANCE DETERMINED BY RADIO ANALYSIS - 215 MILES
DISTANCE DETERMINED BY RADIO ANALYSIS - 170 MILES

SUNRISE 1800

1745

1816

EARHART: "ABOUT 200 MILES OUT"

EARHART: "ABOUT 100 MILES OUT"

HOWLAND

157° - 337°

EARHART: "WE MUST BE ON YOU BUT CANNOT SEE YOU."

EARHART: "GO AHEAD ON 7500 KILOCYCLES." "WE RECEIVED YOUR SIGNAL BUT UNABLE TO GET MINIMUM."

EARHART: "WE ARE ON THE LINE OF POSITION 157 - 337"

...CUDE, DIRECTOR OF POLICE
...AURU IN 1937, WROTE IN 1969
...HE HEARD EARHART BROADCAST
...SHE HAD THE LIGHTS OF THE
...D IN SIGHT.

AFTER SUNRISE, HER RADIO SIGNALS GRADUALLY BECAME MUCH CLEARER AS THE NIGHTTIME STATIC FADED AWAY. THIS IMPROVEMENT BECAME SO NOTICE-ABLE THAT IT LED THE CREW OF THE ITASCA TO BELIEVE SHE WAS MUCH CLOSER THAN SHE ACTUALLY WAS WHEN LAST HEARD FROM.

1745

1816

1912

1928

1933

2014

157° - 337°

FOR SEVERAL NIGHTS AFTER EARHART DISAPPEARED, LISTENERS HEARD A BARELY INTELLIGIBLE WOMAN'S VOICE CALLING ON HER FREQUENCIES. ALTHOUGH THESE REPORTS WERE DISCOUNTED BY THE NAVY, BEARINGS FROM HOWLAND AND THE PAN AM DIRECTION FINDING STATIONS ALL POINTED TO THE GARDNER/HULL ISLAND AREA.

HULL

GARDNER

GARDNER RADIO
400 KHZ. - 750.0 METERS (?)

AT 1928 EARHART GAVE GARDNER A CRYPTIC "GO AHEAD" TO TURN ON ITS RADIO TRANSMITTER SO SHE COULD TAKE BEARINGS. AT 1933 SHE CONFIRMED SHE HAD IT TUNED IN BY ANNOUNCING, "WE RECEIVED YOUR SIGNAL ---". THEN, DURING HER FINAL TRANSMISSION BEFORE SIGNING OFF AT 2014 SHE RADIOED HER LOCATION, "WE ARE ON THE LINE OF POSITION 157 - 337 ---." THE ELECTRA WAS NOW CROSSING A A LINE RUNNING BETWEEN HOWLAND AND GARDNER. UPON REACHING THIS POINT EARHART HAD THREE ALTERNATIVES. SHE COULD: ① FLY DIRECTLY TO HULL BY FIXING HER POSITION WITH RADIO BEARINGS ON GARDNER CROSSED BY SUNLINES, ② TURN TOWARD GARDNER AND USE IT AS AN ENROUTE CHECKPOINT ON A TRACK TO HULL, ③ ABORT THE MISSION AND ASK THE ITASCA FOR A HOMING FREQUENCY TO HOWLAND --- NOT "7500 KILOCYCLES".

Amelia Earhart Photographs

Amelia Earhart poses in front of her newly-completed Lockheed Model 10E Electra in May 1936. The source of the $25,000 spent in reconstructing the airplane in 1937 remains a disputed issue.
Photo credit - Smithsonian Institution's National Air & Space Museum Negative #43033A

Earhart with pilot friends Laura Ingalls and Col. Roscoe Turner
Photo credit - National Archives

Left to right: George Putnam's son, Amelia Earhart, unknown admirer, and George Putnam
Photo credit - National Archives

Amelia Earhart and signature
Photo credit - National Archives

Amelia Earhart and her friend Eleanor Roosevelt were very likely the most photographed American women of the 1930s.
Photo credit - Paul Mantz Collection

Amelia Earhart in 1936 at the peak of her aviation career. Airplane and Cord convertible are fruits of lecture circuit and admirers.
Photo credit - Smithsonian Institution's
National Air & Space Museum Negative #80-3182

Amelia Earhart reviews model specifications of Electra with Hall Hibbard, Lockheed Vice President and Chief Engineer, in 1936.
Photo credit - Lockheed Aircraft Corp.

Amelia Earhart in Link Trainer owned by Paul Mantz in 1936
Photo credit - Paul Mantz Collection

Publicity photograph of Amelia Earhart by one of the engines of her Electra in 1936
Photo credit - Smithsonian Institution's National Air & Space Museum Negative #71-1050

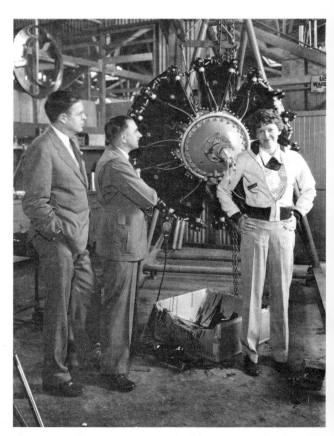

George Putnam, Paul Mantz and Amelia Earhart viewing dependable Wasp engines
Photo credit - Lockheed Aircraft Corp.

Jimmie Mattern's Lockheed Electra Model 12 was rigged for aerial refueling. Amelia Earhart toyed with this idea before Howland Island was converted to an airfield for her use by President Franklin Roosevelt. Jimmie Mattern is on the right.
Photo credit - National Archives

Amelia Earhart sits on main wing spar of her Lockheed Electra. This metal wing spar extends wingtip to wingtip and provides great structural integrity.
Photo credit - Lockheed Aircraft Corp.

Amelia Earhart inspects her Lockheed
Photo credit - Lockheed Aircraft Corp.

Amelia Earhart with table full of National Air Race trophies in 1936. She didn't win any of these.
Photo credit - National Archives

Amelia Earhart in public relations photograph
Photo credit - Lockheed Aircraft Corp.

ACKNOWLEDGEMENTS

Recounting events which occurred half a century previously is by definition historical in nature. During that lengthy period, a conservative estimate would identify well over 100 man-years of recorded research effort by a considerable number of persons devoted to the Earhart/Noonan disappearance of July 1937. This extensive data, with archival records available over two-thirds of the globe as well as worldwide press coverage, comprise the information base one must build on to interpret what history has told us. The trick is to determine how much of this data base is relevant, which isn't, and by interpretation and additional research develop a coherent and logical explanation of transpired events. Although most of the Earhart world flight authors are quite well known, their collective efforts must be acknowledged as supplying backgroud material of some value to subsequent researchers. Frederick Goerner and Joseph Gervais between them have acknowledged devoting more than 50 man years or more or less continuous effort in "the search". Additional authors include later ones such as Paul Briand, Richard "Dick" Strippel, Don Dwiggins, Oliver Skaggs, Vincent Loomis and Jeffrey Ethell, and Robert Myers.

In more than five years of research, I have covered two-thirds of the globe and retreived archival material from South Australia to Kew, England (and many ports of call between). A large number of military personnel have contributed their first-hand "on-the-scene" accounts of what did, in fact, happen. Included in this group are four of the six naval aviators who flew off the U.S.S. *Colorado* on the landing mission on the Hull Island lagoon and others who served on the ships (reported and unreported) known to be in involved in support Earhart's world flight attempts and the subsequent search operation. Four professional radio engineers have at last defined the radio equipment installed in her Lockheed and the significant role radio equipment played in the trans-world flights. Three of the most knowledgeable geographers of the Central Pacific Ocean area opened their files to be (in one case going back 65 years).

MAJOR CONTRIBUTORS

Radio-Electronic Engineers/Operators: Frederick J. Hooven (Bendix Radio), Vernon Moore (Bendix Radio), Karl Pierson (Patterson Radio) Paul Rafford, Jr. (Pan American Airways)

Pacific Ocean Georgraphers: Edwin H. Bryan, Jr. (Bishop Museum), Carlos Hagen (U.C.L.A.), Lee J. Motteler (State Geographer of Hawaii)

Earhart Authors contacted: Paul L. Briand, Don Dwiggens, Jeffrey Ethell, Joseph Gervais, Robert H. Myers, Carol Osborne, Ann H. Pellegreno, Doris Rich, Dick Strippel

Retired Military Officers: Capt. Horace W. Blakeslee, USN; VAdm. Harold T. Deutermann, USN; Capt. John J. Farley, USNR; Naval (Cadet) Aviator Wayne Jordan, USN; Col. Henry A. Myers, USA; VAdm. Lloyd M. Mustin, USN; Capt. William B. Short, USN; Capt. William A. Sullivan, USN; Capt. Charles D. Swain, USN; Aviation Photographer's Mate Thurman Wade, USN; Naval (Cadet) Aviator J. Ashley Wilson, Jr., USN

CONTRIBUTORS

Walter Clark (Eastmak Kodak), Harvey Christen (Lockheed), Keith Dowden (Purdue University), Francis O. Furman (Martin Aircraft), Jeffrey Geiger (USAF), Charles N. Hill, Wallace Jennings (American Samoa), Heather Jones (Australia), Jane Jones (New Zealand), Elinor Jones (Western Samoa), Clarence "Kelly" Johnson (Lockheed), Francis X. Holbrook (Fordham University), Chase Langford (U.C.L.A.), Elgen Long, John F. Luttrell, Kenneth Lum-King (Hawaii), Vernon MacKenzie (Western Samoa), Ruckins Douglas "Bo" McKneely, Claudia Oakes (N.A.S.M.), Wayne Pryor (Lockheed), Frederick M. Rarick M.D., Brewster Reynolds, Moye Stephens (Lockheed), and John A. Ulm (Australia)

Typists: Laura L. Donahue, Kathy B. Willer, Cynthia J. Williams

Publisher: SunShine House, Inc.
Drina Welch Abel, Alan Abel, Greg Abel

BIBLIOGRAPHY
BOOKS

Backus, Jean L. Letters From Amelia. Boston: Beacon Press, 1982.

Bailey, Truman. Polynesian Venture. New York: Doubleday, Doran & Co., Inc., 1939.

Barber, Joseph Jr. Hawaii: Restless Rampart. New York: The Bobbs Merrill Co., 1941. (Chapter: "Propaganda, Hawaii-Style").

Bender, Marylin and Altschul, Selig. The Chosen Instrument- Juan Trippe--The Rise and Fall of an American Entrepreneur. New York: Simon and Schuster, 1982.

Beschloss, Michael R. Mayday: Eisenhower, Krushcev and the U-2 Affair. New York: Harper and Row, 1986. (Discusses British participation with United States in overflying Russia in 1950s.)

Briand, Paul Jr. Daughter of the Sky. New York: Duell, Sloan and Pearce, 1960.

Brooks-Pazmany, Kathleen. United States Women in Aviation: 1919-1929. Washington, D.C. Smithsonian Institution Press, 1983.

Bryan, E. H. Jr. American Polynesia and the Hawaiian Chain. Honolulu: Tonge Publishing Co, 1942.

Bryan, E. H. Jr. Panala'u Memoirs. Pacific Scientific Information Center, Honolulu: Bishop Museum, 1974.

Buckley, K. and Klugman, K. The Australia Presence in the Pacific: Burns-Philp 1914-1946. Sydney: George Allen & Unwin, 1983.

Burke, John. Amelia Earhart--Winged Legend. New York: G. P. Putnam's Sons, 1970.

Cochrane, Jacqueline. The Stars at Noon. Boston: Little, Brown and Co., 1954.

Davidson, J. B. Amelia Earhart Returns from Saipan. Canton, Ohio: Davidson, 1969.

Dorwart, J. M. Conflict of Duty-The U.S. Navy's Intelligence Dilemma, 1919-1945. Annapolis, MD: Naval Institute Press, 1983. (Roosevelt's covert activities in Pacific using civilians before WW II.)

Dwiggins, Don. Hollywood Pilot. New York: Doubleday & Co., Inc., 1967. (Excellent coverage of Paul Mantz/Earhart relationship.)

Eakins, H. R. Around the World in 18 Days. New York: Longmans, Green and Co., 1936. (Flying the Pacific in Pan American Airways Clippers.)

Editor of the Air Force Times. Before the Eagle Landed. Washington D.C.: Robert Bruce, Inc., (Chapter: "The Last Flight of Amelia Earhart" by J. Gordon Vaeth).

Earhart, Amelia. 20 Hours and 40 Minutes. New York: Harcourt, Brace and Co., 1928.

Earhart, Amelia. (Edited by G. P. Putnam, Jr.) Last Flight. New York: Harcourt, Brace and Co., 1938. (Best factual account of Earhart's world flight attempts.)

Goerner, Fred. The Search for Amelia Earhart. New York: Doubleday & Co., Inc., 1966.

Gratien, C. Hartley. The Southwest Pacific Since 1900. Ann Arbor: University of Michigan Press, 1963.

Holmes, W. J. Double-Edged Secrets. Annapolis, MD: Naval Institute Press, 1979.

Hull, Cordell. The Memoirs of Cordell Hull. (Vol. I & Vol. II) New York: The Macmillan Co., 1948.
170

Ickes, Harold L. The Secret Diary of Harold Ickes: The First Thousand Days. (Vol.1) New York: Simon and Schuster, 1953. (Pacific Islands colonizations.)

Ingells, Douglas L. They Tamed the Sky. "We Rode the Stratosphere." New York: D. Appleton Company, 1947. (XC-35.)

Jackson, Ron. China Clipper. New York: Everst House, 1980. (Describes US Navy use of Midway, Wake and Guam for covert activities.)

Johnson, Clarence L. and Smith, Maggie. Kelley: More Than My Share of It All. Washington, D.C.: Smithsonian Institution Press, 1985.

Kahn, David. The Codebreakers. New York: The Macmillan Co., 1974.

Klaas, Joe. Amelia Earhart Lives. New York: McGraw-Hill, 1970.

Knaggs, Oliver. Amelia Earhart-Her Last Flight. Cape Town, South Africa: Timmins, Ltd., 1983.

Loomis, Vincent V. and Ethell, Jeffery L. Amelia Earhart-The Final Story. New York: Random House, 1985.

Manchester, William. The Glory and the Dream. Boston: Little, Brown and Co., 1973.

Markham, Beryl. West With the Night. Boston: Houghton Mifflin Co., 1942. (Reprinted San Francisco: North Point Press, 1983.)

Moolman, Valeria. Women Aloft. Alexandria, VA: Time Life Books, 1981.

Morrissey, Muriel. Courage Is the Price. Wichita: McCormick-Armstrong Publishing Division, 1963.

Morrison, S. E. History of U.S. Naval Operations in World War II. Vol. III, The Rising Sun in the Pacific. Boston: Little, Brown and Co., 1953. (Introductory chapters on events leading to war.)

Morrison, S. E. The Two-Ocean War. Boston: Little, Brown and Co., 1963.

Myers, Robert M. Stand By To Die-The Disappearance, Rescue, and Return of Amelia Earhart. Pacific Grove, CA: Lighthouse Writer's Guild, 1985.

Nyberg, Bartell. "The Search for Amelia Earhart." Excerpts from Empire (Magazine section of the Denver Post) June 28, 1970. (Material on Robert Stanley.)

Oliver, Douglas L. The Pacific Islands. Cambridge, Mass: Harvard University Press, 1957.

Pellegreno, Ann H. World Flight--The Earhart Trail. Ames, Iowa: Iowa State University Press, 1971. (This book contains a great deal of valuable information on investigations of previous researchers into the Earhart mystery.)

Planck, Charles E. Women With Wings. New York: Harper Brothers, 1942, (Chapter: "Amelia Who Likes Icarus").

Polhemus, William L. Howland Island. ETA Thirty Years and Thirty Minutes. Burlington, Vermont: Polhemus Navigation Sciences, Inc., 1971.

Putnam, G. P. Jr. Soaring Wings. New York: Harcourt, Brace and Co., 1939.

Price, Willard. Pacific Adventure. New York: Reynal and Hichcock, 1936. (Discussion of Japanese Mandates and Pacific air routes.)

Safford, Laurance F., Capt. USN (Ret.) Amelia Earhart's Last Flight: A Tragedy of Errors. Unpublished manuscript, date unknown.

Schoolfield, Mason M., Cmdr USN (Ret.) An Air Navigator Studies the Disappearance of Amelia Earhart. Unpublished manuscript, 1971.

Serling, Robert J. The Electra Story. Garden City, New York: Doubleday & Co., Inc., 1963. (Discusses origins of Model 10 Electra.)

Smith, Elinor. Aviatrix. New York: Harcourt Brace Javanovich, 1981. (Mentions G. P. Putnam Jr. and Amelia Earhart.)

Smith, Henry Ladd. Airways Abroad - The History of World Air Routes. Madison: University of Wisconsin Press, 1950.

Snook, Neta. I Taught Amelia to Fly. New York: Vantage Press, 1978.

St. John, Adela Rogers. Some Are Born Great. New York: Doubleday & Co., Inc., 1974.

Strippel, Dick. Amelia Earhart--The Myth and the Reality. New York: Exposition Press, 1972. (Based primarily on domestic sources.)

Taylor, H. A. Airspeed Aircraft Since 1931. London: Putnam and Co., Ltd., 1970.

Thaden, Louise. High, Wide and Frightened. New York: Air Facts Press, 1973.

Thorpe, Elliott R., Brig. Gen. USA (Ret.). East Wind Rain - The Intimate Account of an Intelligence Officer in the Pacific 1939-1969. Boston: Gambit, Inc., 1969.

Toland, John. Infamy-Pearl Harbor and Its Aftermath. New York: Doubleday & Co., Inc., 1982. (The Roosevelt administration's infamy.)

Toland, John. The Rising Sun. New York: Random House, 1970.

United States Coast Guard. USCGC Itasca. Ship's history monograph, undated.

Willoughby, M. F., The U.S. Coast Guard in World War II. Annapolis, MD: Naval Institute Press, 1957. (Discusses development of Navy and Coast Guard direction finding equipment and techniques during the late 1930s as well as Howland and Baker Islands.)

Zacharias, Ellis M., R Adm., USN (Ret.),. Secret Missions. New York: G.P. Putnam's Sons, Inc., 1946. (Discusses case of Capt. "Pete" Ellis, USMC, and pre-World War II USN intelligence activities.)

UNITED STATES GOVERNMENT FILES

National Archives Records Group 26--Records of the US Coast Guard.

A. Correspondence File 601 - *Itasca* for 1937.
   1. Cruise report of the *Itasca* for the period during which it was searching for the Earhart plane, together with a letter and two cables. 14 pages.
   2. Track Chart showing area searched by the *Itasca.* 1 page.

B. Correspondence File 601 - Amelia Earhart
   1. Copy of the radio log of the *Itasca,* June 9-July 16, 1937, together with official remarks and opinions.
   2. Copies of cables and radiograms dated February-April and June-July 1937 relating to preparations for the flight and to the search for the plane. 159 pages.
   3. Transcripts of the logbook of the *Itasca,* June 22-July 23, 1937. 70 pages.
   4. Copy of the communication log of the *Itasca.* 43 pages.
   5. General correspondence dated 1937-1938, including remarks on newspaper articles about the search for the plane.
   6. Photographs of Miss Earhart, the plane, and related subjects. 26 items.

National Archives Record Group 37 - Records of the Hydrographic Office.

Correspondence concerning the flight and the search, weather data for the Pacific Region, and weekly letter of USS *Colorado* on the search. Covers period October 14, 1937-May 13, 1938. 25 pages.

National Archives Record Group 45 - Collections of the Office of Naval Records and Library.

Fourteenth Naval District, Serial 095 of July 31, 1937; Report of the Earhart search. Covers period July 2-18, 1937. 96 pages.

National Archives Record Group 80 - General Records of the Department of the Navy.

Correspondence and Messages. Covers period October 31, 1936-October 21, 1938. 106 pages.

U.S. Naval History Division Archives.

Naval Investigative Service (formerly Office of Naval Intelligence) File. Correspondence and a thermofax copy of the Fourteenth Naval District Report of the Earhart Search by the US Navy and US Coast Guard, July 2-18, 1937. Covers period July 2, 1937-June 9, 1967. 360 pages.

Fourteenth Naval District File, Serial 17527 of December 3, 1938; Search Plan and dispatch reports of the Earhart search. Covers period July 1-25, 1937. 487 pages.

United States Department of States - Correspondence File 800.79611. Putnam.

The Correspondence, Memoranda and Documents of Franklin D. Roosevelt Library, Hyde Park, New York--Various records groups covering the period 1934-1937.

Various U.S. Navy Documentation, 1935-1942 pertaining to Pacific Theater.

H.O. No. 184 Naval Air Pilot - Pacific Islands, Washington: U.S. Navy Hydrographic Office, January 1936. Covers details of Japanese Mandates and Central/South Pacific Islands.

ONI-52 (1) Field Monograph of Islands to Northward and Eastward of Samoa, Washington: Office of Naval Intelligence, May 15, 1942. Extensive information covering Central Pacific Islands including Phoenix Island Group.

Fiju National Archives. Details on Capt. John W. Jones, RNR; Burns Philp (South Seas) Co., Ltd., and M.V. *Makoa* sinking at Hull Island (Phoenix Group).

Various documents, British High Commissioner, Capt. J. W. Jones, A.S. *Makoa,* etc. Sydney, Australia, University of Sydney special collections.

PERIODICALS

1935-1941

Price, Willard. "Japan's New Outposts." Harper's, October 1935.

"U.S. Lays Claims to Some Midocean Stepping Stones." Newsweek, October 1935.

"Howland, Baker and Jarvis; U.S. Claims Islands in Mid-Pacific." Time, October 28, 1935.

Price, Willard. "Asia's New Great Wall." New Republic, April 1935.

"Amelia Earhart's New Flight; Expedition Into the Realm of Academics to Show Women the Pathway to a New Career." Christian Science Monitor, April 29, 1936.

Price, Willard. "Stepping Stones to Destiny." Fortune, May 1936.

"Pacific Airbases; U.S. Security Day." Literary Digest, November 7, 1936.

"Pacific Dots: Islets Converted as Aviation Prepares for the Antipodes." Literary Digest, January 23, 1937.

"Collector's Stamps to Pay for Round-World Trip." Newsweek, February 20, 1937.

"Earhart Wrecks Ship After Setting an Ocean Record." Newsweek, March 27, 1937.

"Mourning Becomes Electra." Time, March 29, 1937.

Williams, J. "More American Air Bases." Asia, June 1937.

"Lost Earhart." Time, July 12, 1937.

"Warships and Planes Sweep Pacific for Lost Flyers." Newsweek, July 17, 1937.

"A Round-the-World Flight Ends in the Pacific." Life, July 19, 1937.

"One in a Million." Time, July 19, 1937.

"The Loss of Mrs. Amelia Earhart Putnam." Flight, July 22, 1937.

"Search Abandoned." Time, July 26, 1937.

Untitled article on US Navy's search for Amelia Earhart. US Navy BuAer (Bureau Newsletter) August 15, 1937.

1943-1944

McCoy, Horace. "Flight for Freedom." Woman's Home Companion, January 1943.

Price, Willard. "Truk-Gibralter of the Pacific." Fact Digest, January 1944.

1966-1981

Goerner, Fred. "My Search for Amelia Earhart." True, September 1966.

Okumiya, Masatke, Lt. Gen., Japanese Self-Defense Force (retired). "For Sugar Boats or Submarines." U.S. Naval Institute Proceedings, August 1968.

Holbrook, Francis X. "Commercial Aviation and the Colonization of the Equatorial Islands." Aviation Historian, Winter, December 1970.

Holbrook, Francis X. "Amelia Earhart's Final Flight." Proceedings, Naval Institute Press, 1971.

Strippel, Dick. "Amelia Earhart's Flight Into Eternity." Air Classics, July 1972.

Riley, Arthur A. "Search For Amelia Earhart Narrows." Air World, July 1976.

Hamill, Pete. "The Cult of Amelia Earhart." MS., September 1976.

Janczarek, Ted. "Amelia Earhart: She Didn't Die in Her Plane." Coronet, September 1976.

Wolfe, Frank. "Amelia Earhart Myths." Houston Chronical Magazine, May 15, 1977.

Thomas, Donald W. "Amelia Earhart's Fatal Decision." American Aviation Historical Society Journal, Summer 1977.

Vaeth, J. Gordon. "What Happened to Amelia Earhart." <u>NOAA Magazine</u>, July 1977. (See also article by the same title in <u>Air Line Pilot</u>, February 1978.)

Vaeth, J. Gordon. "Amelia Earhart...Spy in the Sky." <u>Naval Aviation News</u>, January 1978.

Emmert, Thomas M. and Larkins, William T. "Lockheed's Model 10 Electra." America Aviation Historical Society <u>Journal</u>, Second Quarter 1978. (A highly detailed history of the plane and its variants.)

Smith, Joe, Clements, Max and Clements, Maryke. "Aviation's Greatest Mystery - Amelia Earhart - What Really Happened." <u>Runway 26</u>, August, September, October 1978.

Kock, R. W. "Amelia and the Mystery of N16020." <u>Air Classics</u>, August 1981.

SOURCES ON AMELIA EARHART

Earhart, Amelia. <u>The Fun of It</u>. New York: Harcourt Brace and Co., 1932.

Earhart, Amelia. (Edited by George Palmer Putnam.) <u>Last Flight</u>. New York: Harcourt Brace and Co., 1937.

Putnam, George Palmer. <u>Soaring Wings</u>. New York: Harcourt Brace and Co., 1939.

SELECTED SOURCES ON JAPAN AND THE MICRONESIAN ISLANDS

Borden, Charles A. <u>South Sea Islands</u>. Philadelphia: Macrae Smith, 1961.

Clyde, Paul H. <u>Japan's Pacific Mandate</u>. New York: Macmillan, 1935.

Gayn, Mark J. <u>The Fight for the Pacific</u>. New York: William Narrow, 1941.

Grattan, C. Hartley. <u>The Southwest Pacific Since 1900</u>. Ann Arbor: University of Michigan Press, 1963.

Hobbs, William H. <u>The Fortress Islands of the Pacific</u>. Ann Arbor: J. W. Edwards, 1945.

Thomas, David. <u>The Battle of the Java Sea</u>. New York: Stein and Day, 1969.

SELECTED SOURCES ON THE 1967 FLIGHT

"After 30 Years of Wandering the World TCA Comes Home." <u>Antique Airplane Association News</u>, January-February 1969.

Burke, John. <u>Winged Legend</u>. New York: G.P. Putnam's Sons, 1970. (A biography of Amelia Earhart.)

David, Kiane. "The 28,000 Mile Mission of Ann Pellegreno." <u>Chicago Tribune Magazine</u>, November 19, 1967.

Esch, Marvin L. "Nation Honors Ann Pellegreno." <u>Congressional Record</u>, July 12, 1967.

Pellegreno, Ann H. "I Completed Amelia Earhart's Flight." <u>McCall's</u>, November 1967.

DOCUMENTS

Balfour, Harry J. Letter to Francis X. Holbrook, November 14, 1969.

Central Intelligence, B-2, GHQ. "Report on Amelia Earhart." August 8, 1949.

Collopy, James A. Letter to Secretary, Civil Aviation Board, Territory of New Guinea, 1937.

Cude, T. H. Letters to Francis X. Holbrook. December 15, 1969 and January 4, 1970. Nauru Island Overflight. July 2, 1937.

Detudamo, Buraro. Letter to Paul Rafford, Jr. September 11, 1983.

Dwiggins, Don. Letters and records from personal collection on Paul Mantz/Earhart.

Hooveh, Frederick J. "Amelia Earhart's Last Flight." Unpublished manuscript. Washington: National Air and Space Museum files, 1982.

Kamoi, Special Service Vessel, Japanese Imperial Navy. Log books, 1935-1938.

Koshu, Special Service Vessel, Japanese Imperial Navy. Log books, 1937.

Lexington Group. "Report of Earhart Search." USS *Lexington,* July 1937.

Mitchell, John H. "The Morning Amelia Earhart Ran Out of Luck." Unpublished manuscript, 1983.

"Amelia Earhart-Flight Into Yesterday." Symposium featuring Muriel Earhart Morrissey, Fay Gillis Wells, Rear Admiral Richard B. Blac, USNR (Ret.), Elgen Long, Fred Goerner, Gordon Vaeth, 1982.

National Air and Space Museum, Smithsonian Institution. Amelia Earhart files.

National Archives and Records Service, CAA records, diplomatic record, U.S. Coast Guard files, old Army and Navy records.

Purdue University. Amelia Earhart Collection, Various Boxes. Noonan flight charts.

Rafford, Paul Jr. Amelia Earhart-Her Own Navigator? Unpublished manuscript, 1983.

Rafford, Paul Jr. Amelia Earhart's Tragic Last Flight, Unpublished manuscript, 1981.

U. S. Coast Guard, Office of the Historian. *Itasca* records, Amelia Earhart file.

Washburn, Bradford. Amelia Earhart's Last Flight. Unpublished manuscript, 1983.

Wolfe, Frank H. Jr. Analysis of the Last Amelia Earhart Flight. Unpublished manuscript, National Air and Space Museum Earhart Files.